MULTI-COMPANY PROJECT MANAGEMENT

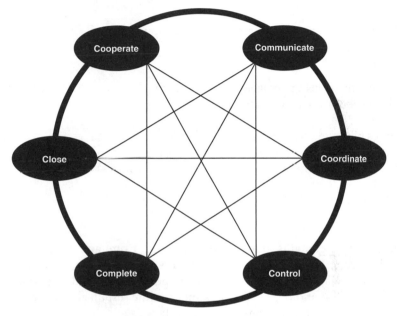

Maximizing Business Results through Strategic Collaboration

Dean A. Baker, PMP

ISBN 978-1-60427-035-8

Printed and bound in the U.S.A. Printed on acid-free paper
10 9 8 7 6 5 4 3 2 1

Library of Congress Cataloging-in-Publication Data

Baker, Dean A., 1945–

Multi-company project management : maximizing business results through
strategic collaboration / by Dean A. Baker.
    p. cm.
Includes bibliographical references and index.
ISBN 978-1-60427-035-8 (hardcover : alk. paper)
    1. Project management. 2. Strategic alliances (Business) I. Title.
HD69.P75B349 2009
658.4'04—dc22

                          2009032549

Phone: (954) 727-9333
Fax: (561) 892-0700
Web: www.jrosspub.com

This book is dedicated to all current and future project sponsors and managers in the hope that the multi-company management concepts, project perspectives, tools, activities and personal experiences presented in this book add value and increase success in their projects and operations.

The MPM process offers a variety of unique new tools and perspectives on existing tools to aid in multi-company projects and operation improvements. The following list details the tools and their purpose:

Situational Matrix—Protects proprietary rights in a multi-company organization
Mission Statement and Goals Card—Provides project focus
Communication Plan with Website Support—Formal communication network plan
Open Issues List—Tool to manage project stakeholders
Milestone Chart—Interface management and project tracking by leadership
Activity Value Technique—More subjective and simpler alternative to Earned Value
Project Scorecard—Drive goal achievement and continuous improvement
Visual Control Board—Visualization of work progress
Lessons Learned Integration Process—Build lessons permanently into process
Process Survey—Evaluate the overall project process
Project Evaluation—Evaluate project results
Operational Assessments—Verify project and operations fit
Opportunity Assessments—Verify potential before starting an improvement
Resource/Results Matrix—Prioritizes areas for improvement
Network Analysis—Plan process improvements

The multi-company approach balancing customer and supplier perspectives while addressing project and operation environments is distinctive. Since emphasis is on application, the book contains more than one hundred illustrations and tables, including twenty-five sample checklists and meeting agendas to aid the reader in implementing the integrated management principles for building an MPM process. The checklists and agendas are available to readers as downloadable files from the publisher's website at www.jrosspub.com/wav.

The first chapter of this book provides an overview of multi-company project management in the typical customer supplier environment covering benefits, process description, application, structure, and initiation. The balance of the book consists of three parts. The first two parts provide a complete explanation of the MPM methodology in a multi-company organization structure involving the customer and supplier. Part I addresses project organization formation as well as project management *Initiate* and *Plan* processes. Part II covers multi-company organization management along with project management *Control, Execute,* and *Closure* processes. Numerous tools, checklists, sample agendas, and actual experiences from the past decade in applying this approach to strategic equipment acquisition projects in the automotive industry support the process descriptions.

The objective is to provide the reader with a detailed plan that is easily adapted for implementing MPM on projects in manufacturing, construction, retail, finance, information technology, or any other business, or industry environment.

Part III applies MPM in an operations environment involving improvements. Using the techniques and methods in Part I and II, it incorporates the Six Sigma DMAIC framework together with the total productive maintenance metric of Overall Equipment Effectiveness to define a modified project-style equipment enhancement process to improve performance. A case study initiated by Automatic Feed Company with itself as the supplier and Kasle Metal Processing as the customer is the framework for describing the application of MPM in operations improvement. Since this case study is manufacturing specific, the detailed checklists and agendas have limited application outside manufacturing, but the concepts employed provide insight into developing other MPM improvement applications.

One- and two-day workshops in designing an MPM process and planning a pilot project customized to your company culture and industry environment are available by contacting the author at the following e-mail address: dabaker@teamimplementers.com

Dean A. Baker, PMP
Team Implementers

ABOUT THE AUTHOR

DEAN A. BAKER is a certified Project Management Professional (PMP), an international certification from the Project Management Institute recognized in more than 125 countries. Baker earned his BS in Electrical Engineering from Kettering University (formerly General Motors Institute) and his MS in Electrical Engineering from the University of Michigan.

Baker acquired much of his project and operations management experience during his successful 40-year career with General Motors Corporation. He gained this relevant experience in a variety of roles such as production manager, assistant plant manager, and Chief Manufacturing Engineer at GM Headquarters.

A few of his many noteworthy accomplishments were achieved while Chief Manufacturing Engineer of Body-in White for the Metal Fabricating Division where he successfully lead the division's plant modernization projects and provided manufacturing engineering support to plants in the United States and Canada. Dean also designed, planned, and implemented team concepts for all major stamping projects. These projects totaled over $2 billion and involved major equipment suppliers from the United States, Canada, Japan, Germany, and Brazil. The projects impacted over 60 percent of all the stamping equipment in GM, and when combined with the plant productivity efforts, resulted in GM's stamping equipment productivity improving from the least productive rating in 1996 to the most productive rating in 2003. Dean's proven record of success in automotive manufacturing operations and on large projects was achieved through the systematic application of strategic planning, detailed project management, disciplined implementation of team processes, and other concepts documented in this book.

In 2005, Baker started a consulting firm known as Team Implementers. He now shares his knowledge and experience with other companies through his

Web
Added
Value™

This book has free material available for download from the
Web Added Value™ resource center at *www.jrosspub.com*

At J. Ross Publishing we are committed to providing today's professional with practical, hands-on tools that enhance the learning experience and give readers an opportunity to apply what they have learned. That is why we offer free ancillary materials available for download on this book and all participating Web Added Value™ publications. These online resources may include interactive versions of material that appears in the book or supplemental templates, worksheets, models, plans, case studies, proposals, spreadsheets, and assessment tools, among other things. Whenever you see the WAV™ symbol in any of our publications, it means bonus materials accompany the book and are available from the Web Added Value™ Download Resource Center at www.jrosspub.com.

Downloads for *Multi-Company Project Management* include free downloadable MPM and MPM² project management checklists, agenda templates, and multi-company project assessment tools.

MULTI-COMPANY PROJECT MANAGEMENT OVERVIEW

By definition, a project is a one-of-a-kind effort with a specified beginning and end that creates a unique product, service, or result. Although a project has a finite duration, it can cover a long timeframe—often several years or more. It has unique deliverables in the form of a product, service capability, or document. Due to its unique nature, it usually involves an iterative planning process called *progressive elaboration*, which evolves over time with the development of more information. Both project management and operations management require people to perform the work, involve resource constraints, and provide detailed planning and control. One difference is that *projects* are one-time unique events while *operations* are ongoing, repetitive processes that sustain business. As a result, *operations* follow "the traditional business organizational form, which is basically vertical and emphasizes a strong superior-subordinate relationship" (Kerzner 2006, 2). In contrast, *project management* employs a temporary management structure that easily adapts to changing conditions and requires a high degree of cross-functional cooperation.

Conventional thinking normally views a project from a single company's perspective. The company assigns a project manager to lead the process and assigns resources to the project manager through direct or indirect (or both) lines of authority. For the most part, the company views the project as internal, to be executed within the company's project management process. On larger projects, the project perspective expands to include companies that contribute major content as well. Beyond the project customer, this could include an engineering design house, original equipment manufacturer (OEM), architect, general contractor, software designer, and its key suppliers. When the content represents sufficient strategic value in terms of size, complexity, risk, or opportunity, a company will assign its own manager and project organization. By looking at this from a broader viewpoint, it is easy to see that each of the project organizations is simply a subset of the overall project. Projects involving multiple companies have the added dimension of cross-company cooperation and require a means for integrating the various project organizations to manage their overall effectiveness and maximize project success for all participants. The integration of multi-company management and project management techniques yields a process referred to as *multi-company project management* (MPM).

MPM involves companies that are unique entities working on a project; there is not one authority with complete control to make decisions. One could argue that the customer has that authority by virtue of its control over the original contract and ability to terminate the agreement. However, the terms of the agreement, the willingness of the supplier companies to accept customer requests, and the level of the supplier's commitment to customer satisfaction limit this authority. Everyone knows the importance of customer satisfaction due to its influence on a company's reputation, growth, and future opportunities. Multi-company projects require a paradigm shift that also recognizes significant value in achieving supplier satisfaction in terms of the benefits a long-term relationship with the supplier yields on future projects and supporting the product throughout its lifecycle. For example, just as a customer makes allowances when evaluating project bids based on prior experiences with a supplier, the supplier considers previous experiences with the customer when preparing its bid and establishing the pricing level. In addition, the operating life of a typical product is far longer (10 times longer or more) than the project and offers significant improvement opportunities when a strong customer and supplier relationship exists. As a result, effective project organizations involving multiple companies require a joint leadership structure and the full collaboration of key companies that utilize a consensus style decision-making approach.

MPM combines multi-company management and project management methodologies into a set of six process groups designated as *Six C*. These Six C process groups include the activities, tools, and procedures to form and manage multi-company project teams and fulfill project management deliverables. MPM divides a project into phases and makes a determination to manage each phase using project management or existing operational processes. Each phase employing project management utilizes the Six C processes to create the team to execute the project phase. Although each team draws methodology from each of the Six C groups, the project teams use different tools and techniques depending on their role and deliverables in the overall project. Further, MPM organizes the project teams and defines a communication plan tying them together in an efficient project network and MPM links project phases managed with existing operation processes to the overall project through critical deliverables and timing using interface events or milestones.

The MPM process is ideally suited for multi-company projects with significant strategic value to the customer and supplier. MPM applications tend to be projects with relatively long durations to meet the required level of significance for most projects. The shortest reported application of the MPM process was just less than one year, with most MPM processes averaging three to four years due to the staggered delivery of multiple systems (there is no limit on the duration). Longer projects do have the potential for carrying greater significance.

Senior executives are a critical component of MPM. Given the organizational barriers, contract language, and past adversarial relationships, senior executives from both the customer and supplier must support the relationship through their words and active participation. This is not a stretch, since the focus is on projects of strategic value to both, which are high on the senior executive's priority list. To accomplish this involvement and provide the required leadership, MPM begins with the formation of a leadership team. The leadership defines the remaining organizational structure, sets goals, aligns business objectives, assists in resolving issues, and oversees the total relationship. The idea of involving the customer in a leadership role with the project supplier in project teams is not original. In 1994, Barkley and Saylor proposed customer leadership in project teams as a core element in their book *Customer Driven Project Management* with a second edition published in 2001.

In addition to integrating project management and multi-company management to increase project success, MPM improves the customer and supplier relationship, which is a key element that spans both the project and operation portions of the product lifecycle. In a highly successful team, the results can be greater than the sum of the individual parts, which defines synergy. MPM forms customer and supplier relationships that add synergy and has dramatic effects on the success of the implementation project as well as on-going operation performance. Effectively implemented, MPM benefits both the customer and supplier; therefore, either party can initiate MPM after securing the agreement and the support of the other. Implementing MPM at the outset of a purchase takes advantage of opportunities over the life of the product and maximizes results. However, initiating MPM in conjunction with an operations improvement effort many years after the product or service has been in production also yields benefits. MPM incorporates strategic customer and supplier collaboration to build synergy in the results.

The advantages of the customer and supplier relationship apply to a wide range of projects and industries. In the retail business, the relationship between Proctor & Gamble and Wal-Mart began with a supplier-initiated meeting between John Smale, CEO of Proctor & Gamble and Proctor & Gamble's executive team, and Sam Walton and his Wal-Mart senior executives to see if they could reach a common ground for mutual benefit. They found that by being more open, communicating more effectively and by establishing trust in the relationship, both companies realized a significant positive impact. Don Soderquist, in his book *The Wal-Mart Way*, cites annual purchases from Proctor & Gamble in 1987 of $350 million just prior to the formation of their relationship compared to $8 billion in 2004 as an example of the mutual benefit gained through their relationship (2005, 167–172).

Outsourcing is a tool used by many companies to contract with an outside party to obtain services, resources, or products. The purpose of outsourcing is to resolve skill shortages, capacity constraints, or competitiveness of specific components. "The root of many outsourcing problems is often that many companies fail to recognize the importance of appropriately managing the relationship between the outsourcing organization and the company that performs the outsourcing service and balancing control and independence between the parties in the relationship" (Johnson, Johnson, & Arab 2006, 78). Whenever outsourcing work is critical to the strategic plans of the company, using the MPM approach to structure and implement the outsourcing project will increase success.

Traditional thinking and organizational structures typically place a wall between the customer and supplier and reinforce it with lengthy contract language designed to protect the respective parties. Oftentimes the relationship between customer and supplier is adversarial. Many customers view the supplier as the bad guy, delivering poor quality, missing schedules, aggravating cost problems, and generally not living up to expectations when supplying goods and services. The customer and supplier relationship is much like the past union and management relationships in the United States automotive industry that negotiated contracts with a win-lose mentality. Now, both unions and management are beginning to see that to survive they must change to a more collaborative relationship. In a similar manner, customers and suppliers need to understand the degree to which they are dependent on each other and the value of working collaboratively to their mutual benefit.

Forming joint teams is an effective approach. However, it is not a panacea for all relationships. In fact, if the participating companies are not adequately committed and involved, the joint team will be ineffective and could become counterproductive. Rather, customers and suppliers need to seek out specific relationships that are strategic to their respective businesses. When both the customer and supplier identify significant value in the relationship, MPM is appropriate and optimizes results.

BENEFITS

Participant Benefits. In the terminology of the Project Management Institute (PMI®)[1], a project sponsor is the person within the company who has ownership of the project with the ability to assign resources, set priorities, and make major decisions on the project. These project sponsors are usually key executives, divisional managers, board members, or presidents within their respective companies. Many project sponsors find themselves in too many confrontational meetings and feel their expectations lack understanding; they struggle with the project's scope and encounter too many projects in crisis. Prior to MPM, I often experienced these frustrations too late in the project to achieve effective resolution to the satisfaction of all participants. The desire to overcome these issues was a prime motivator in creating MPM. Frequently, the project manager reports to the sponsor. The project manager has overall responsibility for the project. In multi-company project environments, project managers often find mixed and confusing priorities, are frustrated with their inability to get commitments from other companies and influence key stakeholders, and get bogged down in complex and inefficient decision-making processes. Implementation of MPM minimizes or eliminates these issues for the sponsor and project manager.

A key difference in applying the MPM approach to multiple companies versus the traditional project management single company approach is the need to form a *leadership team* of representatives from the customer and suppliers. The project leadership team consists of the project sponsors, project managers, and representatives from sales, purchasing, or other functions as appropriate. Each participant brings specific skill sets that enhance the effectiveness of the team. The project sponsors are essential participants since the leadership must deal with intercompany issues and company-specific issues that are often beyond the authority of the project managers. The project sponsors, by virtue of their senior management experience, have broad business experience and company knowledge needed to achieve win-win solutions to complex problems that the individual project organizations cannot resolve. The project managers provide the technical expertise and detailed project knowledge required by the leadership team. The sales or purchasing representatives are the front door to intercompany relationships, provide valuable assistance in interpreting contract language, and are generally required in most companies to seal any agreements. Perhaps most importantly, the purchasing and sales representatives provide a higher level of objectivity than that of the

---

[1]PMI is a service and trademark of the Project Management Institute, Inc. which is registered in the United States and other nations.

project managers or sponsors since they are not as intimately involved in the project details.

The objectivity that sales and purchasing participants bring to the MPM process is extremely valuable in maintaining focus, fostering balanced communication, and resolving significant highly emotional intercompany project issues. For example, both the project sponsor and manager usually have a strong technical background by virtue of their education or experience in the industry. This strong technical focus can result in discussions and decisions that belong to others. Sales and purchasing personnel often bring this form of micromanaging to the leadership team's attention, allowing them to redirect efforts to more worthwhile topics. Another dimension of objectivity occurs whenever the project manager reports directly to the sponsor. This dynamic makes the project manager timid in offering ideas contrary to the sponsor and sponsors may not give ideas from their subordinates the full consideration they deserve. Purchasing and sales, by virtue of being outside the sponsor's functional organization, help to balance the communications; the diverse backgrounds of the personnel promote creativity. Finally, the project manager and sponsor are intimately involved in the project—the project manager through daily project responsibilities and the sponsor through project ownership and expectations of results. The combination of personal involvement and technical background creates a mindset in some issues where they *cannot see the forest for the trees*. The sales and purchasing departments help to minimize this situation, keep the big picture in perspective, and state issues in simple, objective terms; but they are not the only source for this objectivity. Finance personnel, outside consultants, or others with broad business perspectives and strong interpersonal skills can fill this need as well.

Project Benefits. The benefits of MPM to the project are many. It facilitates the coordination and integration of the individual company project organizations. Without the project leadership team, the project sponsors would only meet in confrontational situations when problems arise in the project. The trust and respect built among the leadership along with ongoing project monitoring oftentimes allows project sponsors to resolve issues with a simple phone call. The existence of the leadership team raises the importance of the project within all participating companies by virtue of their organizations observing the personal involvement of their project sponsors in the project. It provides a critical mechanism for expediting or resolving issues that are behind schedule or lack resolution in normal project development. Regular leadership meetings provide a series of events in the project timeline common to all participating companies that drive a sense of urgency in meeting deadlines, resolving problems, and making decisions. In these meetings, the project sponsors see project progress not only from their own company's perspective, but also from the other participant's viewpoint. The leadership team provides a chance to present opportunities that will improve project performance and results. Oftentimes, by virtue of their broad range of involvement across many projects, the participants identify opportunities that would leverage other projects in their respective companies to aid the success of the project. The participants are able to demonstrate the value and capabilities of their respective companies through their creative contributions and performance on the project that can lead to future business opportunities. The relationships developed through this process can also carry over and benefit other activities that the companies are jointly involved with, even after the MPM project is complete.

In the past, project managers defined a successful project as meeting time, cost, and specifications, referring to the specifications set at project onset. As a project progressed over time, project managers lost sight of the customer and showed little concern for the customer's needs or expectations. In the end, project managers discovered that even a successful project produced unsatisfactory results for the customer due to their own failure to treat customer satisfaction as a continuous input to the project (Barkley, Saylor 2001, 63–64). This lack of customer satisfaction negatively affects relationships, project execution, and future business opportunities. MPM overcomes this issue by utilizing the customer and suppliers in joint leadership roles in specific project phases. Thus, the customer continuously provides their voice to ensure optimal customer satisfaction of the project.

Company Benefits. In addition to the participant and project benefits, MPM collaboration drives advantages for the customer and supplier companies. For the customer, a strong relationship with the supplier provides a huge source of knowledge and opportunity regarding the competition. The supplier deals with the competition daily on a firsthand basis, meeting the competition's needs and resolving quality and productivity problems on existing operations. As a result, the supplier has a broad perspective of the possibilities the processes offer, the different approaches for solving problems, and the various industry strategies employed. Frequently, the supplier can become the door for gaining access to the competitor to see competitive operating processes. Of course, this usually requires an agreement for a reciprocal visit by the competition, but the information acquired can be worth it.

For the supplier, a strong relationship with the customer provides direct knowledge regarding the performance of the supplier's products as well as their competitors' products. In general, customers that invest in costly equipment are highly capitalized and are often far larger companies than are their suppliers. For example, the automotive companies' capitalization is in the billions, while many of their equipment suppliers are in only the millions. The customer's size and their ability to specify equipment components allows them to influence the equipment supplier's component supply base to meet the schedule and quality requirements.

In addition, the customers often enjoy significant discounts on components that the supplier can share.

The preceding two paragraphs have touched on only a few of the customer and supplier advantages in the MPM process. Figures 1.1a, 1.1b, and 1.1c offer a more inclusive list of advantages. Figure 1.1a covers the advantages enjoyed by both the customer and supplier. Figures 1.1b and 1.1c cover the advantages unique to the customer and supplier respectively. During the past ten years, I have been involved in MPM processes initiated by customers and suppliers, and these lists are representative of the cumulative advantages that I have personally observed to date rather than of every possible advantage. Other independent research regarding customer and supplier collaboration confirms many of the advantages listed (Boston, Keller, and Rooney 2002; Shuman and Twombly 2006).

- Lessons learned improve both customer and supplier
- Improved communication quality and effectiveness
- Improved efficiency by working smarter not harder with each other
- Leadership links all stakeholders
- Inter-company brainstorming and dialogue creates greater innovation
- Builds trust & respect among participants aiding future problem resolution
- Raises the importance of the activity within the respective company
- Critical mechanism for expediting or resolving issues
- Drives urgency in deadlines, open issues, and decisions
- Valuable insight gained through knowledge of the other company's perspective
- Opportunities surface to improve results
- Leverage other projects, resources, or experiences to increase success
- Relationships carry over to benefit other activities in which the companies are involved
- Improves coordination/facilitation of individual company teams
- Achieves both vertical and horizontal organizational alignment over project life

Figure 1.1a MPM customer and supplier advantages

- Influence supplier equipment development to meet customer technology challenges
- Benefit from suppliers knowledge & experience of competitors
- Ability to tap supplier's technical resources aids in success
- Facilitates integration of new equipment and improvements into customer operations

Figure 1.1b MPM customer advantages

- Leverage the customers influence and size in buying process
- Benefit from customer's knowledge & experience of other suppliers
- Influence customer's assessment of future equipment needs
- Build awareness of supplier capabilities among customer decision makers
- Facilitate new equipment buy offs and enhance customer satisfaction
- Increase requests for service and spare parts
- Generate training opportunities
- Create future business opportunities
- Increase efficiency and utilization of engineering and project management personnel
- Opportunity for longer-term contracts and improved asset utilization
- Faster recognition of customer requirements and reduced change implementation time

Figure 1.1c MPM supplier advantages

Survey Results. During the past ten years, participants of the leadership teams involved in the MPM process completed surveys at the conclusion of each project to provide data to support and improve the process. The projects ranged in duration from one to six years, and in total, cost from $1 million to $100 million. The data in Table 1.1 provides further evidence of the value of an MPM approach. The table is a summary of surveys conducted by the participants at the end of major equipment projects, evaluating the overall effectiveness of the MPM approach in terms of seven parameters. Assessment of the major areas in which the MPM process contributed value provided the basis for parameter selection. Respondents

Table 1.1 MPM leadership team survey summary

Parameter	HELP		NO	HURT	
	2	1	0	1	2
1 Roles & responsibilities	45	38	7	3	
2 Communication requirements	41	41	9	2	
3 Recognizing risk/potential problems	48	32	10	2	1
4 Maintaining/adjusting schedules	37	40	14	1	1
5 Initial timing requirements	34	39	20		
6 Supplying a better product	32	41	19	1	
7 Performance & technical spec.	27	42	24-		

82% positive and less than 2% negative
Source: (93 surveys of 11 projects between 1997 and 2007)

used their own interpretation of each parameter in making a subjective rating. A plus one indicated minor improvement and a plus two indicated major improvement; minus one represented minor detriment and minus two was a major detriment. The surveys represent 11 projects in the automotive stamping industry, which occurred between 1997 and 2007. The survey participants consisted of company presidents, members of boards of directors, vice presidents of operations, engineering directors and managers, program and project managers, and sales and purchasing managers from the United States, Canada, Japan, Germany, and Brazil. In the 93 surveys representing a broad cross section of functions, organizational perspectives, business interests, and cultural diversity, there was an overwhelming 82 percent positive assessment on the merits of MPM with less than a 2 percent negative assessment.

Multiplying the total survey checks for each parameter and column by the respective column value and then adding the results across all columns for a given parameter yields a weighted point value for each parameter. For example, the *Roles and responsibilities parameter* involved the following calculations:

$$45 \times (+2) = 90$$
$$38 \times (+1) = 38$$
$$7 \times (0) = 0$$
$$3 \times (-1) = (-3)$$
$$0 \times (-2) = 0$$
$$\text{Total} = 125$$

Summing the preceding calculations for the *roles and responsibilities* parameter yields a point value of 125. The results shown in Table 1.2, listed in descending order, reflect that the greatest value is in recognizing the risk and potential problems with 126 points and defining roles and responsibilities with 125 points. Communicating requirements is close with 121 points. Overall, the range in values

Table 1.2 Weighted value of survey parameter

Parameter	Weighted value
Recognizing risk/potential problems	126
Roles & responsibilities	125
Communication requirements	121
Maintaining/adjusting schedules	113
Initial timing requirements	107
Supplying a better product	104
Performance & technical spec.	96

is only 30 points. This tight range indicates that all parameters yielded a significant value.

Success Examples. The synergy created through customer supplier collaboration in MPM drives project success that far exceeds the sum of individual companies' contributions. In one case, the supplier initiated an MPM process involving the design and installation of a replacement transfer press de-stack feeder for an automotive supplier; Table 1.3 displays the project results. The de-stack feeder project reduced installation, start-up, and ramp-up times by 69 percent and set new records for both companies. In addition, everyone operated under budget, new equipment ran with better-than-original cycle-time and uptime expectations, and there were no safety incidents.

Table 1.3 Project results de-stack feeder replacement

Activity	Original contract	Leadership goals	Actual performance	Overall record	Time saved
Install	14 days	5 days	4 days	10 days	71%
Start up	5 days	4 days	2 days	3 days	60%
Ramp up	10 days	5 days	3 days	7 days	70%
Total	29 days	14 days	9 days	20 days	69%

In another case, an auto company purchased seven progressive stamping systems that were projected to meet the company's needs for the next ten years. This project was so successful it set a world productivity benchmark that was 25 percent higher than prior benchmarks. This created 25 percent more capacity than expected, and the higher productivity motivated the auto company to process every part possible into these systems. Within two years, the auto company fully utilized the surplus capacity and purchased four more systems from the same *original equipment manufacturer* (OEM) and suppliers.

In a third case, a customer purchased four transfer-press systems from a well-established OEM—the technology leader for that system type. These systems cost over $20 million each. Including site preparation costs, the project exceeded $100 million. The useful life of a transfer-press system is 15 to 20 years. As such, it is a major strategic investment for the customer. The estimated time to design, build, and install the first system was 2.5 years, with the delivery of each subsequent system staggered by three months. Thus, the project duration was over three years. In the middle of installing the first two systems, the OEM declared bankruptcy and closed its doors, causing a contract breach. Normally, shutting down the project would be the only option. Everyone would have lost significantly, the customer would not have had access to the technology, and starting over would have seriously delayed the customer's access to that capacity. In addition, one or more of the suppliers were so heavily committed with material to the bankrupt OEM that they would have had to declare bankruptcy as well. The MPM process, even with the loss of the critical OEM member, successfully completed the two installations and startups, meeting the customer's budget and performance goals with minimal slippage in timing. The ability to complete the project without the OEM clearly demonstrates the synergy possible in the MPM process. In addition, another OEM accepted the original contract for the remaining two systems. The MPM organization reformulated itself with the new OEM and the other original suppliers and delivered the two systems without incident to the customer's revised timeline. The relationships and success the customer and the new OEM had experienced on previous MPM projects was one of the factors in the second OEM taking over the bankrupt OEM's contract.

Project sponsors, regardless of which company they represent, will find their participation in MPM to be very rewarding; it offers a perspective of the project like no other, and it will open up new possibilities and new ways of thinking that might otherwise go unnoticed. MPM allows project managers to surface and resolve issues that were previously outside their control. It elevates the stature of their project within their company as well as the other participants, making them more effective. It also provides a disciplined review process that helps control project quality, timing, and cost. For sales or purchasing representatives, MPM is a huge advantage in building critical customer and supplier relationships. It provides in-depth knowledge about the capabilities of the participants, identifies the needs and wants of the customer, and provides a way to monitor the overall execution of the contract to ensure all terms are complete.

The integration of a structured MPM process with a solid project management process like that spelled out by PMI® significantly increases both the frequency and magnitude of a project's success. Strategically involving the customer and supplier in project collaboration builds synergy that yields results greater than the sum of the individual companies. MPM has no downside. If you believe in the power of collaboration and project management, MPM is an opportunity you cannot afford to pass up!

PROCESS DESCRIPTION

MPM is actually the integration of two methodologies: *multi-company management* and *project management*. In both cases, the methodologies are a collection of activities or best practices organized into process groups. In order to accomplish the desired results, the project manager exercises freedom in selecting the appropriate activity from each process group to provide the maximum flexibility in applying MPM. Imposing a specific structure or procedure on any organization rarely leads to success since it lacks the prerequisite organizational commitment and understanding needed to sustain them. For best results, MPM blends with the existing company culture, business climate, project management approach, and organizational structure. Maintaining this flexibility is essential to avoid dictating a specific structure while using the process design as a means for building the necessary understanding and commitment to ensure success. Ideally, any company planning to implement MPM would use this book in conjunction with a project-organization design workshop to develop the project organization structure for their company. The workshop provides a carefully documented organization structure and project approach that drives consistency and forms a baseline for continuous improvement of the process.

Multi-company management consists of five process groups. Table 1.4 lists these five groups in column one of the table as *cooperate, communicate, coordinate, collaborate,* and *celebrate.* These five process groups do not stand alone, since forming a multi-company organization requires a greater motive or result to drive the formation of the organization and produce value. Consequently, multi-company management must be married with the purpose that created the need for the initial multi-company formation. In the context of MPM, this is the project and its management framework as defined by PMI®.

PMI® details the project management framework in *A Guide to the Project Management Body of Knowledge (PMBOK® Guide)*[2]. To define *project management,* the *PMBOK® Guide* identifies five process groups shown in column two of the table as *initiate, plan, monitor and control, execute,* and *close.* Currently, PMI®

Table 1.4 Six C process map

Multi-company management	Project management	MPM Six C processes
Cooperate		Cooperate
Communicate	Initiate	Communicate
Coordinate	Plan	Coordinate
Collaborate	Monitor & control	Control
	Execute	Complete
Celebrate	Close	Close

---

[2]PMBOK is a service and trademark of the Project Management Institute, Inc. which is registered in the United States and other nations.

has identified 42 activities, processes, or procedures that make up the five preceding process groups; these represent the best methods in project management.

When project management combines with multi-company management, the result is *multi-company project management*, which consists of six core process groups. These *Six C* process groups have the following designations: *cooperate, communicate, coordinate, control, complete,* and *close*. They constitute the core elements of the MPM approach. The third column of the table maps the activities from the multi-company management and project management groups into the Six C process groups. Note that multi-company management's *cooperate* and project management's *execute* elements translate directly into the *cooperate* and *complete* process groups respectively, while the remaining Six C process groups consist of some combination from multi-company management and project management. The *communicate* group includes multi-company management's *communicate* and project management's *initiate* elements. The *coordinate* group integrates multi-company management's *coordinate* and project management's *plan* elements. The *control* group combines elements from multi-company management's *collaborate* and project management's *monitor and control*. The *close* group is a combination of multi-company management's *celebrate* group and the *close* group in project management. Essentially, MPM creates the optimum environment for project management involving multiple companies to operate with maximum efficiency and creativity.

Figure 1.2 illustrates the interrelationship of the process groups as a network with all process groups linked together. Each team responsible for a specific phase of the project follows a sequential implementation of the Six C process groups starting with *cooperate* and proceeding clockwise, ending with *close*. In actual practice, major changes in personnel, project scope, or external variables such as economic climate may necessitate revisiting specific process groups, which can disrupt the sequence. Each process group depends on the deliverables, decisions, and experiential learning from all the preceding process groups. For example, the group norms developed as part of *cooperate* help to guide the team's behavior in all subsequent activities. The communication plan developed as part of *communicate* defines the information flow required throughout the project. Developed as part of *coordinate*, the project schedule forms the baseline for *control*, describes the project task's *completion* elements, and identifies the project's *close* requirements.

The typical project manager generally has an engineering background or technical experience in a field related to the assigned project. Usually, it is through successful application of these talents that brings one to the level of project manager. The project manager typically has special training in project management methodology, but people skills are not the primary area of expertise. Even though there is certainly a broad spectrum of information about people skills, project managers and participants frequently have a difficult time combining interper-

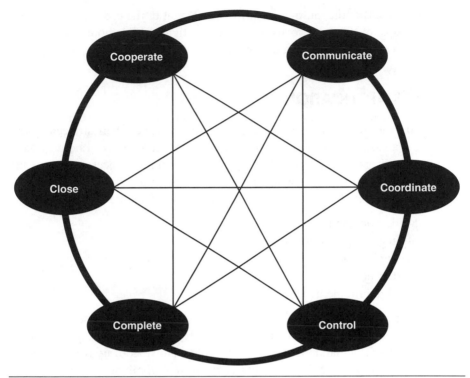

Figure 1.2 Six C process network

sonal philosophy and concepts with project management methodologies in practical applications; it is even more difficult when multiple companies compound the organizational issues. This book provides simple, easy-to-implement activities, techniques, and procedures within the Six C process groups to guide the project manager and participants in implementation of MPM.

This book is like a cookbook that provides detailed tasks, instructions, and tools to assist in the formation, development, and management of projects and their associated individual and company relationships. The tasks in the Six C process groups are standalone activities written for use in a group setting. A project team does not use every task, since different tasks apply to different project phases. Through years of use, all the tasks detailed have proved to yield the desired results in support of MPM. The *PMBOK® Guide* documents the foundation for project management, and thousands of books and articles provide additional support to the subject. Although there is no standard established for MPM, this book provides a foundation based on my experiences as both a project sponsor and a consultant in multi-company projects over the past 15 years. With the emphasis on application, the Six C process discussions in this context do not cover all the possibilities in either the multi-company management or the project management process groups, but instead, focus on selected activities from both that relate to MPM and the tools presented in this book.

PROCESS APPLICATION

Projects are the means through which companies advance their strategic goals. Developing a successful set of company strategies is meaningless without the correct set of projects to implement the strategies. Grouping projects based on the strategic considerations from which they were born creates five categories. The five categories defined by PMI® are as follows (PMBOK® Guide 2008, 10):

- Market demand
- Strategic opportunity or business need
- Technology advance
- Customer request
- Legal requirement

As an example, *market demand* may create a need to either increase or decrease volume on a given product, which might require one or more projects to vary capacity to match demand. These projects could involve adding, reassigning, or idling equipment, personnel, or a facility. A *business need* might consist of specific training to support a strategy such as improved customer service. *Technology advances* such as a new material or process that significantly reduces total cost or improves quality would drive projects to incorporate the technology in order to achieve a competitive advantage or keep up with the competition. *Customer request* is simply a customer who requests a specific product or service from a supplier. Finally, a variety of *legal requirements* ensures the legal compliance of projects. The following are a few examples:

- Sarbanes-Oxley—financial reporting
- OSHA—safety standards
- Industry-specific standards—auto emissions, toy and child-related products standards, food ingredients and handling

Project Portfolio Management. Most successful companies follow a defined process for converting their strategies into specific projects, which they refer to as *project portfolio management*. Project portfolio management uses specific criteria for evaluating and selecting projects and monitors the projects to completion to ensure conformance to criteria and alignment with current company strategy. The selection criteria should maximize the value received for each dollar spent, ensure alignment with company strategies, and yield the appropriate mix of risk, market timing, and resource utilization. Project managers must be knowledgeable of this process and interface their project with it on a regular basis to make sure the project remains aligned with the company strategies.

Although project portfolio management is outside the scope of this text, this book offers the following critical observation as it applies to MPM: Usually, this project portfolio approach applies to the customer who is soliciting projects from suppliers to achieve their strategic goals. However, suppliers, particularly those whose main business is executing projects for their customers, need to use this same portfolio approach when selecting projects to bid on to make sure that the projects they win fit within their strategic goals, maximize profits, and provide a good balance of risk and resource utilization. A supplier's failure to manage their portfolio can have serious consequences on project timing, cost, and satisfaction; this failure was a contributing factor in the OEM bankruptcy cited previously in *Success Examples*. Project performance directly affects both the customer and supplier. Therefore, it is important for customers and suppliers to discuss the project fit within their respective organizations to avoid surprises and problems during project execution.

Strategic Project. A fundamental premise of MPM is that the project has significant strategic value to both the customer and the supplier. All projects by virtue of their role as the means to implement corporate strategy have strategic value. Thus, it is important to have a common understanding of the term *significant strategic value* from both the customer and supplier viewpoints, which defines what MPM calls a *strategic project*. Defining a strategic project begins with selection of the appropriate customer and supplier entities. Company scale is the first factor to consider. For example, a single division within one of the major automotive companies might have an equipment project budget of $200 million per year while the company's total project budget could be in the billions. A project involving equipment valued at $50 million would be insignificant to the automotive company, yet would represent a major strategic value to the division. In a similar manner, a large global equipment supplier of control systems or automation with sales in excess of $3 billion might have a division that sells a project to a customer with equipment valued at $30 million. To the global supplier, the sale would be insignificant, but to the division within that supplier that has annual sales of $300 million, it would have tremendous value. Thus, identifying a strategic project requires defining the appropriate customer and supplier entity.

One offshoot of defining the appropriate customer and supplier entity is that in large companies, an internal project between multiple divisions within the same company can create a de-facto customer and supplier relationship. These relationships qualify as a strategic project and are appropriate for this approach. These have the potential for generating even greater results because everyone is part of the same company. The side benefits on other projects and activities are high as well because the relationships built will carry over into other company activities, further increasing the effectiveness of the organization.

The project organization formed between the GM World Wide Facilities Group (WFG) and the GM Metal Fabricating Division (MFD) is a good example of an interdivisional customer and supplier relationship. The project utilized the MPM process to complete the site work at three GM stamping plants and involved four transfer presses purchased by the MFD. The project required extensive building modifications with combined costs in excess of $20 million to support the four presses that were valued in excess of $120 million. The organizational structure was very complex, since management was under the project management department within WFG, and the labor to perform the work was in another department called the facilities group. In a similar fashion, the manufacturing engineering department within MFD was responsible for ordering the equipment, but the manufacturing department was the final user. The four presses were a critical element in the production of stampings for a new truck program. Both MFD and WFG considered the project significant due to the risk to GM's truck program. In addition, MFD considered the project significant due to its cost and WFG considered it significant due to the organizational complexity.

WFG and MFD implemented the MPM process with WFG's project management department serving as the main supplier and MFD's manufacturing engineering department serving as the customer. The MPM process included the site contractor, press supplier, architect, facilities group, and plants as team participants to cover all stakeholders. The process aided in problem resolution, faster decision making, improved planning, effective project execution, and meeting all project requirements. For years preceding this project, a strained relationship existed between MFD engineering and WFG project management due to MFD's dependency on WFG as its only source for all facility projects. WFG passed on any increased costs it incurred to MFD, which created strained feelings and mistrust. The understanding gained through the MPM process unified the two groups and resulted in the establishment of other joint meetings and working relationships to improve performance.

The preceding example uses project risk, cost, and complexity in assessing strategic significance. The four parameters of size, opportunity, risk, and complexity provide the complete framework for determining strategic significance. Admittedly, size in the form of project cost is the most common and easiest to determine parameter in establishing strategic significance. The customer looks at size in terms of its annual project budget and the supplier looks at size in terms of annual sales. Any time the size exceeds 10 percent of your project budget as a customer or 10 percent of sales as a supplier, it is ripe for MPM application. The 10 percent is somewhat subjective, but whenever projects fell below that level, problems occurred in securing or sustaining the involvement of senior management, which is necessary to start and sustain the process. Conversely, if senior management becomes involved in too many projects, it reduces their availability and effectiveness in completing core organizational responsibilities for their company. Senior management must establish the proper balance of involvement while empowering their employees.

Opportunity and risk parameters require forecasting the potential impact the project will have on the organization if it succeeds (opportunities) or fails (risks) and the probability of each. The customer identifies the opportunity impact as the project payback in the original project submission along with other benefits not quantified in the payback, such as increased customer satisfaction, improved on-time performance and increased durability. For the supplier, opportunity is in the form of profit and other intangibles, such as the introduction of a new technology or customer and resource utilization. In the opportunity parameter, both customers and suppliers tend to be overly optimistic. Thus, you must temper these values with the probability for success. Risk is the flipside of opportunity involving the consequences of a failure, and no one undertakes a project to fail. Consequently, the customer and supplier often fail to consider this aspect. However, both the customer and supplier should complete a risk assessment before taking on any project. The customer should compile data regarding the potential risk and adjust the project portfolio as part of the selection process. The supplier should compile risk data for use in determining the desirability of a project when setting the expected profit as part of establishing the final price submission. There is such a wide variation among industries and businesses regarding risk tolerance, that a simple standard of acceptance is impractical. Each company must develop its own criteria for acceptable risk.

Complexity is the final parameter considered. In many cases, such as the cited transfer-press site-prep project example size and complexity go hand in hand, but not always. Take, for example, an information technology project that would link all machines in a multi-plant organization to a central database for production monitoring, process control, and capacity planning. From the customer's viewpoint, this could be a relatively small project in terms of cost, yet represent major complexity in terms of the amalgamation with all the personnel in the plants and headquarters that would have to use the technology. Similarly, the project may appear small to the IT supplier who already has a similar package on the shelf, but the complexity of implementing the system and getting the desired satisfaction from the customer will be high. The complexity aspect of IT projects makes them particularly good prospects for the MPM approach. Complexity can also take the

A strategic project meets one of the following criteria:

1. Large size based on project cost—greater than 10% of project portfolio or sales
2. High risk—subjective measurement based on company and industry
3. High opportunity—subjective measurement based on company and industry
4. High complexity with medium or greater risk
5. High complexity with medium or greater opportunity

Figure 1.3 Definition of a strategic project

form of new designs, untested or unfamiliar components, and logistical issues driven by global sourcing. A highly complex project is not strategically significant if it has low risk and low opportunity. Thus, a highly complex project is strategically significant only when risk or opportunity is of medium size or greater.

In summary, MPM achieves best results when applied to strategic projects. To be strategic, a project must meet specific criteria for a given set of customer and supplier entities. Figure 1.3 summarizes the strategic project criteria. Size using project cost as a proportion of the total project portfolio or sales is the most common criteria, with any proportion over 10 percent considered strategic. Acceptable risk and opportunity levels are a function of the industry and company in which one works. In these areas, use a subjective low, medium, and high scale of value that fits your situation. If either risk or opportunity ranks high, the project is strategic and MPM is appropriate. Projects that involve extensive training hours, large quantities of people, new technology, or large organizational structures are generally indicative of a complex project. However, to be strategic, highly complex projects must also contain at least medium risk or opportunities.

MPM PROJECT ORGANIZATION

Generally, large projects divide into project phases. Often the phases are similar to the functional groups within the participating companies and follow a natural sequence. In many cases, the phases overlap. The chart in Figure 1.4 is a generic listing of some possible phases potentially encountered in an equipment acquisition or construction project. Project management methodology may not be the best approach for all phases of a project. For example, a supplier might perform the manufacture phase of an equipment acquisition project using its operations organization. This permanent organization structure delivers maximum efficiency and quality of repetitive operations within a controlled environment. Imposing a temporary project organization structure on the supplier's manufacturing opera-

Lead	Manufacture	Start up
Research	Assemble	Train
Specify	Transport	Buy off
Procure	Site prep	Ramp up
Engineer	Install	Warranty

Figure 1.4 Possible project phases

tion would be very disruptive, potentially harming supplier performance and the ability to deliver a quality product to the customer. MPM integrates project management and operation management methodologies by defining the project phases and selecting the appropriate methodology for each phase. MPM links the operation phases to the overall project through milestones or interface events explained in Chapter 4 as part of scheduling.

The following paragraphs provide generalized guidance regarding which phases are appropriate for MPM or operations methodology. The lead phase is required for all projects, always runs for the entire duration of the project, and provides the overall management of the total project. The leadership team discussed previously represents the lead phase. The lead phase is the key for all joint organizations in the other phases of MPM. If the lead phase is not set up as a joint customer and supplier organization, the MPM process reverts to the more traditional, single company perspective with leadership handled by the project manager rather than a joint organization. The MPM approach is applicable to the other phases, but it will lack a portion of the power and synergy that would otherwise be possible with full customer and supplier collaboration. Absence of a leadership team will also make it difficult to acquire and sustain the desired support from participants outside the company leading the project. This is not to discourage joint teams in the other phases, but to encourage realistic expectations. A project phase involving a cross-functional group from multiple companies working together on a daily basis requires an MPM approach to get optimum results. Install and start-up phases are good examples of this type of situation. Project managers who are unable to establish a joint leadership team process or an agreement to multi-company organizations in other phases should not be discouraged. Instead, project managers should consider including participation of a less formal nature from the customer and supplier in appropriate phases to gain some of the benefits.

For an equipment acquisition project research is minimal, usually involving some benchmarking of the competition and investigating available equipment options, which is handled within the operations organization. The customer normally does specification and procurement internally, unless using a single-source approach. In this case, a multi-company approach may be appropriate. Engineering is a fertile area for an MPM process. The manufacture, assembly, and transport phases are common parts of a supplier's normal product delivery process, integral parts of a supplier's organization, and best left to the management of the respective supplier.

Site prep is an area in which the MPM process is desirable. However, the customer or supplier company may change. For example, if the project is a turnkey in which the OEM is responsible for site prep, the OEM becomes the customer and the construction general contractor becomes the supplier, leaving the original customer to play a smaller role. If the customer is responsible for site prep, the construction general contractor is the supplier to the customer and the OEM plays a smaller role in this phase. This was the case in the previous example of the internal customer and supplier relationship between MFD (customer) and WFG (general contractor). In this example, a separate MPM project was set up to deal with the site prep phase.

The install, start-up, train, and ramp-up phases are all excellent areas to establish MPM. In particular, these are areas in which, at a minimum, participation from the customer and supplier should be encouraged even if the project does not have sufficient strategic value to warrant a leadership team. The ramp-up and warranty phases overlap into the normal operation and are often not considered part of the project. However, they can also add value when structured as part of MPM.

Before proceeding with an MPM project, you must layout a preliminary organizational structure for managing the project. This involves looking at all the various phases of the project and organizations involved to identify where an MPM or operations approach is appropriate. In each phase appropriate for MPM, a multi-company team is created to manage the project phase by applying the Six C process groups as explained in subsequent chapters. The phases using the operational approach are then linked back to the MPM organizational planning and review process via specific interface events. The following four steps in conjunction with the two rules summarize the process for identifying the MPM organizational structure:

Four-step process for defining MPM project organizational structure:

1. Using the previous list of phases, delete and add phases as appropriate
2. Identify each phase as unique to the project or on-going and repetitive
3. Review list of unique phases for possible consolidation and renaming
4. Agree on project phases to use MPM according to the two rules listed below and identify participants
   Rule 1—If the phase is customer focused and unique, use MPM
   Rule 2—If the phase is ongoing or repetitive, use company operational framework to manage the phase as part of its ongoing operation and link it to MPM via specified interface events

The typical equipment acquisition project consists of ten phases: *specify, lead, engineer, manufacture, transport, site prep, install, train, start-up,* and *buyoff.* These phases overlap each other, and the time to complete each one will vary depending on the magnitude of the project. For example, Figure 1.5 is a macro timeline for a typical new transfer-press system. The timeline consists of overlapping phases from purchase order to the completion of the start-up phase and is 30 months in duration. In this example, performing each step in sequence without any overlap would cause the 30 months to increase to 54 months. This example provides a baseline for the balance of the MPM process discussion.

The *specify* phase is considered the customer's responsibility, and falls outside the scope of the project. Applying the preceding four-step process to the baseline example yields the generic organizational structure that provides the framework for this text. It consists of a leadership team for the lead phase, an engineering team for the engineer phase, an installation team for the combined install and site prep phases, and a start-up team that covers the start-up, train, and buyoff phases. The chart in Figure 1.6 summarizes the resulting organizational structure, identifies participants, defines relationships, and details approximate timing for each phase. Note that the engineering, installation, and start-up teams all link to the leadership team via the project managers. In addition, the start-up team also links to the engineering team via the lead engineers, who are common to both and to the installation team via the site engineers, skilled tradesmen, and OEM supervisor. The project timeline on the left shows how the various MPM project phases overlap.

The manufacture and transport phases are considered the supplier's responsibility—operations executed within its own organization that use existing operational management processes. Specific interface events will link the manufacture and transport phases to the MPM structure. For the purposes of this discussion, a single OEM and its suppliers provide the project. This assumed organizational structure makes it easier to understand the task explanations and associated terminology. It also provides a structure that project managers can reference when building their own organization process. As stated earlier, this preliminary proposal requires modification and approval by the customer's and supplier's senior executives and the leadership team they create.

It is a good idea to define a set of deliverables for each MPM team to keep the focus on the results and help define roles and responsibilities. The chart in Figure 1.7 is an example of a preliminary proposal of deliverables to support the organizational structure defined previously. The general deliverables apply to all MPM teams, followed by specific deliverables for each of the four MPM teams in the structure.

Project timeline in months

Project phase	-4	-2		2	4	6	8	10	12	14	16	18	20	22	24	26	28	30
Specify	4 Months																	
Lead					30 months													
Engineer					14 months													
Manuf.						13 months												
Transport											3 months							
Site prep										6 months								
Install												8 months						
Train														4 Months				
Start-up																4 Months		
Buy off																		2 mo

Figure 1.5 Typical new transfer-press project timeline

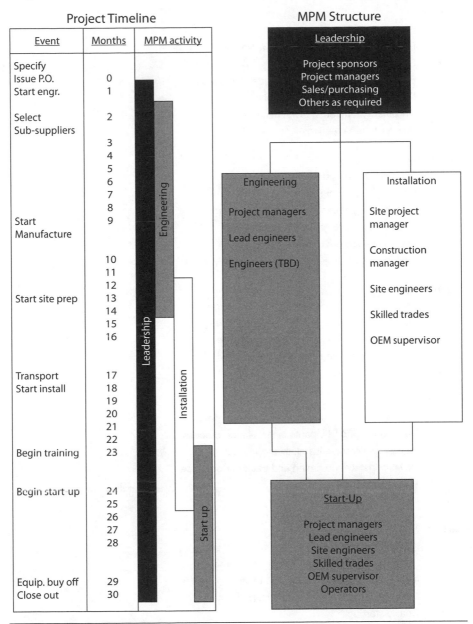

Figure 1.6 MPM project team structure

General

- Establish group norms
- Build trust through individual awareness
- Share organizational structures
- Build team participation and leadership skills
- Meet project timing requirements
- Document all meetings with minutes
- Plan for future meetings

Leadership

- Establish mission statement and goals
- Create and maintain situational matrix
- Establish engineering and installation teams
- Ensure issues are resolved or delegated
- Assess risk factors to project
- Monitor overall project xecution

Engineering

- Adhere to project mission statement and goals
- Identify and resolve engineering open issues
- Elevate unresolved issues to leadership team
- Develop engineering timing and track performance
- Quality system design

Installation

- Adhere to project mission statement and goals
- Define roles of participants in installation process
- Identify and resolve installation open issues
- Develop installation timing and track performance
- Plan visit to OEM
- Quality installation

Start up

- Adhere to project mission statement and goals
- Define roles of participants in start-up process
- Identify and resolve open issues related to start up
- Develop start-up timing and track performance
- Quality start up

Figure 1.7 MPM project team deliverables

PROCESS INITIATION

Initiation of MPM begins with a study of the process and methods outlined in this book followed by a workshop to define the basic project phases, organizational structure, and deliverables to fit the specific company's business and organizational culture. In addition to defining the organizational structure, the workshop builds understanding among key leader participants, provides experiential learning of techniques employed in MPM, and defines a pilot plan to test the workshop results in an MPM environment. Next, project selection requires assessing the strategic value of each project for appropriate customer and supplier entities to identify projects that meet the definition of a strategic project for the customer and supplier. After identifying a strategic project, the initiating company follows the pilot plan developed for MPM, starting with the formation of the leadership team.

The leadership team membership described in the MPM project team structure is one possible combination. Project sponsors and managers are required. However, the balance of the leadership membership is subject to the culture and business circumstances prevailing at the time. The role and authority of sales and purchasing personnel with respect to the sponsors varies between companies. For example, in large organizations, the sponsor and purchasing representative carry equal authority and issuance of a purchase order requires approval of both. Purchasing provides a form of check and balance to ensure orders follow company procedures. While in a smaller company the purchasing agent functions more like an administrative resource following the direction of the sponsor. Frequently in smaller companies, the sponsor has a dual role of sales agent. Thus, it is a good idea to conduct an internal workshop with representatives from all key disciplines to define the specific membership that is right for your company; it may be that many workable variations are possible. For example, other leadership participants might include department heads from engineering, service, planning, manufacturing, maintenance, construction, or finance. When replacing sales or purchasing personnel, project managers should remember their objectivity value and ensure that objectivity exists in the project organization. Care is required to establish sufficient participation that will allow flexibility to such an extent that one person's absence does not inhibit effectiveness, the number of participants enables efficient use of everyone's time, and the group has the ability to meet regularly in varied locations while avoiding exorbitant travel expenses for the participating companies.

The customer frequently carries out initiation of the leadership team because the customer has the greatest influence over the project. However, other key parties that assume the role of project supplier such as the OEM, architect, general contractor, or engineering house can also initiate the process, provided they have the full support of the customer. Unlike internal company projects that have assignments made within the company organizational structure, participation on the project leadership team is purely voluntary, particularly for the project sponsors. Since this represents a role that is out of the ordinary for the typical project sponsor, the initiator must identify and meet personally with each sponsor. The purpose of the meeting is to outline MPM and secure their voluntary commitment to participate.

Once all parties agree voluntarily to participate in MPM, the leadership team formation process can begin. Since leadership teams consist of sponsors who are peers, it is best to structure the initial meeting with cochairs and rotate the assignment in subsequent meetings. The customer sponsor is one of the cochairs, and the other cochair is the initiating company's sponsor. In cases where the customer is the team initiator, the customer selects a cochair at their discretion. The cochairs choose the critical suppliers together and invite them to join the leadership team. The initiating company has responsibility for all planning related to the leadership formation event, while the cochair provides the facility and acts as host for the event. The event requires a face-to-face meeting for all participants that generally lasts for two days. The initial meeting design provides experiential learning of selected Six C techniques and covers the first three of the Six C process groups: *cooperate, communicate,* and *coordinate.* During this event, leadership completes most of the leadership responsibilities related to project initiation and planning.

Every team formation regardless of type follows this pattern, but the type of team formed determines the techniques to use from the three process groups and the specific project management deliverables. As each MPM team goes through its formation event using these three process groups, it generates deliverables contributing to project initiation and planning requirements. It is important to maintain a good pace that adds value while allowing everyone to contribute. Covering this content in one day is not practical since it restricts the sharing of ideas, limits the time needed to build relationships, and severely curtails any action-plan development. Trying to extend it beyond the two days increases the difficulty in scheduling participants—particularly senior management—lacks urgency in following the agenda, and is not an efficient use of resources (e.g., time). The checklist in Figure 1.8 is a guide for setting up the initial leadership meeting and can be adapted to the other team formation events.

Project title _____

Customer _____ **Supplier** _____

Key executive _____ **Key executive** _____

Project manager _____ **Project manager** _____

#	Activity	✔
1.	Establish strategic value of project to your company & secure support from your key executive	
2.	Schedule meeting between initiating company and the other customer or supplier key executives	
3.	Present merits & requirements of MPM & determine strategic value to partnering organization	
4.	Secure agreement between customer and supplier to implement the MPM approach	
5.	Agree on leadership team participants	
6.	Agree on place, date, and duration for leadership formation meeting	
7.	Verify meeting facility and equipment (checklist Chapter 4)	
8.	Arrange refreshments, lunch	
9.	Finalize leadership agenda (template Chapter 4)	
10.	Prepare & send invitations signed jointly from both customer & supplier	
11.	Customer & supplier assign agenda topics to participants	
12.	Review available materials on agenda topics from text & other sources as appropriate with assigned topic leaders	
13.	Review final presentation content	

Figure 1.8 Pre-leadership formation checklist

This book has free material available for download from the
Web Added Value™ resource center at *www.jrosspub.com*

PART I: MULTI-COMPANY PROJECT ORGANIZATION, INITIATION, AND PLANNING

Applying MPM Process Groups

Chapter 2: Cooperate

Chapter 3: Communicate

Chapter 4: Coordinate

OVERVIEW

Chapter 1 provided an overall concept of multi-company project management (MPM) in terms of benefits, process design, application, and organizational structure. Part I describes the activities involved in forming project teams for each MPM phase, which encompass the first three MPM process groups, *cooperate*, *communicate*, and *coordinate*. Many project organizations leave activities from the *cooperate* and *communicate* groups to chance without providing a structure to build these elements into the organization. MPM provides specific activities and structure for cooperation and communication to develop organization maturity and effectiveness.

In MPM, there are three basic types of teams: *manage*, *design*, and *work*. Generally, there is one manage and one design team, with all others being work teams. In our equipment acquisition project example, leadership fulfills the manage function, engineering the design function, and installation and start-up the work functions. Each of the next three chapters covers a specific process group, which addresses activities for all three types of teams.

Project management teams perform work in a variety of configurations such as individual assignments, subgroups by function or company, and subgroups or total group that are cross-functional and cross-company. The initial formation activities employ these configurations to build experiences with the different modes. The activities start with individual assignments and gradually build to the more complex cross-functional, cross-company configuration. Each activity places a heavy emphasis on collaboration and consensus decisions, which provide important experiential learning for the participants. One objective of the team formation process is to get each project team functioning in a total cross-functional, cross-company configuration when developing action plans and schedules to take maximum advantage of the collaboration opportunities in a multi-company project.

During formation, organizations are in their infancy and require direction, structure, and training. To meet this need, the exhaustive explanations of activities and tools enables project managers and other project participants to lead their facilitation and use them without further training or support. Thus, the descriptions may appear unnecessarily detailed in construction, but this is vital for the practical application objectives of this book.

Chapter 4 contains a *Putting the Organization Together* section that assembles all the ideas using a set of recommended agendas for applying the activities to each team type. Any project organization can use the agenda designs by simply assigning project-specific participants to the agenda topics. A summary matrix identifying the activities to specific process groups and team types provides an overview.

Thus, understanding how all the elements fit together in the final MPM team-building formula becomes crystal clear by the end of Chapter 4.

From a project management perspective, Part I encompasses project initiation and planning, which are critical to any successful project. Project leaders and participants, in their desire to get started on the project, frequently fail to recognize the importance of initiation and planning in terms of the effect they have on the project results and the customer's overall satisfaction. As a result, they do not give initiation and planning the necessary time and attention that would ensure success. The formation of the various project teams occurs over the life of the project. In the project timeline discussed in Chapter 1, the leadership team forms the first month, engineering forms the second, installation forms month 12, and start-up forms month 23. Each project team as part of the MPM team-building process must contribute to the project initiation and planning activities that drive the progressive elaboration aspect of project management. Therefore, initiation and planning activities still occur 23 months into the project. The MPM process makes sure that the initiation and planning activities receive sufficient time and thoroughness by making them an integral part of the structured MPM team-building process.

As the MPM team-building progresses, the activities generate the deliverables for creating the project baseline schedule. These deliverables are:

- Project charter
- Project phases and organization structure
- Work breakdown structure
- Task dependencies network
- Task list (estimated time and resource)
- Interface event or milestone chart
- Project schedule baseline

## 2

COOPERATE

This chapter covers the activities, tools, and techniques involved in building multi-company cooperation for all types of MPM teams. This particular process group translates directly from multi-company management, and thus contains primarily the interpersonal aspect of team building. In the context of the two-day organization formation event, this represents the first half-day. Cooperation is a core ingredient of any successful personal or business relationship. In a multi-company process, it is important to design it into the relationship from the start. Thus, it is the first of the Six C process groups addressed. Mandating cooperation between organizations is not practical since it lacks the personal element needed for true cooperation. Building bonds among individuals within the organizations based on trust, respect, understanding, and mutual goals develops cooperation. Once cooperation is established, truth, integrity, and commitment provide the nourishment to sustain and grow cooperation. This chapter addresses the use of various tools for creating cooperation among the individuals of customer and supplier companies and discusses the variations that are appropriate for the different project teams. It covers the objectives and associated tasks listed in Table 2.1 along with identifying the appropriate team application.

Each task description follows a common format that begins with an overview of the task as well as any prework requirements. Then, the task description explains the overall process in detail along with listing the expected deliverables. In many cases, sample charts or other aids are included. Readers can go to the publisher's website for a free download of any checklists or agendas presented in this text for the reader's use in building their teams.

Table 2.1 Cooperation objectives and tasks

Objective	Task/tools	Team application
Defining the environment	Norms	All teams
Building linkages	Personal history	All teams
	Personal history alternate	All teams
Roles and responsibilities	Organizational chart	Leadership
	Situational matrix	Leadership
	Responsibility chart	Engineering
	RASIC chart	Install/startup

DEFINING THE ENVIRONMENT

Any group meeting requires a set of norms to guide their conduct. At one extreme, a group may adopt a formal set of rules such as *Robert's Rules of Order*. At the other, there may be no documentation at all. Even at the extreme of publishing nothing, in reality, each person has his or her own code of conduct based on culture, experience, and individual beliefs. In the latter case, the unwritten personal norms can vary substantially among the group members. This difference in norms can cause irritation and conflict, reducing the effectiveness of the group. Simple things such as dress codes, meeting timeliness, and phone interruptions can cause small issues, and other areas can cause major conflicts. Some examples of areas that have the potential to cause major conflicts are disrespect, withholding information, dishonesty, lack of participation, hyperparticipation, and lack of discretion or breach of confidentiality.

Establishing and posting a set of norms from the start when organizing a group minimizes and perhaps avoids many conflicts that often occur within groups. When conflicts do occur, referring to the posted norms can resolve the conflict quickly and objectively without the destructive and lingering effects of a perceived personal confrontation. A formal set of norms has the added benefit of enabling a new member to quickly be a productive participant of an established group.

Think of norms in terms of four categories: *structure, interpersonal, communication*, and *attitude*. A complete set of norms addresses all four categories. The following are a few examples of the type of items in each category:

- *Structure:* dress code, agenda, minutes, timeliness, breaks, pagers
- *Interpersonal:* respect, trust, equality, honesty, hidden agendas
- *Communications:* listening, asking questions, building on other's ideas
- *Attitude:* outlook, support, risk, humor, commitment

Figure 2.1 lists typical norms that have proven to serve as successful foundations for effective organizations. Terms should not be forced on a group when developing the norms. Groups should come up with ideas in their own words. Further, it is unproductive to try to capture every item on the list. Instead, only the norms that are most critical to the group and situation should be captured. The list should also be kept open-ended to allow for future additions. However, it is necessary for each group to identify the items in each of the four categories. Structure is the easiest item, is the type of item usually offered first, and is lowest on the scale of

Structure

>   Start and end meetings and breaks on time
>
>   Prepare ahead of the meeting
>
>   Issue agenda ahead of meetings
>
>   Maintain focus on the agenda items
>
>   Minimize disruptions (phones & pagers on vibrate)
>
>   Document with minutes approved by the group

Interpersonal

>   Open and honest
>
>   Avoid hidden agendas
>
>   Treat others as equals
>
>   Encourage everyone to participate
>
>   Treat each other with respect and trust
>
>   Complete assignments as promised

Communication

>   Follow practices of a good listener
>
>   Never criticize another's idea
>
>   Encourage building on other's ideas
>
>   Encourage questions to build understanding
>
>   Maintain confidentiality of group discussions
>
>   Avoid the use of sarcasm in all communications

Attitude

>   Express optimism and be positive
>
>   Treat problems as opportunities
>
>   Willingness to take measured risks
>
>   Keep an open mind
>
>   Utilize humor and have fun
>
>   Commit to organization goals

Figure 2.1 Typical norms of effective teams

The main deliverable is the establishment of a list of norms for the group that are published with the minutes. The group then reviews these norms at each meeting, updates them as required, and uses them to regulate behavior to keep the group on track. This exercise helps to break the ice and gets people talking. It encourages participation, demonstrates a consensus process, and allows everyone to contribute to the process.

BUILDING LINKAGES

Differences between individuals are beneficial when creating ideas and a weakness when building cooperation. There are many sources creating differences such as culture, personality, family background, education, religion, work experience, individual skills, fundamental beliefs, etc. Every project organization needs creativity and innovation. Therefore, embracing these differences and structuring the organizations to take full advantage of them is a requirement. The two most effective ways to bridge the gap between these differences and achieve cooperation is to build an understanding of the differences and identify common linkages between the individuals. Each difference is tantamount to posing a barrier or filter that inhibits the flow of information and each common linkage is comparable to an information path. Building an understanding of the differences reduces the barriers and opens the filters that inhibit information flow, while building linkages creates additional information paths. This combination of understanding the differences and building linkages increases communication quantity and quality, thus fostering cooperation and creativity.

After the norms define the environment, the next step toward cooperation is creating both linkages and understanding between the participants. Anything individuals have in common such as personal interests, culture, business interests, or beliefs will establish linkage, which helps individuals to identify with each other, aids in understanding, and encourages respect. The three elements of identity, understanding, and respect create a platform from which trust grows. In the normal multi-company business environment, this requires a lot of one-on-one contact between specific individuals over a long time. The personal history exercise provides an efficient means of building connections and understanding between participants in a short time at the start of the project to realize benefits over the entire project. By doing this exercise as a group activity, everyone gains awareness of the group's collective skills and experiences while acquiring insight into each individual's values and motivation.

Personal History. The personal history task requires that each individual describe themselves in terms of their family, education, work experience, likes, and dislikes.

A facilitator leads the process by giving out the assignment and organizing the report.

The process starts with the facilitator instructing everyone to use colored markers and one sheet of chart paper to create a personal history. They can use pictures, letters, and numbers, but cannot use words. The facilitator should allow participants to organize the chart to suit their individual tastes. Differences in the chart are typical, such as variations in orientation (portrait or landscape) and in presentation (sequential, quadrant, or storyline). Some may use a variety of colors to liven the chart's visual impact. All this creativity adds individualism to the charts and value to the exercise. The task should take 30 to 45 minutes to complete. When done, participants place their first name in the upper right corner of the chart and tape or pin the chart on the wall.

Facilitators or project managers may find themselves repeating this task multiple times for each group that they manage. The tendency to make a single chart for reuse in this exercise should be avoided, as this disengages the facilitator from the rest of the group. It is important that the facilitator or project manager demonstrates the same commitment to the task as does everyone else. Instead, the facilitator's goal should be to add more creativity to improve on previous efforts.

Once everyone has completed the chart, each person stands up to present his or her personal history. It is best to ask for volunteers and let the group determine the sequence of the presenters. The facilitator explains that the personal history charts will remain on the wall for the remainder of the two-day session and then discarded. Figure 2.2 is a sample personal history chart drawn in a sequential format. The time constraints, skills, and creativity of the participants produce a wide range of results. Artistic skills are not a requirement for this exercise, and can run the gamut from the child-like drawing in the example to more sophisticated drawings that one might expect from a professional artist. The importance of the need to explain the drawings should be obvious from the sample. In this example, the top row of pictures represents the individual's family consisting of his wife of 40 years, two married daughters, four grandchildren (ages 14, 6, 3, and 6 months), and an unmarried son. The second row describes his education and experience, which include degrees from General Motors Institute and University of Michigan in electrical engineering, military service as a construction electrician, and work experience in engineering and manufacturing in automotive stamping facilities in Michigan and Ohio. The third row symbolizes *Likes,* including golf, sailing, water-skiing, and tennis. The fourth row covers *Dislikes,* such as people working in different directions, raw meat, and eating with chopsticks.

The main deliverable of this exercise is building personal awareness among the participants, which helps to create trust and respect within the cross-company, cross-functional organization. The use of pictures (as opposed to words) levels the playing field, since it is unlikely that everyone will be at the same level of education,

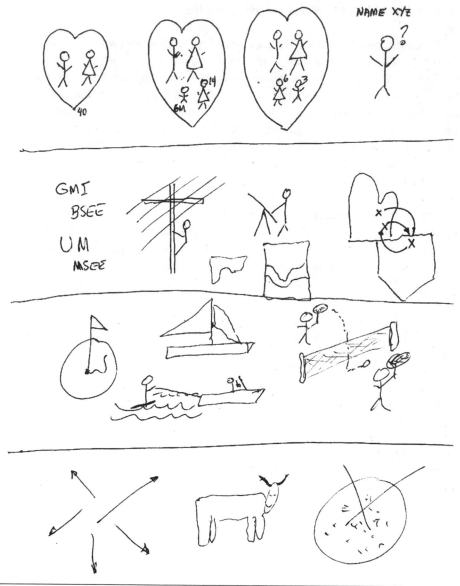

Figure 2.2 Personal history chart

and some participants may be from foreign countries where English is not the primary language. The pictures depict an individual's primary thoughts to help others remember. During each presentation, participants identify elements of commonality between themselves and everyone else. As everyone presents their education and experience, they help build a level of respect with each other. The structure of this exercise requires everyone to participate equally, which sets a good example for the remainder of the two-day event. Generally, through the pictures and presentations, there is some lighthearted joking and fun, which sets a good environment.

This exercise has a few areas of sensitivity. Depending on an individual's personal circumstance, certain family aspects may be delicate. Thus, let each person provide his or her own definition of family and be careful in asking questions that delve into areas not shown on the chart. Another area of sensitivity is education. In all my experience with leadership and engineering groups, this has never been a problem. These participants are highly educated or have credentials due to their experience. In general, they all take pride in their educational accomplishments. However, the educational backgrounds of each team should be considered to determine if education could be a potential sore spot and if so, participants should be asked only about experiences and not about formal education.

Personal History—Alternate. The personal history task described above can become rather repetitious for the project manager who is also involved in the leadership, engineering, installation, and startup; there may be multiple installation and start-up events if multiple sites are involved. This alternate method is one of many variations employed to add variety to this exercise. In this alternate, the group divides into pairs. The task is to describe each person's assigned partner in terms of family, education, work experience, likes, and dislikes.

The facilitator starts the process by pairing off the group, being careful to put together those who do not know each other where at all possible. The facilitator has each person fill out a chart that describes his or her partner's family, education, work experience, likes, and dislikes. The facilitator uses his own discretion in determining if words may be used. When the chart is complete, the facilitator asks each pair to write the creator's name in the lower right corner of each chart, the partner's name in the upper left corner of each chart, and then post the two charts on the wall.

Once everyone is done, each person stands and presents the completed chart, which should detail the personal history of their partner. It is best to ask for volunteers and let the group determine the sequence of the presenters. Personal history charts remain on the wall for the duration of the two-day session, at which point the charts are discarded.

Like the original personal history task, the main deliverable of this exercise is building personal awareness among the members, which helps to create trust and respect. It gets participants to open up, requires full participation, creates the desired linkages, and sets a good mood. In both personal history tasks, the education and experience helps build awareness of the skills and experiences of other members of the group. This becomes beneficial in the later stages of the project's planning and execution. On many occasions, participants have expressed amazement at how much they learned about personnel from other companies and from their own personnel as well. It is surprising that a simple exercise such as personal history reveals things about people you have worked with for many years. The resulting linkages benefit all participants.

There are many techniques offered under the heading of icebreakers for a meeting to help build cooperation, and facilitators are encouraged to try others. There are three key requirements for our purpose; (1) it must cover a broad range of topics to increase opportunity for linkage, (2) include work experiences, and (3) provide visual documentation of the results for referral during the balance of the workgroup formation.

One final thought on building an understanding that could prove useful when working on international projects: Cultural differences can take many different forms, but those driven by geographical continents such as North America, Asia, and Europe are the most significant. In one project using MPM with Japanese and American companies, the leadership held a one-day cultural training session taught by an outside expert in cultural differences. Participants from both the leadership and engineering teams attended. Even though most participants had traveled internationally, the training was eye-opening for all participants. The increased understanding of differences improved cooperation. For companies involved with international projects using the MPM approach, an investment in basic cultural training on a company or multi-company basis will yield improved understanding and cooperation on the current and future projects. Doing it on a multi-company basis has the added benefits of spreading training costs, building shared experiences, and linking the training to immediate application.

ROLES AND RESPONSIBILITIES

Lack of understanding the roles and responsibilities (R&R) is a major source of problems in project organizations that escalates exponentially when multiple companies are involved. A thorough job of clarifying these issues before the project begins reduces conflict and ensures coverage of all known aspects. It avoids problems that involve the management of people and the work they perform by identifying the individual and company responsible for each task. Before beginning the roles and responsibility exercises, it is beneficial to review project organizations from a big-picture perspective, as well as the advantages each offers. Understanding basic project organization structures helps to interpret the authority level of the project managers and the companies they represent.

Project Organization Structures. There are three basic types of project organizations: *functional*, *project*, and *matrix*. The matrix project organization has three
versions: *weak*, *balanced*, and *strong*. Figure 2.3 is a comparison of the *functional*
and *project* organizations that represent the two extremes. In the following organizational examples, the same letter designation for staff means they have the same
functional expertise, and the number differentiates the individuals. Staff with the
same letter designation report to the same manager in a functional organization.
In the project organizations, each staff person reporting to the project manager
has a different letter designation indicating different functional expertise.

Functional organizations are typical of companies that manufacture and sell
standard products involving repetition. The organization divides into groups that
perform the same function, hence the name *functional organization*. Projects are
a means for implementing company strategies in support of the company's mission. Members assigned to projects are normally part time since they have regular
job functions as well. Project leadership and coordination, as indicated by the
dashed-line box in the functional organization, is the responsibility of the functional managers. This is a fundamental structure representing most customers
involved in MPM. For small in-house projects, they employ this structure.
Generally, the importance of the strategic project and the range of functions
impacted will cause them to adopt one of the matrix-style structures for the specific project. The functional organization has the following advantages:

- Flexibility in staff assignments for fluctuating workloads
- Same experts can work multiple projects
- Functional expertise is concentrated for development
- Maintains commonality in the organization
- Reduces duplication, overlap, and repeat problems

Project organizations are typical of companies organized for the sole purpose of
completing major projects. The project is the company's product. Large construction firms undertaking multi-year building programs is one such example.
Government programs such as the space program and new military weapons systems are other areas where this form of organization is appropriate. The companies usually work on multiple projects at the same time and follow a specific
project management methodology. The project manager has full supervisory
authority over the project members who tend to be isolated, focusing only on their
project. In our equipment acquisition scenario, if the equipment supplier focuses
exclusively on large systems with high cost and multi-year time durations, it will
lean toward the project structure, but usually ends up with one of the matrix

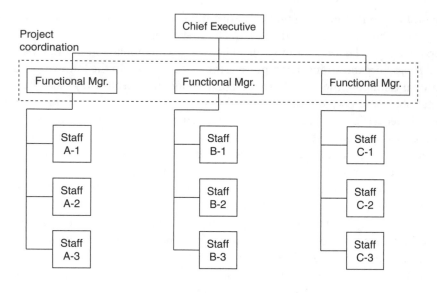

Functional organization

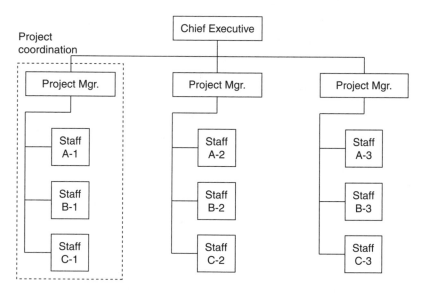

Project organization

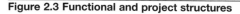

Figure 2.3 Functional and project structures

versions such as strong or balanced. The project organization has the following advantages:

- Dedicated project manager focusing on the project needs
- Dedicated project organization with central authority
- Simple organization with clear accountability
- Customer- and project-focused
- Fast communication, problem solving, and decision-making
- Aids cooperation and eliminates gaps between functions

As one might expect, the opposite of advantages for the functional and project extremes are the disadvantages for the other. For example, the functional structure has the advantage of staff flexibility but lacks a project manager. The project structure has the advantage of a dedicated project manager but lacks staff flexibility.

The matrix versions combine the advantages of the functional organization and project organization in varying degrees to aid in execution. The three versions of matrix organizations fall between functional and project. Figure 2.4 displays weak and balanced matrix structures and Figure 2.5 is a strong matrix structure. In all matrix structures, the project team is multi-functional and handles coordination. The major difference in structures is the existence and organizational position of the project manager. A weak matrix lacks a project manager, leaving the team to work as peers. In a balanced matrix, management selects one of the participants to fulfill the functional role of project manager. A strong matrix includes a dedicated project manager with a reporting relationship equal to or greater than that of the functional managers. The matrix structure provides both project and customer focus while maintaining functional expertise and company interests. Both project and functional managers have responsibilities. The project manager serves as an intermediary between the customer and supplier, and the functional manager decides how specific tasks are accomplished. The advantages are simply the sum of the functional and project advantages. However, the degree of achievement for each advantage is naturally lower than in the extreme structures. The matrix also introduces some new disadvantages that require careful management to avoid problems. The disadvantages are:

- Balance of power issues between managers
- Project members have more than one boss
- Accountability, mixed directions, and priority conflicts
- Must coordinate project and functional managers

In strategic projects utilizing MPM, the matrix structure is the predominate mode. The two critical points that affect the functioning of the entire process are the level of authority each project manager represents and their project management skills. Due to the existence of multiple companies, this authority varies between project

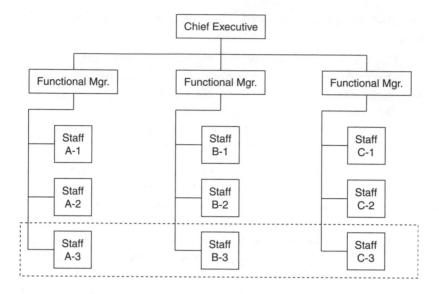

Weak matrix organization

Staff coordinates among themselves
One staff member is designated by management to coordinate

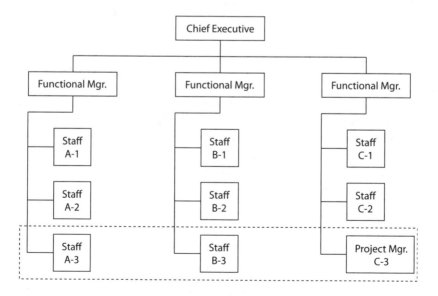

Balanced matrix organization

Project manager appointed with specific project authority

Figure 2.4 Weak and balanced matrix structures

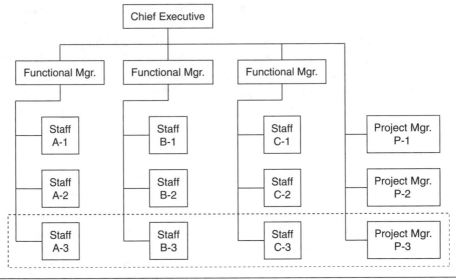

Figure 2.5 Strong matrix structure

managers based on the version of matrix structure that their company has adopted. Project management skills are a function of the individuals selected. Project managers with high-quality skills in a strong matrix minimize the leadership's intervention and decision-making requirements over the project's lifecycle. The leadership role will be mostly reviewing status, demonstrating interest, and cheering the project teams. If even one of the companies selects the weak matrix, leadership intervention and decision-making increases due to the stronger project manager's inability to secure the required agreements from the weak matrix team peers without leadership involvement. The weak matrix team peers—even with strong skills—simply do not have the authority to close agreements or fulfill commitments. If all the organizations utilize the weak matrix, it further compounds leadership's intervention and decision-making.

In the customer company, the importance of the functional organization in providing technical expertise and maintaining commonality for the plant operations precludes structuring projects in a pure project organization. In the equipment supplier company, functional organizations provide the most efficient utilization of technical resources and fit well with the traditional functional manufacturing operations, making pure project structures impractical. Thus, for both customer and supplier, a strong matrix structure is recommended for strategic projects, and a balanced or weak matrix structure is recommended for lesser projects, depending on the amount of cross-functional involvement. The lesser projects provide training opportunities for future functional and project managers.

The strong matrix structure places a heavy burden on the executive responsible for both projects and functional managers, yielding spans of control in the 15 to 20 range. Restructuring executive assignments into project and functional groups achieves a lower span of control, but drives coordination of functional and project managers as well as decision making higher into the organization and aggravates the problems associated with matrix projects. The MPM process is a major enabler for managing a large span of control involving diverse projects and sites. It provides an efficient way for the executive to focus energy on one project at a time in a regularly planned manner that easily integrates with other responsibilities.

Organizational Chart. The Project Management Institute uses a tool called the *Responsibility Assignment Matrix* (RAM) to link the organizational structure to the project work breakdown-structure. Large projects develop several RAMs in various levels of detail (*PMBOK® Guide* 2008, 221). The application of the RAM varies with the project phase and its location in the project lifecycle. Employing the RAM concept using a variety of tools tailored for each project team provides improved results and increases effectiveness. At the leadership level, the single-line organizational chart and situational matrix tasks provide the required R&R clarification. The engineering team uses a responsibility chart tool. The installation and start-up teams utilize the higher level detail provided by the RASIC chart.

The leadership formation occurs at project onset, and its role is to lead the project, The participants must understand the big picture; for them, it is critical that they understand the organization structures involved and the responsibilities of the participants within the organizations. The single-line organizational chart exercise fills this need.

The organizational chart exercise creates a single-line organizational chart for each company represented in the leadership from the top officer in the company to the key participants on the project. All participants in the leadership must appear on their company's organizational chart. It only shows reporting relationships related to the project. There is no prework required to avoid companies using their corporate charts, since it is desirable to create charts with the project as the centerpiece of thought. For example, assume that Company A decides to implement MPM for a $30 million system allocated to Plant 1. The Plant 1 manager assumes the role of *project sponsor,* and the project manager and purchasing agent participate on the leadership team with the plant manager. Figure 2.6 is a single-line organizational chart. It displays only the direct reporting relationships from the leadership participants and up. Obviously, the plant manager has many more reporting relationships, but only those directly related to the project appear. In this example, the engineering director was not included in the leadership. An alternative case is for the engineering director to fill the role of project sponsor,

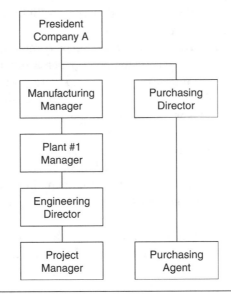

Figure 2.6 Single-line organizational chart

thus replacing the plant manager. In another case, both may participate, particularly if their future availability may be a problem.

Smaller, privately owned companies have more stable organizations with fewer personnel changes. Small companies will create organization charts in a few minutes and explain them just as easily. The organizational complexity of large companies can be overwhelming at times, and the frequency of changes can be staggering. For large companies, the organizational chart task can be challenging for the participants. In many cases, the participants from a large company may have debates with each other regarding the exact organizational structure and the presentations often require multiple charts and presenters. If it is difficult for the people who work within the company, then imagine how confusing it must be for outsiders. In one extreme case, a drive and control systems supplier was a participant on three different MPM projects over a five-year period. Each time the supplier presented their organization, it was a revelation with very little resemblance to prior presentations, both in structure and personnel assignments. In this age of mergers and acquisitions, this type of change is the norm.

The focus of this exercise is the leadership itself and the organization the participants report through to the top of their respective companies. This yields insight regarding the authority and influence each person has within their organization and collectively represents the power of the multi-company leadership.

Understanding the leadership role, individual responsibility, and authority greatly enhances cooperation and team effectiveness.

The process starts by dividing the leadership by company. Each company creates their own organizational chart using chart paper and markers. For this exercise, the groups are spread into breakout areas to work on the assignment. Each group posts their organization chart on the wall in the main conference room when complete and decides who will present the chart. Generally, it requires 45 minutes for this exercise.

Once the group reassembles, volunteers explain their organization charts to the group. Each group determines their method of delivery (e.g., single presenter, multiple presenters). During each presentation, the main group asks questions to gain an understanding of each organization. The charts remain up for the balance of the leadership formation event.

The main deliverable of this task is a set of single-line organizational charts. It is a good idea to transfer the charts to 8 1/2″ x 11″ sized sheets of paper and include them in the minutes. The presentations help participants to understand the roles and responsibilities of the various participants within their respective companies. This understanding of roles by the leadership members also helps to bring the group closer together. The process demonstrates the use of self-directed subgroups in accomplishing a simple, nonthreatening task and reporting to the main group.

Situational Matrix Chart. At the outset of project team-formation events, participants may have a certain amount of concern regarding what they are getting into and what is expected. The norms and linkage building followed with roles and responsibilities put most of this alarm to rest. However, in the leadership meeting, the company sponsors also have a concern regarding what they are committing their company to and how they are going to protect proprietary information. After all, how can one be open and avoid hidden agendas without disclosing company secrets or competitive strategies?

This was exactly the situation in my first MPM project. Four companies— General Motors as the customer, a Japanese press manufacturer as the supplier, and two U.S. suppliers of drives and controls as sub-supplierss to the press manufacturer—were the participants. The two U.S. sub-supplierss were fierce and capable competitors on the drives and controls. One had all the drives and the other all the controls on the multi-press project. Discussing their concerns lead to the realization that in any MPM project, even when direct competitors are not involved, the participants must serve two parties: the team and their company. In certain situations such as proprietary rights, competitive strategies, and pricing negotiation, the interest of the company supersedes the team. If one participant is protecting company interests while another is making a sacrifice for the project, the participant sacrificing for the project is at a great disadvantage and the other participant is violating the leadership norms. Think of the leadership environment as a network where everyone is linked, directly sharing information equally. However, the company interests such as proprietary information, strategies, and pricing are best represented by the traditional hierarchical business arrangement between a buyer and seller. Figure 2.7 illustrates these two relationships for this particular case. Note that in the hierarchical structure, communication exists only between the sub-supplierss and their customer—the press manufacturer. Whereas, in the network structure, everyone communicates on an equal basis. There are only three lines of communication in the hierarchical. In theory, sub-supplierss never talk to each other in the hierarchical. In the four-company network, six lines of communication enable everyone to talk directly to any participant or company.

For the case in question, all parties mutually agreed that both structures had their value and avoided trying to subvert the project or company interests to the other. It is necessary to agree on which structure to use in any given situation so that everyone is on an even playing field, and this led to the creation of the situational matrix. The situational matrix chart is a tool designed to solve this problem, and is a critical deliverable that is unique to MPM. The situational matrix tool addresses the specific need in MPM to identify when the participants work in a network structure and when they work in the traditional hierarchical structure. In addition, the situational matrix fills a secondary function by providing more insight of roles and responsibilities since each company also identifies a lead person for each of the situations defined in the situational matrix. Only the leadership

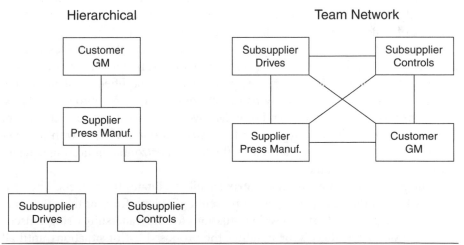

Figure 2.7 Hierarchical and team relationships

uses this tool since the other project teams take their direction from the leadership and this type of decision belongs to leadership.

Note that the situational matrix used to sort out network and hierarchical relationships in MPM, also has a parallel application in internal company teams involving a strong union. Many times unions will fear a partnership with management, thinking they will lose bargaining power, while management often fears a loss of authority. By using the situational matrix, union and management can define when to use the network process and when to use the traditional process, alleviating the fears of both parties and establishing a viable team process supported by both.

The purpose of the situational matrix task is to address concerns that companies have regarding the protection of their proprietary and negotiation rights as a company when working in a multi-company environment, as well as further clarifying roles and responsibilities. It involves listing all possible situations in which the leadership will have to operate over the life of the project, then agreeing on those situations in which the leadership will function as a network, and those that will require the traditional hierarchical relationship. It also identifies the point person in each organization for each situation. It is a self-directed, small-group company exercise. To aid facilitation, a designated person, usually from the company initiating MPM, prepares a mock situational matrix form containing a sketch of the hierarchical and network structures and a spreadsheet. Table 2.2 is a generic spreadsheet assuming a four-company project consisting of a customer, OEM, and two suppliers to the OEM. On the left, the spreadsheet lists situations that the leadership is most likely to encounter. Each company is assigned a vertical column to identify the point person for each situation. The last vertical column identifies the type of structure (network or hierarchical) for each situation.

A matrix for a specific project is created by modifying the network and hierarchical structures for the number of companies and the hierarchical relationships. The specific situation listings on the spreadsheet are modified to fit individual circumstances, then the company names are entered in the appropriate places. When there is only a customer and supplier involved, there is only one channel of communication to draw. In the hierarchical structure, it is vertical with the customer on top. In the network structure, the line is horizontal, indicating equality between the two companies.

The person who prepares the matrix usually facilitates the process. The process starts with the designated person presenting a blank form of the situational matrix with a proposed list of possible situations for the leadership. Using consensus, the group adds, deletes, or modifies the proposed list of situations until all possibilities are covered. Once the list of situations is agreed to, each company fills out its company's information in a breakout session. Each company fills out its own company's column with the prime contact person and designates the style of

Table 2.2 Situational matrix spreadsheet example

PROJECT ACTIVITY	Customer	OEM	Supplier #1	Supplier #2	Type
Improve the project management process					
Remedy unresolved delivery and performance variation					
Approve macro schedules					
Negotiate customer/OEM purchase/sales order changes					
Negotiate OEM/supplier purchase/sales order changes					
Approve purchase order alterations (POAs)					
Initiate purchase order alterations (POAs)					
Approve detail schedule changes					
Remedy cost, delivery, and performance variances					
Resolve disputes over technical issues					
Resolve mechanical engineering issues					
Resolve electrical engineering issues					
Manage the start-up process					
Manage the site preparation process					
Manage plant responsible installation					
Interface for turnkey installation					

relationship as *hierarchical* or *team network*. When each company completes its form, the entire group reassembles and reviews the results. The leadership must then reach concurrence on a single style of relationship for each situation.

The main deliverable from this task is a completed situational matrix chart with consensus agreement on the situations and relationship style that the companies will use with each other as well as the point person from each company for each situation. The group reviews and updates the matrix as required—incorporating new situations, organizational changes, etc.—during the course of the project. Similar to the organizational chart, it is a simple, small-group assignment, but the decisions are far more significant and the subgroup must get concurrence with the larger group to complete the matrix. This is typical of one type of approach that the leadership will utilize in some of its issue-resolution situations. The matrix chart also helps to clarify roles and responsibilities because of the specific assignments in the matrix.

Responsibility Chart. This task creates a responsibility chart for each company participating in the organizing event, which represents the facets of the organization associated with the engineering, installation, or startup of the equipment. All participants in the project team must appear on their company's chart. Only reporting relationships related to the project are shown. This is a self-directed small group exercise performed by each company. The responsibility chart differs from that of the organizational chart done by the leadership because the upper management relationships are less critical, and it provides more detail for the respective engineering, installation, or start-up organizations. In this exercise, peer relationships across the organizations are critical, and the focus is horizontal. This is particularly effective for the engineering group to establish a more cooperative design process. For example, using the previous Company A organization, assume the engineering team is comprised of the customer's project manager, electrical engineer, mechanical engineer, and safety manager. Then, Figure 2.8 represents the responsibility chart for Company A on the engineering team. Note that the chart spans more functions and does not show any levels above the engineering director. However, it does show the immediate supervisor for all Company A participants on the engineering team.

The facilitator begins the process by dividing the group by company. Each company uses transparencies with the appropriate markers. Transparencies have

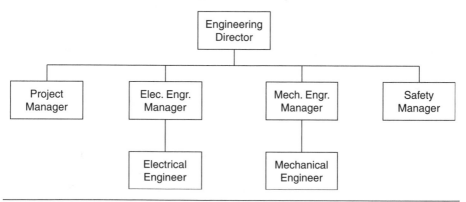

Figure 2.8 Responsibility chart

an advantage in ease of copying, and the participants will have the key information when the workshop is over. Generally, 30 minutes are required for this exercise. High-tech participants may elect to use computers to generate electronic copies and display them with an overhead projector.

The facilitator instructs the company-groups to draw the responsibility charts, showing the people who will be directly associated with the project, along with one or two levels of supervision. Responsibilities are listed for each person represented on the chart that detail their role in the project. The goal is to provide the other participants with a picture of the people who will be directly involved with the engineering, shipping, installation, and start-up aspects, and the people—usually supervisors of the participants—who will be involved when problems arise. Companies may elect to show upper levels of management to illustrate significant organizational links. An example of this is for the customer to show enough of the divisional organization to highlight the link between engineering and the plant. Companies may also elect to add phone numbers to the chart.

Once the group reassembles, volunteers explain their charts to the group. Each group determines their own method of delivery (e.g., single presenter, multiple presenters). The main group asks questions to gain an understanding of each organization. The charts are left up during the rest of project phase organizing event.

The responsibility charts are the main deliverables from this exercise. Participants should receive copies of these charts before the meeting is over. The presentations help the participants understand the roles and responsibilities of the various participants within their respective companies. The process also demonstrates the use of self-directed subgroups to accomplish a simple, nonthreatening task and report to the main group.

RASIC Chart. The installation and start-up phases generally need detailed information on specific roles and responsibilities as related to the work breakdown structure to avoid duplicating efforts, conflicting executions of multiple activities, and skipping activities. Chapter 3 explains the work breakdown structure in more detail as part of the scheduling process. For now, think of it as all the tasks required to complete the project. Since the installation and start-up team formations occur farther down the project timeline (e.g., installation at month 12 and startup at month 23), the project is better defined and project tasks are easily identified. This improved level of project detail makes this a useful tool for installation and start-up teams. The *PMBOK® Guide* suggests the use of a tool called a RACI chart, which identifies persons or groups who are responsible, accountable, consulted, and informed for a given activity (*PMBOK® Guide* 2008, 221). MPM adds *support* to this tool, and refers to it as a RASIC chart. It identifies key project stakeholders or groups and determines their level of involvement in the project. It is a full group exercise lead by a facilitator. A project manager can create a mock RASIC, which the group can then modify to fit their needs as prework prior to the meeting, expediting the exercise. This looks at everything related to the organization's assignment, including individuals or groups not represented. The focus is on looking at the actual project execution as defined by the work breakdown structure.

The project manager who prepares the mock RASIC usually leads the process. It is an important planning step to develop a complete list of project participants as well as their role and involvement within the project. The use of a RASIC model or chart is an effective tool used to document roles and responsibilities. Another benefit of the RASIC is that it helps to clarify communication channels for the project. In the RASIC matrix, the following code identifies each participant's involvement:

R = *Responsible* for completing the work
A = Authority to *approve* the work
S = *Support* in completing the work
I = *Informed* before, during, or at the conclusion of an activity without playing an active role in executing the project
C = *Consulted* to provide expert or technical information pertaining to an activity

The RASIC model identifies each step or activity of the project. The level of detail identifies either individuals or groups. A macro-level RASIC identifies departments or groups for components of the project, while a micro-level RASIC identifies individuals for specific activities. For both installation and startup, it is best to do a micro-level RASIC. In practice, the final RASIC is usually a combination of individuals and groups, since listing individuals beyond those represented in the organizing event may not be practical.

Every activity requires an *R*. The matrix allows one *R* for a given activity. If two *R*s are identified, the activity needs to be further divided or defined until only one responsible party is identified. Activities may or may not require an *A*, *S*, *C*, or *I*. Table 2.3 is a partial generic RASIC chart for an installation project phase. The model is utilized, updated, and referenced to define new activities or changes during execution of the project.

The main deliverable of this task is a *roles and responsibilities* chart (RASIC model) that identifies the involvement of the participants in executing the activities associated with the completion of the project, and represents agreement of all participants. This is a very effective tool in resolving conflicts, getting questions answered, and keeping the project moving in general.

Table 2.3 Sample partial RASIC for generic installation

Item #	Installation activity	Site				Constr.	OEM	
		PM	Engr	Skilled	Suprv	Contractor	PM	Engr
1	Agree on final equip layout	A	R	I	S	C	S	
2	Define miscellaneous plant items	A	S	R	C	I	I	
3	Define plant facility requirements	A	R	I	S	C		S
4	Estimate plant facility costs	A	R					
5	Estimate installation costs					S	A	R
6	Develop resource requirements	A		C	S	R	S	
7	Review plans with union	S		I	R		S	
8	Develop schedule for facilities	R	S	I	S	C	I	
9	Develop schedule for installation	A	C	I	S	S	R	S
10	Define in plant staging area	A	S	I	R	S	I	S
11	Supply mechanical parts list						A	R
12	Supply electrical parts list						A	R
13	Order spare parts	C	A	R			I	
14	Verify equipment delivery to plant	A	R	I	I	I	I	
15	Technical direction for installation	A	S	I	I	I	S	R
16	Manage installation personnel	A	S	I	S	R	I	S
17	Define plant logistics	A	R	I	S	S	S	C
18	Set up trailer for installation	I	I	R	A	I	I	I
19	Procure special tools for installation	I			A	R		
20	Conduct daily line up meetings	I			A	R		

SUMMARY

The *cooperate* process group defines the environment, builds linkages, fosters an understanding of differences, and defines roles and responsibilities. The methodology employed for the various activities utilizes the following group and subgroup combinations to provide the participants with experiential learning:

- *Define environment*—Full group using freewheeling brainstorming and consensus decision making
- *Building linkages*—Individual work requiring creativity and presentation to full team
- *Roles and responsibilities*—Subgroup work by company with presentation and consensus decisions by full group
- *Situational matrix*—Subgroup work by company with presentation and consensus decision making by full group

The activities in *Defining the environment* and *Building linkages* apply equally to all project phases with only minor adjustments to address educational concerns as required. However, the *roles and responsibilities* exercises are more project-phase specific and introduce the situational matrix for the leadership. Although the situational matrix only applies to the leadership team and is a subset of *roles and responsibilities*, the major purpose is to protect proprietary and negotiating rights of the companies working in MPM. This tool is unique to MPM and is a key enabler in building collaboration among multiple companies working in any project environment.

## 3

COMMUNICATE

Building cooperation among the project participants sets the stage for optimal communication—the second of the multi-company project management (MPM) process groups. When forming project teams, the activities associated with communicating occur during the second half of the first day and the first part of the second day. Project initiation occurs as a part of communication and involves the creation of the project charter, which consists of a *mission, goals, specifications*, the *scope of work, deliverables, assumptions*, and *resources*. Throughout these activities, customer and supplier expectations are essential to ensuring the maximum project satisfaction on behalf of all parties. This chapter also covers key communication tools including Internet conferencing, videoconferencing, and the communication plan that ties together all project teams and participants.

Figure 3.1—with apologies to General Motors—illustrates the importance of communication in the hypothetical situation of a father purchasing a car for his son. In this example, each person has an ideal car concept based on individual desires and needs. The father values economy, the dealer covets higher profits, the engineer craves all the latest technological gadgets, the manufacturer seeks higher volume, and the son desires speed and status. Multi-company organizations are no different; each individual has a view of reality based on individual perspective and company allegiance. For any project to be successful, it must effectively communicate to align the wants and needs of all the stakeholders. Failure to achieve alignment at the beginning of the project results in lost customer satisfaction. The humor in this illustration quickly fades when communication problems appear in a project.

In organizations, the number of communication channels grows quickly as participants increase. Figure 3.2 represents the communication network in a six-person team. The ovals represent the individuals on the team, designated as *A*

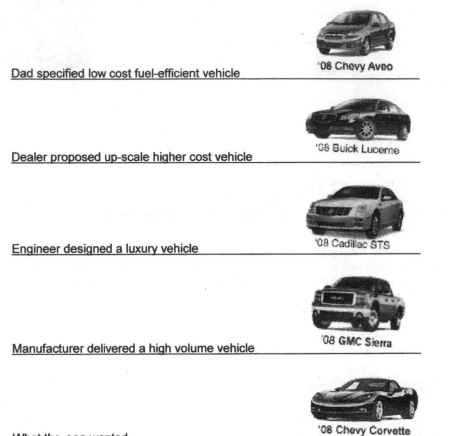

Dad specified low cost fuel-efficient vehicle   '08 Chevy Aveo

Dealer proposed up-scale higher cost vehicle   '08 Buick Lucerne

Engineer designed a luxury vehicle   '08 Cadillac STS

Manufacturer delivered a high volume vehicle   '08 GMC Sierra

What the son wanted   '08 Chevy Corvette

Figure 3.1 Father purchasing son's first car

through F, and the connecting lines represent communication channels between individuals. Counting the lines yields 15 communication channels. If N is the number of participants, the following formula represents the relationship:

$$\text{Communication channels} = [N\,(N-1)]\,/\,2$$

Communications involving multi-company organizations during the execution of projects are complex. Applying the formula to a typical twelve-person leadership group brings the number of communication channels to 66 per the following calculation:

$$N = \text{number of individuals in the group} = 12$$
$$\text{Communication channels} = [N\,(N-1)]\,/\,2$$
$$= [12(11)]\,/\,2 = 66$$

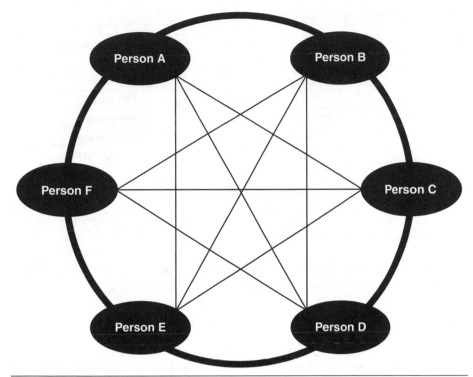

Figure 3.2 Communication channels in a six-person team

Factoring in the impact of the communication channels within the engineering, installation, and start-up teams; the channels between project teams; and the possibility of multiple sites that require multiple installation and start-up teams; the communication channel counts exceed one thousand. Considering the number of communication channels on a large project, it should be no surprise that project managers spend as much as 90 percent of their time on communication issues (Kerzner 2006, 233). The subject of communication is a field of study in itself and is beyond the scope of this book. The objective of this chapter is to present simple tools to facilitate communication in multi-company projects.

Communicate is a combination of the multi-company management's *communicate* and the project management's *initiate* process groups. The tasks used to support communication take different forms depending on the type of project team formed. This chapter covers the communication objectives and associated tasks or tools detailed in Table 3.1. The last column of the table identifies the team application for the task or tool.

The chapter organization is similar in format to the prior chapters in terms of task description. The task begins with an explanation of purpose followed by an

Table 3.1 Communication objectives and tasks

Objective	Task/tools	Team application
Mission and goals	Brainstorming	Leadership
	Categorization	Leadership
	Mission statement and goal setting	Leadership
Scope definition	Specification and engineering review	Engineering
	Statement of work	Install/startup
	Fact finding	Install/startup
Communication	Website	All teams
	Conferencing	All teams
	Video conferencing	Leadership/engineering
	Communication plan	All teams

overview of the process and pre-work requirements. The task finishes with a detailed process explanation and description of deliverables.

MISSION AND GOALS

Leadership is responsible for establishing the overall project objectives to focus all project phases on a common set of goals to maintain project alignment throughout the project lifecycle. They accomplish this responsibility using three tasks: brainstorming, categorization, and a mission statement and goals.

Brainstorming. This technique has been around a long time, is an excellent way to generate ideas without criticism, and is a common practice in many organizations. The speed of idea generation and the focus on quantity without judging causes participants to more freely express themselves. The leadership's broad business perspective and experiences brings significant value to the MPM process. The brainstorming exercise is a means of tapping into that information to augment the overall project. Using a structured activity with the full group and requiring open participation by everyone maximizes the ideas and encourages building on the ideas of others. Unlike most brainstorming, which focuses on a particular problem, the only requirement for leadership brainstorming is that it be applicable to either the project or final product. This keeps it as broad as possible and avoids limiting the topics generated. There are several variations on the brainstorming task, but I consider this specific approach to be the most effective in the leadership formation event.

The brainstorming task generates a list of concerns, risks, open issues, good ideas, questions, and recommendations directly related to the specific project or product. The task design encompasses the entire group with a facilitator leading the process; the intent being to get everyone to put forward all their thoughts and concerns—both positive and negative—related to the project or final product. The brainstorming rules ensure all ideas are treated with respect and without critique. The facilitator begins by reviewing the brainstorming guidelines in Figure 3.3.

1. Avoid criticizing ideas

2. Ask questions only for clarification

3. Avoid attempts to respond to items

4. Facilitator ensures he has properly captured each item

5. Facilitator goes around the room in order

6. Each person offers one item per turn

7. If not able to think of something immediately you "Pass"

8. Facilitator maintains a brisk pace

9. Record all items even if they are repeat or re-worded

10. Each item is numbered

11. Facilitator does not offer items

12. Rotate facilitation so the facilitator may input his ideas

Figure 3.3 Brainstorming guidelines

Once everyone understands the guidelines, the facilitator uses a round-robin approach, soliciting input from one point in the room and then proceeding in sequence around the room until everyone has had a chance to contribute one idea. The facilitator repeats the process until all ideas are exhausted. This encourages everyone to participate and prevents any one person from monopolizing the session or offering all ideas at once. The facilitator numbers the input sequentially in front of the group using a flip chart or preferably, an electronic board. Through this process, members see that others in the group share similar thoughts. Recording the results in front of the group is essential to providing visualization of the idea and ensuring recording accuracy. Admittedly, the round-robin exercise applies a small amount of pressure on everyone to come up with ideas, and searching for ideas only gets more difficult as the process continues, after the more common ideas have been used. This is precisely the atmosphere needed to gather everyone's thoughts, concerns, and improvement ideas for team consideration. When possible, a clerical resource (separate from the leadership) captures the brainstorming list using a spreadsheet during the session. This provides real-time minutes of the brainstorming, which will assist with subsequent tasks and provide a means to sort the data during categorization. If one of the participants performs the clerical task during the brainstorming, the participants rotate between this assignment and other functions as is done with the facilitator.

Looking for ways to build on previous ideas is a good technique to exploit. In brainstorming, the group is working toward the goal of generating as many ideas as possible; not only is using another's idea to create items okay, it is an essential part of maximizing the group's results. Here are four approaches to consider when building on another's idea (Harrington-Mackin 1994, 96–97):

- *Modify*—Using an idea already provided, modify or change the issue or concept to yield a new idea or perspective
- *Multiply*—Take the original thought and apply it on a larger scale
- *Subtract*—Take the original thought and apply it on a smaller scale
- *Substitute*—Apply the principles in the original idea to something else

Generally, a group of 15–20 people will develop 100–180 items in a 2–3 hour period. This equates to about one idea every minute, including the time it takes to record the idea to the originator's satisfaction. Facilitation should be shared with at least one or two others since the fast pace does not allow time for the facilitator to think of ideas while recording the thoughts of others. If an idea does not immediately come to mind on a person's turn, that person must pass. If there is no idea forthcoming on subsequent turns, that person must pass again. The process continues until everyone is out of ideas and everyone passes. Then, the facilitator opens it up to the group, asking if anyone has any other items to offer. The facilitator waits 20–30 seconds and asks again, pausing a second time. If there are no responses to the inquiry, the brainstorming session is closed. Usually, this last-chance process will yield several more ideas. Copies are then made of the brainstorming spreadsheet and distributed to everyone.

This completes the first day, although the brainstorming is not yet complete. Dinner and a night's sleep will allow time for the group to formulate additional ideas. The brainstorming session resumes the next morning, capturing any remaining items. It takes an additional one to one and a half hours before the group is exhausted of ideas and yields 25–50 added items. Repeat items during this time are to be expected.

A list of 125–230 brainstorm items representing concerns, open issues, good ideas, questions, or recommendations directly related to the project is the main deliverable from this task. This brainstorming process generally brings out basic project assumptions and many issues related to resources that become a part of the project charter. This brainstorming often uncovers side agreements, specification deviations, and scope modifications that occurred during negotiations prior to issuing the final purchase order. It is critical for everyone on the leadership team to have a common understanding of the issues in order to begin the process of aligning expectations. When using an electronic board, the deliverable is a package containing copies of the handwritten items from the board. Each member should receive this package immediately following the brainstorming. If available, a clerical resource can produce the list of items in the form of a typed spreadsheet.

Categorization. A list of more than 200 items can be overwhelming to any group. To make the ideas more manageable, the leadership must organize them into workable groups, summarize, prioritize, and create action plans. The categorization task fulfills the organizing function. The affinity diagram technique may be a more familiar term to readers. Categorization is a variation that does not use the sticky-note approach and creates the group headers before assigning items to a group. The results are the same but the methods are different.

This task provides a structured review of each item generated during brainstorming by assigning them into 3–6 major groups. It is a full group exercise lead by a facilitator. The process begins with the facilitator soliciting a list of general categories to classify all brainstorming items. This is not the time for the group to start generating the brainstorming issues all over again; these categories need to be broad concepts into which the brainstorming issues can fit. This requires the participants to consider all the issues with a big-picture perspective and is a key orientation needed when developing the mission statement. The group must reach consensus on six or fewer categories that will cover all brainstorming items. The facilitator then gives each category a number or letter designation.

The actual categorization involves the facilitator reading each item as quickly as possible and asking the participants to assign it to a single category. If there is a disagreement as to which category an item belongs, the originator is designated the subject-matter expert of the item and makes the call. *Each item is assigned to one category only.*

This process makes certain that everyone understands each item equally since, during brainstorming, people are thinking up ideas and may not have heard what others were saying. It also serves to refresh memories since there is usually a night between the beginning and end of the brainstorming session. Categorization is also a good time to consolidate duplicate items. The process of agreeing on a category serves to generate discussions to better clarify the item to others. Reviewing all the items collectively provides a complete overview of all issues immediately prior to establishing the mission statement in the next step. Finally, the grouping of all the items helps to facilitate subsequent tasks when dividing them into subgroups.

The task deliverable is each item assigned to a specific category. At a minimum, each participant will have a handwritten list with categories assigned. If a clerical resource is available, the list will be typed and sorted by the agreed upon categories.

Mission Statement and Goals. Trust, a sense of belonging, an understanding of interdependencies, and a commitment to a common purpose are the main differences that distinguish an effective team from just a random group of people. Setting the environment, building linkages, and defining roles and responsibilities addresses the first three items. The essential element in establishing the multi-company organization is commitment to a common purpose. The leadership mission and goals exercise defines the common purpose and generates commitment. The mission is a broad statement of the project's purpose, and the goals identify detailed objectives. The prior brainstorming and categorization tasks provide the requisite ideas and organization of thoughts to support this activity.

This task design divides the leadership into smaller workgroups consisting of multi-company representation and cross-functional skills. The task is to develop the overall mission and goals for the total project to guide all project teams and anyone else involved in the project. The facilitator starts the process by leading the group in dividing the categories previously identified into two or three workgroups, representing equal amounts of content. The key executives assign participants or take volunteers from their company for a specific workgroup. The facilitator and key executives ensure each workgroup is as functionally diverse as possible and contains the greatest mix in company representation. The key executives are spread equally among the groups, as are the respective project managers and sales personnel. The ideal configuration is to have groups which are balanced in size as much as is practical.

This task consists of two parts. First, each workgroup develops a mission statement for the total project. Mission statements should consider the diverse audience that the project covers—from equipment operators to company presidents—in all the organizations represented by the leadership as well as by selected suppliers. The mission statement should have value for all participants while clearly stating the project's objective.

In part two, each workgroup reviews the assigned categorized brainstorming items and develops specific quantifiable goals to ensure project success. The number of goals should be kept at a manageable level. Each goal must represent a significant facet of the total project. The acronym SMART is a useful tool to use in developing these goals (Kerzner 2006, 290). It stands for the following:

- *Specific*
- *Measureable*

- *Aggressive/achievable*
- *Realistic/reach*
- *Time bound*

In addition to proper structuring, the goals need to represent the span of the entire enterprise. I suggest setting goals in the following five major facets of the project represented by the letters SPQRC and defined as follows:

- *Safety*—First priority in any project
- *People*—Communication, relationships, organization
- *Quality*—Specifications, performance, deliverables
- *Responsiveness*—Timing and problem resolution
- *Cost*—Budget, profit, ROI

When each workgroup has completed their proposed mission statement and goals for the assigned categories, the full group assembles to reach consensus. Each group presents their mission statement, then the entire group blends all the mission statements into a single mission statement that everyone agrees to support.

Next, each group presents the goals they developed for their assigned categories to get buy in from the rest of the team. Compiling the goals from each workgroup makes the final list for the project. The goals should be simply stated, easy to understand, and measurable. The number of goals should be reasonable and significant to the total project.

The main deliverable from this task is a consensus mission statement and a clear set of goals for the total project. A second benefit is that through this process, the members experience working in cross-functional and cross-company subgroups. The mission agreement encourages the members to reach a consensus on words, while the goals require each of the groups to sell their ideas to the rest of the leadership.

It works well if someone from the leadership volunteers to make laminated pocket cards that include the mission statement and goals. Using laminated cards for the mission statement and goals gives them substance, makes them permanent, improves visibility, facilitates communication, and is an effective way to distribute hard copies to the participants. During the creation of these cards, the individual that accepts the assignment should have as much liberty as possible, being careful to remember that these pocket-sized cards have a maximum size of about 4" x 6". Figure 3.4 shows the card for the tandem press line project with mission and goals on the front (as shown on the left) and company logos of the participants on the back (as shown on the right). Figure 3.5 is the two-sided card representing the mission and goals for the AA5X interdivisional MPM site preparation project between General Motors' World Wide Facilities Group and Metal Fabricating Division referred to in Chapter 1. Here the front of the card on the left side displays the mission with the goals on the back or right side of the figure.

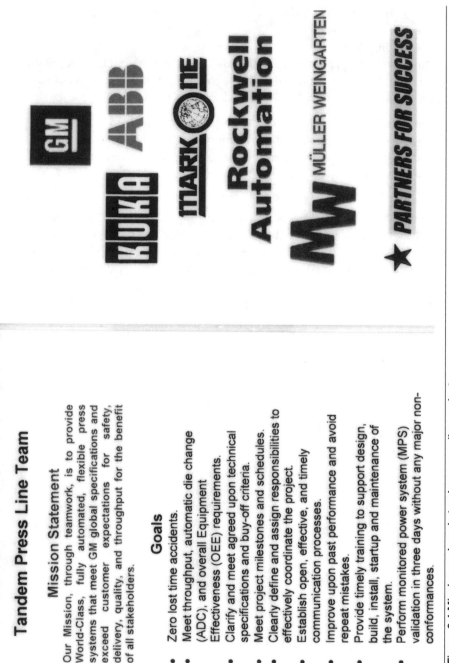

Tandem Press Line Team

Mission Statement

Our Mission, through teamwork, is to provide World-Class, fully automated, flexible press systems that meet GM global specifications and exceed customer expectations for safety, delivery, quality, and throughput for the benefit of all stakeholders.

Goals

- Zero lost time accidents.
- Meet throughput, automatic die change (ADC), and overall Equipment Effectiveness (OEE) requirements.
- Clarify and meet agreed upon technical specifications and buy-off criteria.
- Meet project milestones and schedules.
- Clearly define and assign responsibilities to effectively coordinate the project.
- Establish open, effective, and timely communication processes.
- Improve upon past performance and avoid repeat mistakes.
- Provide timely training to support design, build, install, startup and maintenance of the system.
- Perform monitored power system (MPS) validation in three days without any major non-conformances.

Figure 3.4 Mission and goals tandem press line project

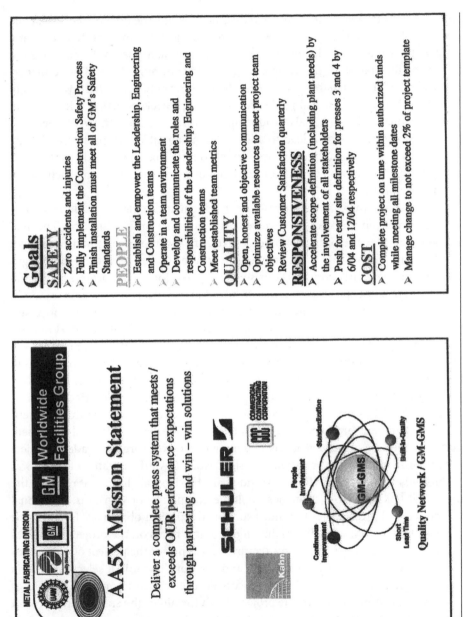

Figure 3.5 Mission and goals AA5X site preparation project

Unfortunately, the black and white text does not provide the full effect of the actual cards in color. In another case of the AA retrofit project, the mission statement and goals on the front or left side of Figure 3.6 repeats in Japanese on the back or right side of the illustration of the sample card to help communicate and build ownership with the OEM's Japanese workforce. It is common to see a slight variation in size between the mission and goal cards for each project reflecting differences in the companies and individuals producing them. In one case, the volunteer produced a 6" x 9" card, which lead to a lot of joking about which participant's shirt pocket was the template. It is also important to note that these cards are targeted for everyone in the project and do not contain team-specific items such as the leadership norms.

To maximize the value of the mission statement and goals, the leadership must communicate them to everyone involved over the entire project lifecycle. The mission and goals for the project should be fixed and promoted by publishing them with the minutes, posting them on a jobsite or website, and reviewing them regularly in meetings. This provides consistency of direction for all project teams and helps to align all people and activities involved in the project.

A major benefit of the MPM approach is its ability to maintain and foster organizational alignment throughout the project lifecycle. "In the context of capital facility projects, alignment may be defined more specifically as: The condition where appropriate project participants are working within acceptable tolerances to develop and meet a uniformly defined and understood set of project objectives" (Griffith and Gibson 2001, 70). Griffith and Gibson further describe organizational alignment as involving three dimensions. In our context, the three dimensions of alignment are vertical, horizontal, and time-based. Vertical alignment relates to the organizational levels of senior executives, project leaders, project participants, and project users who must all work toward the same objectives as established by the mission statement and goals. Horizontal alignment refers to the horizontal linkage across strategies, multiple companies or divisions, functional disciplines, and project sites that must support the project objectives. Finally, time alignment refers to the need to maintain this single focus on the project objectives throughout project execution. This requires constancy of the project objectives for all project teams: lead, engineer, install, and start-up. The initial selection criteria of a strategic project for the MPM process ensures the horizontal alignment of strategies and companies with the project. With the aid of the sponsor, the project manager should check this alignment at regular intervals to ensure that changes in the project or company strategies have not caused a misalignment, requiring corrective action. The mission and goal development, by the leadership and subsequent handoff to the project teams, supports the vertical alignment and aids functional, cross-company, and site horizontal alignment. The existence of the

AA レトロフィット ミッション ステートメント

GM向けIHI AAシステムの信頼性の向上

目標：：

パフォーマンスと信頼性

- システムの信頼性を向上し、機械の問題に依る停止時間を5%未満にする
- 2SPM速度アップ（14SPM W/10" LIFT、12SPM W/14" LIFT）
- 最大1時間で、交換可能な主要コンポーネントを交換する。
- 10年寿命（4000万 HIT）で、コンポーネントを設計する。
- 日本でのIATで、全ての適正テストを実施する。
- 最終目標：ハーバーレポートのNo.1を達成する。

コスト と 出荷

- スケジュール厳守。
- コストを上げない。
- 1号機で、マニュアルを配布し、トレーニングを実施する。
- 1号機で、予備品を準備する。
- 最終目標：2003年7月に、1号機を出荷。

据付工事

- 最小の停止時間で改造を完了する。（40日以内で）
- 安全上の問題で、時間をロスしない。

AA Retrofit Mission Statement

Mission
To improve the reliability of the GM-IHI AA systems.

Goals

Performance and Reliability
- Increase system reliability to less than 5% machine-related downtime
- 2 spm increase (14 spm w/10" lift, 12 spm w/14" lift)
- 1 hour maximum time to repair replaceable major components
- Components sized for 10-year life (40 million hits)
- Design fully validated with IAT in Japan
- Stretch goal: achieve #1 in *Harbour Report*

Cost and Delivery
- Meet schedule
- No cost creep
- Manuals and training delivered with first system
- Spare parts available with first installation

Installation
- Achieve minimum downtime conversion (<40 days)
- No lost time due to safety issues

Figure 3.6 Mission and goals AA retrofit project

leadership team for the entire project timeline combined with fixing the mission and goals for the course of the project drives the time alignment.

SCOPE DEFINITION

The leadership team provides the big-picture perspective of the project. The subsequent project teams dive into the details through the specification and engineering reviews, statement of work development, and fact-finding, which further defines the project scope. This information supports the subsequent *coordinate* process group, which involves the development of the work breakdown structures and creation of detailed schedules for managing the project activities.

Specification and Engineering Reviews. The first MPM applications used identical agenda and tools for all project teams regardless of the project team type. Although this works well for the norms and linkage building, it is not as effective in roles and responsibilities, and fails in brainstorming. The error in this identical approach was most obvious in the brainstorming activity. Using an identical brainstorming technique with engineering generates a huge number of duplicate items with the leadership brainstorming, which is wasted effort and causes confusion when referring to the brainstorming list. Repeating the brainstorming for the installation and start-up teams compounds the problem. The engineering, installation, and start-up teams must focus on specific details related to their responsibilities and need to devote their time to those issues to maximize value. The recognition of the three basic team types—manage, design, and work—resulted in the creation of specific tools for leadership, engineering, and the work teams of installation and startup. Specific tools for each team type first appear in the roles and responsibility section of the prior chapter on *cooperate*. This differentiation in tools flows throughout the balance of the MPM Six C process descriptions.

The specification and engineering review task involves the review of specifications and engineering status to ensure a common understanding. This task also generates a list of issues for engineering to address. Figure 3.7 is a generic agenda for conducting a specification and engineering review.

The specifications review provides understanding and seeks to discover any unknown pre-award conversations, additions to the purchase agreement, or any other expectations that might materially affect the project. The engineering review is necessary; even though the multi-company engineering team is formed early in the project lifecycle, since there is usually some engineering that has already been completed, and everyone should know this status. For example, the customer's engineers spend considerable time developing the specifications for the bid package, and the supplier's engineers perform preliminary engineering or reuse engi-

Specification and engineering review agenda

Specification overview	
Mechanical	Customer mechanical engineer
Electrical	Customer electrical engineer
Key points from pre-award meeting	Customer project manager
Customer processes	
Engineering change requests	Customer project manager
Documentation	or as assigned
OEM presentations	OEM project manager or
Mechanical engineering concept and status	as assigned
Controls architecture and status	
Timing of engineering reviews	
Subsupplier presentations	Supplier project manager or
Mechanical engineering concept and status	as assigned
Controls architecture and status	
Timing of engineering reviews	
Open issues review and assignments	

Figure 3.7 Sample specification review agenda

neering from prior projects when developing their response to the request for quote. To review the engineering status, each company must complete prework for this task. The customer must prepare a presentation on the specifications to the OEM. The OEM must report on the engineering status and on any specifications for its suppliers. The suppliers need to report on their engineering status. As part of the prework, the project manager from either the customer or OEM prepares the agenda for this portion of the meeting. Whoever generates the meeting agenda also takes responsibility for ensuring the preparedness of all parties.

In accordance with the prework agenda, the customer starts by presenting the primary aspects of the specification in an overview format. Next, the customer covers the key points from the pre-award meeting, engineering change request process, documentation requirements, and approval process. Then, the supplier and sub-suppliers present the status of the basic engineering mechanical concepts and electrical architecture in an overview format, along with the anticipated time-table for engineering reviews. During each presentation, the group generates a list of questions or issues. After each presentation, the group reviews all questions and attempts to answer all of them to everyone's satisfaction. The entire group—not just the presenter—answers the questions. For example, a sub-supplier might raise a question during the supplier's presentation concerning a particular component or functionality issue that require answers from the customer, or the presenting company may have representatives who raise questions that require answers from the other participants. Any unanswered questions and unresolved issues are then consolidated into an *open-issues list*. This task is great for soliciting group suggestions that might improve the overall project. These suggestions are also added to the open-issues list for follow-up. Chapter 4, *Coordinate,* discusses the open-issues list in more detail as part of action planning.

Just as was done in the leadership brainstorming, the facilitator needs to record all the issues and questions in front of the group using either a flip chart or preferably, an electronic board. This captures the issues to the satisfaction of the group. In addition, a clerical resource, if available, simultaneously records this information using a spreadsheet as was done in the brainstorming session. If a clerical resource is not available, the information should be recorded into a spreadsheet as soon after the session as possible. This is an excellent item to keep current and post on a project website for everyone to see.

The key deliverable from this task is an open-issues list for engineering. This process clarifies any technical questions, increases the supplier's understanding of customer specifications, and results in everyone having the same expectations of the engineering process. The open nature of the discussion with all participants fosters collaboration and gives the voice of the customer proper consideration. It helps avoid many problems in the future and sets a solid direction for engineering. It also helps the engineers to see how their own work fits into the total project picture.

Statement of Work. The leadership and engineering team formations occur early in the project, while the installation and start-up team formations occur closer to the middle or end of the project. The time between the engineering and installation team formations is when the design and manufacture of the equipment occurs. This represents a significant portion of the project lifecycle. In this interval, the project acquires a great deal of information and answers many questions. Leadership and engineering use the mission, goals, and specifications to determine the initial scope. Work teams such as installation and startup need a more structured scope definition to meet their unique requirements. The extensive information available at this time enables this scope definition. The statement of work task provides the structure.

The statement of work task defines the scope of the installation or start-up phases of a project. This establishes group expectations and understanding of the boundaries, deliverables, and measures of success. This is a group exercise, since everyone must contribute and understand its content. The *statement of work* form in Table 3.2 offers a structure to assist the facilitator in this task. Prior to the exercise, the facilitator needs to be comfortable with the statement of work form, format, and definitions.

Table 3.2 Statement of work format and definitions

Statement of work
Date: _____
Team participants: _____
Project title: A short, concise statement identifying the project usually found in the mission statement.
Purpose: The purpose of the project explains why the work is required. It relates directly to the mission statement and goals.
Project background: Describe the history of the project. Supply information that explains the philosophy of the project. The project background should include information on the history, justification, consequences, and uniqueness of the project.
Deliverables: Describe the output of the project in terms of promises to the customer. These are usually found in the goals.
Measurable success indicators: Concise, measurable characteristics that demonstrate project success. These indicators should substantiate any statements made in the background section. The success indicators should address cost, schedule, and quality and relate to mission and goals.
Support required from the participants: List the items and services required of the participants to ensure the success of the project.
Risks: Risk plans are "If–Then" statements which describe significant risks and reactions.

The process starts with the facilitator explaining the form. The customer's project manager usually facilitates the group in completing this form, similar to the customer's presentation of specifications in the engineering review. The primary difference is that the statement of work is more interactive in its development.

To expedite the task, the designated project manager fills in the title, purpose, and background sections of the form in advance. Key areas are the deliverables, measurement indicators, support requirements, and risks. It is important to stay within the guidelines of the contracts and specifications already agreed to with all suppliers. The task deliverable is a completed *statement of work* form. This provides a clear understanding regarding the responsibility of all parties involved in the project. In addition, it provides a big-picture perspective of the installation or start-up phase of the project to orient the participants for the fact-finding task. The facilitator captures and displays to the group any questions that arise during the creation of the statement of work for review after the fact-finding presentations, which frequently provide some of the answers.

Fact Finding. The fact-finding and statement of work tasks perform the same function as the specification and engineering review task did for the engineering team. This task should be tailored to the needs of the respective installation and start-up work teams. The task involves each company making formal presentations to the team to build a more in-depth understanding of the total systems installation or start-up requirements. Customer personnel need to see the total picture, and the various equipment suppliers need to see how their equipment fits into the total system. As part of the prework, the customer's or supplier's project manager prepares the agenda for this portion of the meeting. Figure 3.8 is a fact-finding agenda for a generic press system project. It can be modified as required to fit specific project needs. As with the specification review, the person creating the agenda takes responsibility for ensuring the preparedness of all parties.

The process follows the agenda with each equipment supplier presenting an in-depth description of installation or start-up requirements. The presentation should include at least a macro timeline and forecasted resources. It should explain

Installation or start-up fact-finding agenda

OEM press system   Press supplier
- Macro timeline
- Resources (quantity and type)
- Pre-conditions
- Special tools
- Supplier support

Front of line   Front of line supplier
- Macro timeline
- Resources
- Pre-conditions
- Special tools
- Supplier support

End of line   End of line supplier
- Macro timeline
- Resources
- Pre-conditions
- Special tools
- Supplier support

Site preparation planning   Customer project manager

Summarize questions   Designated project manager
- Review questions
- Assign responsibility
- Set response date

Figure 3.8 Fact-finding sample agenda

any preconditions, special tools, or other unique issues to help the comprehension of installation or startup. After each presentation, the floor is open for questions. As done previously, the facilitator displays the questions in front of the entire team, seeks an answer from the team, and records responses. Unanswered questions require an action plan, a person accountable, and an estimated completion date, which the next chapter addresses. The facilitator then enters the resultant data into the open-issues list. Third-party facilitation of this part of the meeting, perhaps someone from the leadership or engineering team not assigned to the installation or start-up teams, allows all team participants to focus on the issues. If this is not practical, the project managers share facilitation, freeing each other to participate. A clerical resource records the information and expedites the entering of information into the project's open-issues list.

The deliverables from this task are a set of macro timelines and estimates of resources from each participating company, along with a list of questions requiring action plans, accountability, and promised response times. This process clarifies and answers technical questions and increases the supplier's understanding of customer site issues. This case assumes a relatively simple site preparation situation, which allows site issues to integrate as part of the installation team process. Cases involving major architectural and construction work complicate site preparation, and usually require the formation of a separate site prep team; it would follow the installation team process, but involve different people and issues. All work teams use the same basic agenda, but the content of the discussions and issues vary to fit the specific work team's responsibility. This task ensures that everyone has the same expectations of the installation or start-up process. It helps avoid many problems in the future, and sets a solid direction. It also helps everyone see how specific work content fits into the overall scope of the installation or startup. This task usually generates many site-specific issues, which when answered in advance, help to avoid future problems and delays. The *coordinate* process group discussed in the next chapter addresses action planning for the open-issues list and uses the timeline and resource estimates gathered during this task for scheduling.

COMMUNICATION TOOLS

As indicated previously, a 12-person team has 66 communication channels, and a full set of teams in the MPM process can easily exceed 1000 communication channels. After establishing teams and defining their formal meeting frequency, it quickly becomes apparent that more communication beyond the team meetings is required. The leadership team typically meets quarterly over the course of the project. The engineering team has frequent meetings (typically monthly or weekly) during the initial engineering and design approvals, which are less frequent at other times. Language, culture, and many time zones often create intractable separation issues for teams with globally dispersed members. A few additional tools and a formal communication plan are vital elements in an effective team process.

Website. The website is one of the most valuable and successful communication tools to aid teams in proactively implementing their communications as quickly and efficiently as possible. Website functionality and cost effectiveness has improved to the point that it has become an absolute necessity on any major project. The MPM process involving multiple multi-company teams is no exception, and the use of a project website is required. The value of the project website grows each year as operating costs decrease and functionality continues to improve. A website aids internal team communications, communications between teams, and general communications to anyone on the project with website access.

A website provides a powerful tool to enhance the team environment. It enables a large global-based, multi-company team to collaborate in an open communications environment. The asynchronous environment solves the problems of different time zones and varying levels of verbal language skills. It promotes information sharing and discussion forums that are unavailable in other formats. Additionally, it provides the project management group with a tool to ensure the existence of effective communications during the appropriate project cycles. If used effectively, Internet applications can provide a means to enhance project output. The key to utilizing the Internet effectively is to have an easy-to-use, highly flexible tool for implementing, maintaining, and utilizing websites.

Today, most companies have their own website and related server space. Depending on the security issues, one of the participating company websites may agree to host the project website with the consensus of all participants. Company websites are frequently special-purpose structures for tracking information. Many are internal to the customer, supplier, or sub-suppliers, while some interface with outside suppliers for specific purposes. Using any of these systems will result in communication needs becoming secondary to the original purpose of the base system, which will affect team communications. It is best to go with a third-party source such as QuickPlace or any other system specifically designed for team communications and discussion threads. These website hosts allow for the easy creation of a secure, browser-accessible workspace, providing teams with the means to reach consensus through discussions, collaborate on documents, and coordinate plans. It also provides a central reference and storage point for data and information. There are other Internet tools available; the company and individuals who create the website decide which tools to use. The selected site should have a great deal of flexibility in its architecture, structure, and use. This flexibility allows it to fit the nature of the project's communication. The following are some tips that should prove helpful for project websites:

1. In the ideal situation, all users have the ability to input information into the website. At a minimum, upload information going into the website through multiple persons. Setting up a system that relies on a single person severely restricts the information's effectiveness, discourages usage, and adds administrative costs.

2. Chose a website that generates a report automatically that lists all new postings for the last 24 hours (or some other set number of days). By funneling all communications through the website, the project manager has the ability to see all communications occurring on the project. (This was never possible before the web.)

3. Use the website for all drawing transmittals; it is much more effective and avoids limitations on file transfer capacity. It is important to verify the capacity of the website to handle these large files.

4. Structure the website format to facilitate transfer into the project documentation file when the project is completed. This greatly reduces project documentation efforts and enhances the documentation results.

Conferencing. The conference call is another communication tool that reduces travel costs and promotes communications among team members. It is often the tool of choice for limited discussions; generally less than one hour when a face-to-face discussion is not required. The conference call is very common and this text assumes that readers are familiar with the processes for setting up and conducting an effective conference call.

One variation of the conference call is supplementing it with an additional Internet tool that either allows users to connect remotely to each other's computers in order to share documents in real time over an Internet connection, or provides access to an electronic white board that allows everyone access to it. Windows NetMeeting is an example of one communications software package available on all Microsoft Windows computers, and allows remote file sharing. Using NetMeeting in conjunction with a conference call may be effective when collaborating on items such as documents and drawings.

Another variation of the conference call is the incorporation of full-motion video. Videoconferencing may become the tool of choice when face-to-face discussions are preferred but the time and cost of travel are prohibitive. The full-motion video is more an efficiency tool that reduces project costs and the time wasted in traveling, and facilitates more communication. The business case for the use of full-motion video will vary between projects, depending on the location of the team members and compatibility of existing infrastructure within each of the participating companies. The technology exists to conduct full-motion video meetings literally anywhere in the world. The barriers are availability of hardware and costs. Future technological advancements will continue to enhance the functionality and cost benefits of this tool to where this will be commonplace, and thus this section covers videoconferencing in more detail. The discussion covers various approaches when arranging videoconference capability, as well as general practices and lessons learned before, during, and after the videoconference that will make your communications more effective.

Videoconference Implementation. The first task required after recognizing the need for holding a meeting via videoconference is investigating what resources are available to all parties, and which are best suited for the meeting. There are four basic ways to implement a videoconference:

1. Internal use of the customer, supplier, and sub-supplier's existing equipment
2. Purchased videoconferencing equipment funded by the project
3. External use of third-party provided facilities
4. Internet-based video call

Method 1: Internal. The parties involved must have access to a facility with compatible videoconferencing equipment. In order for personnel to participate via this method, they have to travel to these available sites. It is possible to link dissimilar customer, supplier, and sub-supplier videoconferencing equipment, but experience has proven this cumbersome, and therefore is not recommended. For the most effective conferencing, keep the number of sites to a minimum and use common equipment, even at the expense of additional travel.

Method 2: Purchased equipment. It is possible to purchase low-cost videoconferencing equipment. Generally, this is set up at mutually agreed upon locations that minimize the number of unique sites and amount of travel. Since all parties benefit, the funding should come from participants based on a business case for the specific project. In order for personnel to participate via this method, they travel to the nearest videoconference site.

In 2005, $7,000 per site bought and installed the complete system, which is about the cost of one intercontinental round-trip business-class ticket. An additional $300 per month was spent on monthly communication line costs (ISDN). Hourly communication costs ran about $55. In this particular case, the technology employed limited the number of sites on the videoconference to four. With the rapid advance of technology, videoconferencing costs will continue to decline while travel costs increase, further improving the business case. The gain in availability of participant time is also an important bonus to videoconferencing. Every hour spent not traveling is another hour available for more productive assignments. Typically, fully burdened executive and engineering time is valued at $1,000 per day or higher. These figures were accurate at the time of writing, but the exact costs given here will obviously change as time progresses, requiring a personalized analysis for each business case with current costing data. As indicated earlier, the business case will only improve with time.

Method 3: External source. Using third-party provided facilities is potentially the most flexible way to hold a videoconference, though more inconvenient than using dedicated systems owned by each site. For this method, a videoconference is arranged through a third party such as a FedEx office or other providers. Many FedEx office locations in North America have videoconferencing rooms available, and they have the ability to dial into many other companies' videoconferencing systems for a fee. The cost is determined by the number of sites in use at the time and whether it will be necessary to convert to an off-FedEx office network system. In 2009, the fees ranged from $225 to $350 per hour, per location.

Method 4: Internet-based call. If costs are a problem, one Internet site you might be interested in is www.skype.com. Skype offers free video calls for anyone with access to a computer with a webcam and high-speed broadband service. Security issues are the same as with an open wireless phone call—the possibility exists that anyone could be listening. The quality of the video with just two sites participating is good, but the webcam definitely has limitations. As technology advances and these systems improve, this approach will become more viable.

Regardless of the chosen method for implementing a video call, the following considerations prior to the call, during the call, and after the call should prove useful.

Prevideoconference. In these days of working with a global supplier base, it is often more difficult to find times that fit all parties' normal business hours. This is not necessarily a difficult hurdle, but some understanding of time zones and cultures is helpful. For example, you would not want to schedule a 2:00 p.m. Eastern Standard Time videoconference on a Friday afternoon with a supplier in Japan (unless you wanted to force them to be at work at 3:00 a.m. on a Saturday morning). Meeting notices should be clear about the time for the conference. In order to reduce the possibility of confusion, the time for the meeting should be stated for each location. For example:

Start times: *Thursday* 6:00 p.m. in Detroit, Michigan
                Friday 7:00 a.m. in Yokohama, Japan

In selecting the number of locations to participate in the videoconference, there is a law of diminishing returns. Some technologies limit the number of possible locations. Minimizing the number of locations makes the meeting more effective and easier to control. In a videoconference with two locations, the screen at each location shows one other party. Participants see the images clearly, avoiding confusion about which participant is speaking. If more than two locations are on the call, the screens split and show persons from multiple locations simultaneously, or a switching method displays the location of the person currently speaking on the screen. One way to reduce the number of locations is to have some attendees travel to the video site. This is only practical if some locations are a relatively short distance from each other, or if there is another business need that justifies the travel.

In many ways, a videoconference is just like any other meeting. All parties must be notified well in advance. The conference initiator prepares the agenda, makes topic assignments, and follows up on creation and distribution of presentation materials.

Regarding agendas and presentation materials for the call, it is helpful to have this information available to all attendees prior to the meeting. Having this information available early in hardcopy form at each location will make the conversation more productive. This avoids wasting time trying to capture the material on the camera for attendees at the other locations to see. Attendees can prepare ahead of time to increase understanding of the presentation content, reduce the time spent on the actual presentation, and free up more time for holding meaningful discussions.

During the Videoconference. Regarding facilitation, note taking, recording minutes, and making assignments, videoconferences are just like any other meeting. The following are some tips that are more specific to videoconferences:

1. There is often a slight transmission delay, typically lasting one or two seconds. It takes a while to adapt to the delay. In order to avoid confusion and cross-talk:
   a. Attendees should be courteous and should avoid interrupting another speaker at another location. Interrupting another speaker will result in a much longer delay than the delay that would have been caused by waiting for the speaker to finish the sentence.
   b. It is important to speak clearly and deliberately, aiming into the microphone. Mumblings can be misunderstood or not understood at all. Having to repeat oneself wastes time.
   c. Sidebar discussions should be avoided. Not only is this rude to the speaker, but the microphone picks up a part of the conversation (but perhaps not all), and it may confuse people at other locations. Internal discussions that are not meant for all attendees should be discussed only after pressing the *mute* button.

2. On occasion, there may be meeting participants that have difficulty understanding or speaking English. In this case, it is wise to make extra effort to use clear and direct language, avoiding idioms that non-native English speakers may be unaccustomed to. Speaking slowly and with pauses may also be beneficial.

3. Actively listening to other speakers, particularly when finalizing assignments or decisions, is essential to the success of a meeting. Repeating what was heard to the others on the call avoids any misunderstanding and assures the others that everything has been understood. This also gives the speaker a chance to clarify a point and draw out further discussion if necessary.

4. Participants should silence all cell phones and pagers. Phone calls, if they must be taken during the meeting, should only be answered outside the meeting.

Post-videoconference Activities. After the meeting has ended, the following items will require closure:

1. It is important to thank the host whenever holding the videoconference at another participant's facility. At any location, it is customary to leave the room exactly as the host presented it; taking care that participants do not leave a mess for someone else to clean up.

2. All interested parties should receive presentation materials and meeting minutes. The necessary modifications to these materials (reflecting any changes made during the meetings) must take place prior to distribution and posting on the project website.

3. All decisions and assignments made during the videoconference require follow-up. Being prompt with your own assignments sets a great example for the group.

4. As appropriate, facilitators post new items and update old items on the open-issues list.

The installation and start-up teams are a workgroup at the site, thus they communicate and interact with each other face-to-face on a daily basis. Their need for communication tools is more for the team to communicate to the leadership, engineering, and other site installation and start-up teams. The website previously discussed, along with conference calls, are the tools best suited to provide the team-to-team communications.

Communication Plan. The number and complexity of the communication channels in the MPM teams require a specific communication plan to make sure that participants are getting the information needed in the required format, at the appropriate time, and without information overload. With electronic communication and the ease of using large distribution lists to send information, the potential for information overload is high. Many times, individuals take the easy way out, sending copies to everyone for fear of leaving someone out. This mentality drives information overload that results in the required party overlooking critical information. Tailoring the information to the needs of the receiver offers the best results, making the issues obvious and the need for their involvement clear. For example, sending a detailed 20-page Gantt chart or an incomplete software document to a key executive requesting more resources has little value. It is clear, however, to send a brief (less than one page) e-mail stating that engineering is two weeks behind schedule creating a situation requiring two additional software engineers for one month to recover the schedule. Send that same one-page request to the functional manager in charge of software development and he will probably ask for the detailed Gantt chart.

With the electronic technology of today, the choices available for communicating have grown significantly. For example, the following are some of the media choices considered when planning communications:

Formal letter	Formal report	E-mail
Informal memo	Web posting	Telephone
Voicemail	Teleconference	Videoconference
Web conference	Meeting presentation	Face-to-face

Individuals now have different biases toward the form of media communication. One person partial to verbal communication might prefer face-to-face, telephone, teleconference, voicemail, formal letter, and e-mail communications—in that sequence of priority. Another more computer literate person who is partial to written communication might prefer e-mail, Web posting, Web conferencing, voicemail, telephone, and face-to-face communications.

I had one boss with the irritating habit of always giving priority to the telephone, regardless of the caller or topic. Any time I wanted to talk face-to-face with my boss, I could bet that a 10-minute conversation could last 30 minutes due to phone interruptions. Our offices were side-by-side, and on some occasions, I called my boss so we could talk uninterrupted. There are many different individual preferences; and so the form of communication must target the priority of the individual to get the desired results.

As stated previously, a project manager can easily spend 90 percent of his time on communication; thus, common sense dictates that every project has a communication plan for all stakeholders to deliver the information needed with maximum effectiveness. In communication, both senders and receivers have specific responsibilities. "The sender is responsible for making the information clear and complete so the receiver can receive it correctly, and for confirming that it is properly understood. The receiver is responsible for making sure that the information is received in its entirety and understood correctly" (*PMBOK® Guide* 2004, 229). The communication plan is a guideline to assist the sender in meeting the needs of the receiver. Assembling the communication plan is the responsibility of the project managers. The plan is dynamic with reviews and adjustments to fit individual needs made over the project lifecycle. The installation and start-up teams meet face-to-face on a daily basis, and the bulk of their internal team communications are simply face-to-face. However, the leadership and engineering teams meet only monthly or quarterly, making communication planning more critical. Interteam communications require careful planning as well, since in some cases the teams do not exist at the same time within the project lifecycle. Other environmental issues to consider in the plan are language, culture, time zone differences, project organization structures, and project manager skills.

The website discussed previously can be a huge advantage in any communication plan. It provides central storage for all project information. It controls access, data entry, and modification of the information through passwords. Distribution of information to participants is a pull system with each person drawing or entering the information they want, when they want, 24 hours a day, 7 days a week. It does require all stakeholders to be highly computer literate. In an ideal world, everything would be on the website and everyone would pull whatever information he or she desired. Since we are not in an ideal world, full utilization of the website is essential along with other distribution methods as needed to meet the needs of the stakeholders as defined in the communication plan.

The communication plan is created in two parts. The first part lists the information details consisting of team source, content, frequency, format, and responsible person. The second part is an exception distribution list identifying the method of distribution for each individual or team if other than the website. Tables 3.3 and 3.4 are examples of a two-part communication plan showing information details and distribution respectively. Part I, containing the information detail, is self-explanatory.

The distribution page shown in table 3.4 only has headings for the key executives, project managers, and each team type. It may be necessary to list specific individuals if their information priorities vary greatly. In particular, the key executives or project managers on the leadership team may have very different information priorities that require detailing in the plan by an individual. The distribution page is an exception table identifying tools other than the website for distributing information. An empty box identifies the website as the primary distribution method and a solid black box indicates the information is restricted and not available for distribution. Consider the following examples in interpreting this table.

Table 3.3 Communication plan information details

Team source	Content	Frequency	Format	Responsible person
Leadership	Mission/goals	Each meeting	Pocket card/web	As assigned
	Meeting minutes	Each meeting	Word document	Agenda leader
	Organization chart	Once	Excel chart	Initiating PM
	Situational matrix	As required	Standard form	Initiating PM
	Open issues	Each meeting	Excel chart	Agenda leader
	Action plans status	Any changes	Excel chart	As assigned
	Individual discussion	As required	E-mail/telephone	Discussion participants
	Escalation items	As required	Teleconference	PM initiator
Engineering	Responsibility matrix	Once	Excel chart	As assigned
	Open issues	Each meeting	Excel chart	Agenda leader
	Action plan	Any changes	Excel chart	As assigned
	Schedule baseline	Once	Gantt/milestone	Supplier PM
	Schedule status	Bi-weekly	Gantt/milestone	Supplier PM
	Design reviews	As planned	Drawing mark up	Design reviewer
	Meeting minutes	Each meeting	Word doc	Agenda leader
	Individual discussion	Daily	Web posting	Discussion participants
	Engineering change requests	As required	Standard form	Requesting PM
	Performance & forecasts	Bi-weekly	Earned value	Each PM
	Punchlists	Weekly	Excel chart	Supplier PM
	Photos (manufacturing)	Weekly	JPEG	Supplier PM

Install/startup	RASIC chart	Once	Excel chart	As assigned
	Statement of work	Once	Std form	Agenda leader
	Open issues	Weekly	Excel chart	Agenda leader
	Action plan	Weekly	Excel chart	As assigned
	Schedule baseline	Once	Gantt/network	Lead PM
	Schedule status	Bi-weekly	Gantt/network	Lead PM
	Meeting minutes	Each meeting	Word doc	Agenda leader
	Individual discussion	Daily	Face-to-face	Discussion participants
	Change requests	As required	Standard form	Requesting PM
	Performance & forecasts	Bi-weekly	Earned value	Lead PM
	Punchlists	Weekly	Excel chart	Supplier PM
	Photos	Weekly	JPEG	As assigned

Table 3.4 Communication plan distribution method

Information	Key executive	Project manager	Leadership	Engineer	Install/startup
Leadership					
Mission/goals	Team meeting	Team meeting	Team meeting	Team meeting	Team meeting
Meeting minutes	E-Mail				
Organizational chart			Team meeting		
Situational matrix			Team meeting		
Open issues			Team meeting		
Action plans status			Team meeting		
Individual discussion	Telephone	E-mail	Team meeting		
Escalation items	Teleconference	Teleconference	Teleconference		
Engineering					
Responsibility matrix				Team meeting	
Open issues				Team meeting	
Action plan				Team meeting	
Schedule baseline				Team meeting	
Schedule status				Team meeting	
Design reviews				In Person	
Meeting minutes					
Individual discussion					
Engineering change requests	Team meeting	E-mail			
Performance & forecasts	E-mail	E-mail	Team meeting		
Punchlists					

Photos (manufacturing)			
Install/startup			
RASIC chart		Team meeting	Team meeting
Statement of work			Team meeting
Open issues			In person
Action plan			Team meeting
Schedule baseline			In person
Schedule status			
Meeting minutes			In person
Individual discussion		Team meeting	
Change requests	E-mail	E-mail	
Performance & forecasts	E-mail		
Punchlists			
Photos			

The primary method for distributing the mission and goals is the team meeting, but this does not prevent posting them on the website as well. The website distributes leadership meeting minutes to everyone with special e-mail copies sent to the key executives. The leadership team individual discussions occur during the team meeting through e-mails and phone calls. Leadership or specific executives and project managers involved have access, but there is no distribution of these discussions to the other teams as indicated by the solid black boxes. In contrast, the individual discussions conducted by the engineering team use the website discussion threads and are available to everyone. This is a common form of asynchronous communication within teams separated by large differences in time zones. Finally, individual discussions on the installation and start-up teams occur in person and are not distributed to anyone else. The large amount of blank space represents information that is available on the website for participants to pull and highlights the value of the website. The minimal use of solid black areas indicating restricted information demonstrates the example of a very open communication system.

SUMMARY

The *communicate* process group defines the project charter—a key deliverable in project management initiation. Once communication is complete, the teams are functioning in the cross-company and cross-functional groups as necessary to perform the activity planning and schedule development in the subsequent *coordinate* process group. The methodology employs various activities utilizing the following group and subgroup combinations to continue the participant's experiential learning:

> *Brainstorming*—Full team using the round-robin technique
> *Categorization*—Full-team decisions using an expert for split decisions
> *Mission*—Cross-company, cross-functional subteams with full-team consensus
> *Goals*—Cross-company, cross-functional subteams with full-team buy in
> *Specification*—Cross company, cross functional involving full team
> *Fact finding*—Cross company, cross functional involving full team

The leadership team uses brainstorming and categorization tasks during the team formation event. These tasks are prework to developing the mission and goals for the project, which are critical in defining the overall project scope. Many of the leadership brainstorming issues become assignments for the other teams. Engineering substitutes the *specification review* for *brainstorming* to develop design specific issues and then categorizes prior to action planning. The work teams substitute the *scope of work* and *fact-finding* for *brainstorming* and *categorization* to develop their concerns and define work content. The project managers gain experience in brainstorming during the leadership formation and facilitate brainstorming in all teams during project execution as a means to develop solutions for problems they face.

The leadership provides the mission and goals to the other teams, and they become the foundation on which the other teams build their more traditional scope definition tasks. It is a good idea to review the mission statement and goals on a regular basis in the leadership meeting. The other teams use the mission and goals to provide guidance for resolving their scope-definition issues and require regular reviews in their meetings as well.

Communication is a critical activity throughout the life of the project. Project managers spend 90 percent of their time communicating. It is important to document a communication plan that is timely and targeted to the specific needs of the teams and participants. The plan must be as open as possible to increase the information sharing among the teams. Technology simplifies the communication plan and offers tremendous opportunity to improve communication efficiency.

## 4

COORDINATE

Coordinate is the third of the multi-company project management (MPM) Six C process groups and consists of the integration of multi-company management's *coordinate* and project management's *planning* process groups. The primary emphasis is on the tasks associated with action planning and project scheduling. In simplistic terms, the action plans manage project participants and other stakeholders, and the schedules manage the project activities. These activities create assignments for team members to follow-up on as they set about the work of implementing the project. These activities complete the second day of team building. Everything up to this point has focused on preparing the team to work in cross-functional and cross-company teams for action-plan development and the creation of schedules. Failure to achieve substantial progress on action plans and schedules is like a Big Mac without the beef. The facilitators must ensure that action plans and schedules receive proper attention in order to claim success from the two-day event. This chapter follows the same format as the previous two chapters to address the action planning and scheduling tasks for each of the respective team types. The section *Putting the Organization Together* organizes all activities from *cooperate, communicate,* and *coordinate* into agendas for each team type to help the reader apply these concepts to their own MPM projects. Finally, the last section provides a brief summary of the team and project accomplishments through Part I.

ACTION PLANNING

Everyone can cite experiences of investing time and energy in meetings, discussing a set of topics, and reaching a basic agreement, only to have the same discussions rehashed at the next meeting—without results. These meetings involve endless hours of discussion and fail to produce concrete results. The difference between these meetings and value-added meetings is action planning with follow-up. Generating results from a meeting requires individuals within the team to agree to either perform the work themselves or take accountability for getting someone else to do it. Talk is cheap, but action requires commitment. To achieve an effective meeting, one must define each action to the entire team's satisfaction, identify the responsible team member, specify an acceptable completion date, and ensure that documentation supports the specific action-plan baseline. The responsible party can be identified through many means, such as by volunteer or team negotiations, assignment from a supervisor, or a natural owner. However, the person accountable sets the completion date (with team approval), ensuring his or her commitment to the completion date. Effective teams put discipline in place to review the status and completion of action plans to the baseline at each subsequent meeting. The combination of action-plan baselines and follow-up makes things happen.

Open-issues List. The need for documentation using the open-issues list is paramount. The open-issues list is an active document for the entire project lifecycle. All teams contribute items and assist in finding a resolution to the issues. A single open-issues list avoids duplicate information, minimizes conflicting responses, provides an excellent record of the project and lessons learned, and is available

Project Title

Issue #	Date		Description	Owner	Action	Due date	Status %

Column 1—Issue #: Original number given to the item when it is created

Column 2—Date: Date the item created

Column 3—Blank: Use this column to enter the originator or categorize it

Column 4—Description: Describes the issue in terms everyone can understand

Column 5—Owner: Identifies the individual, group, or company responsible for taking action to resolve the issue, or answer the question

Column 6—Action: Describes the action taken to resolve the issue

Column 7—Due Date: Expected date the described action is complete

Column 8—Status %: The percentage of completion for the assigned action

Figure 4.1 Open-issues list

to everyone in the project. Open-issues lists come in many formats. Figure 4.1 is one possible spreadsheet format. In this example, the topic headings represent the recommended items captured in the list. Using a spreadsheet provides a common cost-effective tool that can archive completed items and sort open items in a variety of ways. Many companies utilize database management systems, which provide more detailed information and more powerful sorting capabilities, but these systems require additional administrative effort and limit user access, since database software is not as common as spreadsheet software. It has been my preference to keep the information simple and available to all. Any loss of information detail or sorting capability that comes with using a spreadsheet is more than offset by the increased accessibility, ease of input, and overall ownership by the team. Also, the information in a spreadsheet is usually more succinct than that found in a database, and therefore more efficient.

A key task of all teams is a set of actions with assigned responsibilities and estimated completion dates that address the issues identified by the respective team or delegated by another team. Initially, the teams derive the issues from the leadership brainstorming process, engineering specification review, and the installation or start-up fact-finding processes. In subsequent meetings, additional issues arise as part of the normal project execution. Generating issues without the discipline of establishing actions, assigning responsibility, and setting target completion dates has little value. Thus, all teams must document the action baseline and establish regular follow-up to ensure that the project moves forward successfully. Companies frequently want to apply their existing format to MPM, which helps to create buy in and commitment during the action planning process. Provided the other participants buy in, this is an excellent approach. This approach contains the following seven basic elements: *tracking reference, date created, issue description, action plan, action owner, date due,* and *status percent.* The last column on the open-issues list titled *status percent* provides a means of tracking progress against the forecast completion date during regular follow-up meetings and then documents the status. Without this column, there is a tendency to wait until the completion date before checking the status, which invariably leads to missed dates.

Leadership Action Planning. This task design splits up the team into the cross-functional, cross-company groups that are identical to the mission statement and goal development. The division continues building individual relationships in the group, develops plans faster, promotes intercompany camaraderie, and multiplies the number of issues addressed in a given time period. Each cross-functional, cross-company workgroup uses the same set of categories that they used to develop goals. This improves efficiency since the prior goal discussions usually covered possible actions or methodologies for achieving the stated goals. In many cases, the brainstorm items within a specific category are action recommendations or suggestions the group may consider when establishing the action plans. The task is to develop action plans to address the most critical issues in the categories assigned to their group, and prepare a presentation for the total team. The idea is to get team concurrence for the action plans and establish a process and expectation of action planning with follow-up for every leadership meeting.

Each group reports on proposed action plans that support the respective goals. The facilitator then works with the total group to reach consensus. When pushed for time teams have, on occasion, added the action-plan task to the mission and goal tasks and then covered everything in one big report session. This approach usually ends up with the action planning being short-changed and is not recommended. It is best to identify a specific time segment exclusively for action planning. There is insufficient time to develop actions on all issues, but it is critical to develop and document at least some actions using the open issues generated from brainstorming. In some cases, a team will use all their available time on mission and goals, leaving insufficient time to address action plans. Without action plans, a major objective of the two-day team building is lost, and the value of the two days is limited. In this situation, the facilitator needs to push the total group to agree on some actions immediately after the goals are set and give the cross-functional, cross-company groups assignments to work critical action plans outside the meeting and report to the team at an agreed date. The agreed date is usually a few days or weeks after the formation event and is generally coordinated using a conference call.

Due to the total project macro viewpoint of the leadership team, all issues may not be addressed and it is a mistake to attempt resolution to all of them. Many issues are too far away in the project timeline. Such things as installation, logistics, training, and start-up support may be over a year away and it is best to place this on hold until the timing is right. The engineering, installation, or start-up teams are better equipped and staffed to address many issues. Retain these items on the leadership brainstorm list until formation of the respective teams. Then, delegate the items to the appropriate team for resolution. The idea is to keep all issues on the list, and address them in future meetings or delegate to the proper team at the appropriate time.

The key deliverables from this task are detailed actions, responsibility assignments, and estimated completion dates for the issues generated from brainstorming. One issue that is a normal and required output of the action plans is agreement on the overall team structure and implementation timetable. This is where the leadership discusses, modifies, and finalizes the initial template of project phases and MPM teams. This, in turn, requires action plans and timing for establishing the teams with a high priority on the engineering team. The leadership team uses subsequent meetings to follow-up on the action plans until completion, address issues on hold at the proper time, and delegate issues to the appropriate team.

Engineering Action Planning. The engineering action planning task develops action plans to address all the open issues assigned to or generated by the team. As prework, one of the project managers needs to list the issues the leadership team has delegated to engineering. Then, during the specification and engineering review, the project manager crosses out issues the engineers identified and listed. This minimizes the number of issues the leadership must delegate to the engineering team. This typically eliminates over 75 percent of the items from the leadership team. If engineering has identified an issue on their own, they will have greater ownership versus the delegated items.

The facilitator starts the engineering action planning by asking the designated project manager to present a reduced list of issues from the leadership team as explained above. The issues generated during the specification and engineering status review and the reduced list of delegated issues become the new open-issues list for engineering. The engineering team then uses the categorization process to consolidate and sort the issues without regard to any categorization the leadership team has done. This removes any possible duplicate issues and provides for a greater understanding. (See Chapter 3 regarding the categorization task.) The engineers will categorize in a way that fits their natural engineering process, which is often very different from the leadership thinking.

The facilitator leads the group in dividing the categories into two or three groups representing equal amounts of work. Then, individuals volunteer or are assigned by their project manager to a workgroup. The project managers and facilitator balance the workgroups by size and skills, and as much as possible, make sure each group has representation from all parties. The facilitator may divide or concentrate functional skills into particular groups based on the category division, but must ensure that each group contains cross-company representation. Next, the subgroups develop action plans for all the issues in their assigned categories, starting with the highest priority. If time runs short, for each issue they are required to assign a specific person to develop a resolution plan and commit to an estimated time to present the plan to the group.

The main deliverable from this activity is consensus on all the action plans to address the open-issues list. In some cases, a few issues may belong to the leadership or another team; these should be communicated to the leadership via the project managers for disposition or delegation to the appropriate team. If unable to address all remaining issues, at a minimum, all issues will have an owner and due date for an action plan to be established. This minimum requirement for all engineering issues is necessary, since engineering is a critical activity at the beginning of a project. This is the first opportunity for the engineering team to work in smaller cross-company groups. The smaller group session reinforces personal relationships and builds trust. This smaller group setting is a model that the team will use in the future to expedite the resolution of issues.

The criticalness of engineering should not be underestimated early in the project. Failure to address engineering issues early can result in major delays of weeks or months, creating excessive expenditures that are difficult to recover later in the project. The OEM from Chapter 1 that went bankrupt in the middle of the MPM project was only the second project to use the MPM approach, and formation did not start until eight months after placing the purchase order. This particular OEM did not start engineering until eight months after receiving the purchase order. As a result, the OEM had to expedite, work overtime, and add resources to meet project deadline dates in every project phase. This cost the OEM millions they did not have. This is one of the many hard lessons that have been incorporated into the MPM process, and is one reason why MPM works best when implemented immediately after the purchase order.

Installation and Start-up Action Planning. This task follows fact-finding, and assigns, with due dates, all questions raised during the fact-finding as well as any issues delegated by the leadership team. At the time of the installation or start-up team formation, most of the unknowns are resolved and a great deal of information exists on the system. Thus, the number of open issues is minimal and the use of subteams is not required. In addition, the installation or start-up teams typically work as a complete unit on a daily basis, and modeling the subgroup approach is not necessary unless the team is too large to work effectively. As a result, the full-team setting is best suited for this task. As prework, the leadership team designates a project manager to make a list of any issues that the leadership team decides to pass on to the installation or start-up team. During fact-finding, the project manager crosses out duplicate issues identified by the installation or start-up team to minimize the number of delegated issues.

The prior fact-finding presentations generate an open-issues list, which are recorded on a flip chart or electronic board for the group to see. The facilitator starts this task by asking the designated project manager to present a modified list of issues from the leadership team. After all the issues have been consolidated on the open issues list, the facilitator must get an owner and due date for each question. Finally, the facilitator seeks team verification that the due date meets the team's expectation. This fact-finding results in only a few items falling outside the responsibility of the respective teams. The project manager is responsible for communicating items deemed outside the team's responsibility to the leadership for disposition.

The action planning for installation and start-up teams is much less intense than the leadership and engineering teams because the project is far more mature and the unknowns are minimal. The serious action planning of installation and start-up teams is the subsequent detailed schedule, which actually becomes their action plan to meet their deliverables of either quality installation or quality startup.

The main deliverable of this task is a documented issues list with an assigned owner and due date for each item. Teams should post and maintain the open issues list on a website to give everyone involved in the project access to its status.

SCHEDULES

Schedules are just a more evolved form of action plans. Schedules take the action plans and add in dependencies, resources, and durations to build a network that establishes the early and late start and finish dates for the activities, as well as providing a budgeted cost baseline. All teams are involved with project schedules. The engineering, installation, and start-up teams develop and use schedules at a detail level, while the leadership team reviews schedules developed by the other teams at a macro level. It is important to follow a proper process for building the schedule.

Schedule Development. Table 4.1 details the seven steps used in the Six C process to build the overall project schedule. Leadership provides the mission statement and goals that establish the project objective, which is the first step in the process from which the other teams build their schedules. In step two, leadership defines the project phases as part of developing the MPM organization. This is really just a part of developing the *work breakdown structure* (WBS) in normal project schedule development. MPM identifies it specifically because of its importance in mixing operational and MPM phases within projects, developing the team structure, integrating schedules, and managing the overall project.

In step three, the other teams start building their schedules by defining the activities for their particular responsibility. The team inputs these activities into the WBS. An important distinction to make in creating the WBS from this level down is to create each level in the subset based on product rather than function. Leadership used a functional division because they were primarily concerned with

Table 4.1 Seven steps to build a project schedule

Step	Description	Team responsible
1	Define project objective	Leadership
2	Define project phases	Leadership
3	Define WBS and work packages	Engr/install/startup
4	Identify network and dependencies	Engr/install/startup
5	Estimate activity duration and resources	Engr/install/startup
6	Define interface events and dates	Leadership
7	Create integrated schedule and budget	All teams

methods of management. All other teams need a product focus because that is the essence of their responsibility. For example, a product focus begins by dividing the product into subsystems. In our example, the elements in the next level for a transfer press acquisition might be front of line, press, press automation, and end of line. This drives a cross-functional structure in all the activities of engineering, installation, and startup, which the product needs if it is to yield a fully integrated system in the end. A functional breakdown might be electrical, mechanical, hydraulic, pneumatic, structural, etc. A functional breakdown is extremely difficult to correlate with the product and project status. For example, knowing that the total electrical portion of the project is 25 percent complete is not as effective as knowing that the front of line is complete. In actual practice, the subsets are much more descriptive on the product breakdown, and the differences are more apparent. A given functional group aligns naturally and speaks a common language. Thus, the interface within a function is not as critical as the interface between functions. Using a product WBS is a major enabler in closing the gap between functions, resulting in a much higher quality project with greater customer and supplier satisfaction.

The activities in the WBS define the project scope for each team phase and become the foundation for many project management functions including budgeting, scheduling, resource allocating, tracking, and evaluating. It is important to link the cost and schedule using the WBS. The benefits of this linkage are as follows:

- Synchronizes cost and schedule
- Facilitates funds release as needed per the schedule
- Closely links financial and project personnel
- Facilitates documentation and auditing of costs
- Cost structure conforms to phases in project execution

The development of the WBS will require significant attention. A poor-quality WBS may have some or all of the following characteristics:

- Too much or too little detail
- Insufficient team involvement
- Insufficient team commitment
- Constantly changing schedule
- No relation to the cost system
- Requires extensive interpretation

The WBS displays activities in a hierarchical structure similar to an organization chart or document outline with each level representing a breakdown of the activities in more detail. The project is level *0* and the project phases defined in the development of the team structure become level *1*. Each phase divides into elements that are again subdivided as many times as necessary to reach the work package. Figure 4.2 is the partial WBS of a simple kitchen replacement project that involves only two levels of breakdown. The first level is by function and consists of *design, purchase equipment, contract for labor, tear out and preparation, install,* and *close*. The partial WBS only shows the product-oriented level-two breakdown for the tear out and preparation phase, which consists of twelve tasks shown in the illustration.

The lowest level activity in the WBS is the *work package*, which is the point at which the team defines dependencies and performs an estimation of resources and durations. There is no specified number of levels required for the WBS. The level of breakdown must fit the individual project phase and system subset needs in terms of yielding a work package that is easy to define, estimate, and track. Three to four levels of breakdown is common in equipment acquisition projects. In the kitchen tear out and preparation example, it would not make sense to breakdown the level-two task of *removing the sink* further, since that is the expertise of the plumber who is employed to perform the work, and therefore might adversely affect the result. Too much detail is never efficient and often results in failure of the tracking process due to the excessive follow-up and reporting burden it creates. Too little detail results in missed budgets due to poor estimates, surprises due to not thinking the task through completely, and late identification of problems due to insufficient detail in tracking. In the context of equipment acquisition projects, work packages that span less than a few days or more than several months usually represent too much or too little detail respectively. In the kitchen replacement example, most individual tasks span a few days at most.

A well-defined work package includes a set of inputs, a task description, and deliverables. The inputs are a list of activities that must precede the work package; preconditions to doing the work; resource requirements in the form of labor, material, tools, and equipment; the initial contract order specifications; and any other requirements identified for the project. The task description includes a statement of work, the time required to complete the task with specified resources, the cost, the identification of the responsible individual or group, and the means for quality verification. The deliverables are clearly identified measurable results, achieved upon completion of the work package (Nicholas 2004, 170).

After defining the work packages, in step four, the predecessors provide the information to create the network diagram that displays graphically how all the activities fit together. Dependencies are mandatory, discretionary, or external. Mandatory dependencies involve physical constraints such as not erecting a building until the foundation is complete. Discretionary might be the team electing to perform two activities in sequence rather than in parallel. External relates to items outside the project plan such as material provided by an outside source. These dependencies drive the final network logic and contribute to the project dates.

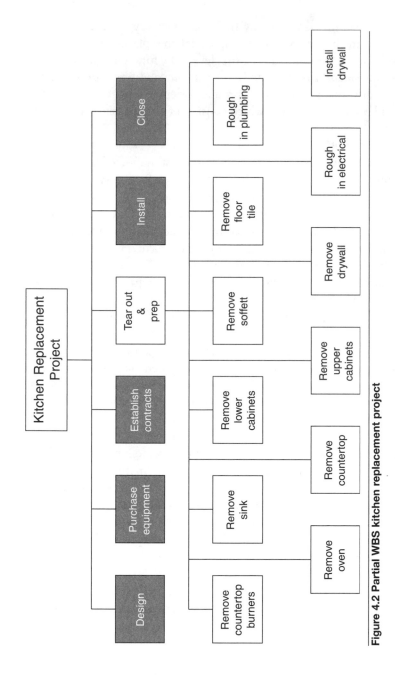

Figure 4.2 Partial WBS kitchen replacement project

Leaving mandatory dependencies out or introducing too many discretionary dependencies results in inaccurate schedule dates. Building a schedule with the network logic makes it possible to determine the critical path as well as ascertain how a change in one activity will affect all other activities in the project. The *Schedule Management* section in Chapter 5 discusses network theory in more detail. There are also many textbooks devoted to network theory, and most software packages provide instructions for creating the networks as part of their deliverables.

Once the network is complete, in step five, each team first determines the resources for each activity and estimates the duration. Applying this information to the network yields the final schedule for that specific project phase. Frequently, this final schedule does not meet project objectives, and so requires the team to reassess resources, activity durations, and network logic. Work methods, tools, and equipment may also provide added efficiency to improve timing. In this area, the MPM process with the diversity of talent, experiences, and seamless interface between companies can really make a difference. A critical aspect of the scheduling process is identifying the individual or group responsible for creating the schedule. For best results, the work team actually doing the work is an integral part of the schedule creation, since they are the most knowledgeable in its execution and their involvement builds commitment.

The leadership team via the project managers performs step six, which involves identifying all the interface events and dates as well as the milestones needed to integrate all the plans. The interface events or milestones are specific points in time that allow integration of all project phases. This is particularly important for phases managed as operations rather than phases that are project oriented, since they are the primary means of tracking and controlling the operational phases such as equipment manufacturing in our template.

In step seven, the other teams create their specific schedules, and the leadership team integrates the schedules from each phase using the interface events, milestones, and project-phase-to-project-phase dependencies to yield the overall *master project baseline schedule* and budget. Each team is responsible for tracking its own performance and taking corrective action when required. The leadership provides oversight, sets priorities, and adjusts team resources as needed to support the other teams in their schedules.

This schedule-building process requires an individual skilled in these steps. Many textbooks, college courses, and user training for a variety of scheduling software applications address the subject of scheduling in detail. Proficiency in scheduling is a prerequisite for project managers. Each organization should have these skills and should make them available to all MPM teams.

Leadership Schedules. The role of leadership in building schedules is different from that of the other teams. Referring to the seven-step schedule, leadership is solely responsible for steps one, two, and six, while the other teams are responsible for three, four, and five. All teams are responsible for step seven, but leadership performs integration while the other teams create specific phase schedules. It is also the role of the leadership to see that schedule creation follows the proper process, involves the appropriate team, and meets the project goals. In the leadership formation meeting, establishing the project objective with mission and goals, as well as defining the project phases through the team structure completes steps one and two. It also ensures agreement on preliminary interface event dates such as project phases, expected delivery dates, and buyoff dates. These dates are more in the form of project goals stated in the purchase agreement. For example, a leadership team involving three new press systems might specify dates as shown in Figure 4.3.

Activity	System A	System B	System C
PO issued	1/1/07	1/1/07	1/1/07
Acceptance	4/1/08	6/1/08	8/1/08
Delivery	7/1/08	9/1/08	11/1/08
Install complete	2/1/09	4/1/09	6/1/09
Final buy off	4/1/09	6/1/09	8/1/09

Figure 4.3 Project dates for typical three-press order

As part of their oversight responsibility, leadership reviews the project schedule at each subsequent team meeting to identify timing shortfalls and ensure the development of contingency plans to keep the project on schedule. Typically, such issues as engineering resources or technical skills, supplier manufacturing capability and resources, customer tool-and-material readiness, material deliveries, approval drawings, software development, and initial acceptance expectations can be hot topics that affect schedules. It is important to remember that it is much cheaper to solve a timing problem at this phase than it is in the later installation and start-up phases. Experience has also shown that jumping into the manufacturing phase without giving sufficient priority and development time to the engineering phase results in rework that adds cost, increases time, and causes conflict.

The engineering, installation, and start-up schedules contain details to plan the respective activities. These highly detailed schedules make for inefficient leadership tools. Thus, the project managers need to roll up these detailed schedules to the appropriate macro level for the leadership's review. Proper construction of the WBS facilitates this rollup. The biggest mistake most project managers make when interacting with senior management is providing too much detail. Providing too much detail makes it difficult to identify the key issues and consumes meeting time that is not value added. This frequently results in the leadership going off on scheduling detail tangents, which are the responsibility of other teams. For best results, project managers should report only the detail required to highlight the issues, and have supporting detail available to answer any questions that may arise.

The leadership-schedule task consists of the approval and ongoing reviews of all schedules at a macro level to maintain timely project execution. It is an exercise performed by the full leadership team. One key deliverable of this task is the definition of all project milestones and interface dates with either agreed dates or tentative dates with specified dates for finalizing them. The prework requires the project managers to select a set of milestone and interface dates from the existing, proposed, and future schedules of the engineering, manufacturing, transportation, site prep, installation, and start-up activities. The next deliverable is the approval of the milestone list and subsequent updates by the leadership. The final deliverable is a plan for ongoing reviews of the key milestone dates by the leadership team.

Milestone Chart. The milestone chart is a useful tool for regulating the level of detail given to the leadership team. It is a chart identifying key milestone dates for the leadership to track. These milestone dates are specific points in time linked to the WBS that represent the completion or start of an activity or project phase. Proper construction of the WBS using a product orientation in the engineering and work teams facilitate this activity. Usually, the project managers work as a subgroup from the leadership team to establish and reach consensus on the milestone dates off-line. The project managers need to ensure there is an even distribution of key milestone dates. In the early stages of the project, it may be too early to establish a particular milestone date due to lack of information. In this situation, the tentative date for that particular milestone is established and a future date is set to review, modify, and finalize the milestone date when more information is available. Using milestone charts as the primary tool for reviewing schedules and Gantt charts for the back-up detail facilitates issue identification and resolution.

As discussed previously, some phases of the project follow a project management methodology while others follow the more traditional operations environment. The use of interfaces link the operations phase to the project management schedule. The interfaces are the inputs or outputs between the project management activities and the operations activities. For example, the manufacturing phase requires software design outputs from the engineering phase as inputs to operate and test the equipment. The installation team needs the packaging plan output from manufacturing as input to detail the installation plan. Using the interfaces allows the functional organization to manufacturer the equipment following the operational procedures and just report the interface dates to manage the project as one integrated plan. Just like the milestone, the interfaces represent significant points in the project and operation phase timelines. The project managers select these interfaces and fold them into the final milestone list.

Table 4.2 is a partial milestone chart for the previous typical three-press project order. This includes the milestones derived from the engineering schedule as well as the interface dates from manufacturing, highlighted in grey. Note that milestones 1 and 15 are the purchase order and acceptance testing dates from the original project order. It is extremely important that everyone understands the content of each milestone. Thus, a description is included to increase that understanding. The activity descriptions from the WBS develop the milestone description for the dates taken out of the schedule. The interface descriptions require separate development. There is a 15-month gap from the original purchase order to acceptance testing for System A. During this period the design and manufacture of the first system is completed. The engineering schedule will easily exceed 200 activities and the supplier's entire operations organization is involved in the manufacturing. The milestone chart identifies 15 events over this timeframe for the leadership to monitor both engineering and operations phases in its oversight capacity to keep the project on track.

The milestone dates actually evolve over the project timeline as more information is available and teams develop detailed schedules. Looking at item number 10, *establish install and start-up dates,* from Table 4.2, approximately eight months into the project, the project managers revise the timing for the install and startup after gaining knowledge of the system design. Essentially, these dates replace the initial install and final buyoff dates in the original project, subject to customer approval. When the install and start-up teams develop their detailed schedules, the dates are updated again. *Progressive elaboration* is the term applied to updating the project schedule as the detail evolves.

Once the project managers complete the milestone chart, the leadership reviews and approves it at their next meeting. The milestone dates should represent clearly understood accomplishments distributed across all project phases that are easy to see and measure. The leadership team's co-leaders guarantee that the milestone dates represent the commitment of the entire leadership team.

Engineering Schedules. The OEM engineering activity, along with its project management group, develops the initial schedules for engineering. Manufacturing and transport use the OEM's operations approach and integrate with the project management plan through interface events. Typically, the engineering schedule provided by the OEM incorporates and tracks the manufacturing and transport interface events as part of the engineering schedule. Development of this schedule

Table 4.2 Partial milestone chart

#	Milestone	Date	Description
1	Purchase order issued	01/01/07	
2	Press content defined	03/26/07	Solidifies press content, deliverables, expectations Deviations resolved and approved by customer Major subsystems defined by customer, including C/B, transfer system, cushion, lube, etc Control architecture, network, and protocols Long lead items detailed
3	Front of line defined	04/01/07	Detail FOL system criteria for press
4	End of line press interface defined	04/19/07	Detail EOL system criteria for press
5	Long lead press components ordered	05/15/07	Long-lead items confirmed with delivery dates; Design, build, testing, & delivery dates approved
6	Proposed sequence of operations documented	06/01/07	Documented sequence of operation to include press startup, e-stop recovery, automatic, ADC, etc
7	Long lead FOL and EOL components ordered	06/26/07	Long-lead items confirmed with delivery dates; Design, build, testing, & delivery dates approved
8	Controls software program defined	07/01/07	Programming file structure, file definitions, etc
9	System facility requirements defined	08/01/07	Press, FOL, & EOL facility requirements to allow system layout and foundation designs to begin
10	Establish install and start-up dates	09/01/07	Tentative dates to be verified by respective teams
11	Mechanical design complete	11/30/07	Includes major subsections for cushion, transfer, clutch brake, lubrication, and counterbalance
12	Controls hardware design complete	12/06/07	Includes hardware architecture, panel layouts, cabling, communication network, etc
13	Press pre-assembly complete	01/14/08	Major press mechanical subsystems preassembled for fit
14	Installation drawings approved	02/01/08	All installation drawings approved by customer
15	Acceptance testing for System A complete & approved by customer	04/01/08	Testing documentation complete All punch list items, action plans, & target dates agreed upon Fifteen month gap from the original purchase order

constitutes the prework for the engineering schedule task. The OEM is responsible for integrating its engineering plan and the plans of its subsuppliers into the master plan. The OEM owns the plan and submits it to the customer and engineering team for approval.

The interface events for manufacturing and transport are relatively easy to develop and track, while the engineering process is often difficult to visualize and track. The OEM's project manager needs to work collaboratively with the customer and suppliers—particularly on the engineering activities—so that all parties understand the expectations and measure the percent complete in the same way. The development of this schedule generally takes several weeks immediately following the engineering team formation, and includes a lot of interaction between the project managers and engineers. One method to help visualize software engineering is to require simulation testing to demonstrate the effectiveness and completeness of the software. The task deliverable is an agreed upon detailed engineering schedule with a common understanding of expectations and measurement of percent complete.

The engineering-schedule task consists of ongoing reviews of the engineering schedule at a detailed level to maintain project timing. The engineering team performs this exercise following the team formation event at each subsequent engineering team meeting with the entire team. The process starts with the OEM project manager's review of the engineering schedule. This schedule is developed as prework with the engineering team to ensure that it meets the format requirements of all participants, achieves the project objectives, and is detailed enough to effectively track progress. At each meeting, the team compares completed activities and the percent complete of the activities in progress to the plan to identify deviations. The team evaluates all deviations to determine where corrective action is required. The team assesses corrective action options, selects the appropriate correction, and updates the plan. The final engineering schedule reflects actual work complete and the current schedule as well as the original base plan. Posting this schedule on a website makes it available to everyone.

Gantt and Network Charts. The Gantt and network charts are two ways of presenting the detailed schedule. Most scheduling software generates these charts and provides a variety of formats for displaying information. Figures 4.4 and 4.5 illustrate a Gantt chart and the corresponding network chart respectively for the tear out and prep phase of a hypothetical kitchen replacement project using MS Project software. In the example, *tear out and prep* consists of 12 activities identified as items 4–15. Item three is the rollup (or summary) of the 12 activities, and item two, *establish construction contracts*, is a predecessor project phase to beginning the tear out. The Gantt chart displays column headings of *Id, task, duration*, and *resource names*. Selecting other column names displays additional information.

ID	Task Name	Duration	Resource Names
1	Kitchen replacement	10 days	
2	Establish constr. contracts	1 day	
3	Tear out old & prep for new	9 days	
4	Disc & remove countertop burn	2 days	Elec
5	Disc & remove sink w/faucets	1 day	Plumb
6	Disc & remove oven	1 day	Elec
7	Remove countertop	1 day	Carp
8	Remove lower cabinets	2 days	Carp
9	Remove upper cabinets	1 day	Carp
10	Remove soffit	1 day	Carp
11	Remove drywall behind cabinet	1 day	Carp
12	Remove floor tile	1 day	Carp
13	Rough in electrical	2 days	Elec
14	Rough in plumbing	1 day	Plumb
15	Install new drywall & paint	1 day	Carp

Figure 4.4 Gantt chart—kitchen tear out & prep phase

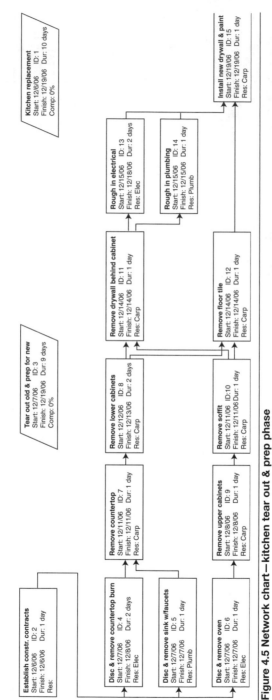

Figure 4.5 Network chart—kitchen tear out & prep phase

The length of the bar represents the activity duration drawn to a timescale. The bars represent the early start and end of each activity. Arrows connecting the bars in the chart represent the activity dependencies. The network chart contains the same information. The network chart states the early start and finish dates in each activity box, while the Gantt chart requires interpretation of the timescale bars. The Gantt chart is the most common and provides a good visualization of the project timing. Engineering and start-up teams find the Gantt chart the most useful format. The network chart does not have a timescale, but its strength is in the visualization of the network dependencies. Installation teams tend to use a network chart because it displays the erection sequence and dependencies involved in installation. The typical major press project lasts a couple years with the intense portion of each project phase ranging from three to nine months. Activities in the range of 100–300 make up a specific phase. Therefore, a complete project with multiple phases and systems quickly exceeds 1,000 activities. Computers and the software scheduling programs make efficient management of this quantity of information possible. Creating the initial schedules is not as daunting as it might first appear, since suppliers have templates for generic engineering, installation, and start-up schedules that they adjust for the specific project and customer circumstances. The input from the team ensures that it represents the experiences, best practices, and commitment of all participants.

Installation and Start-up Schedules. This task involves the development of a detailed schedule with resources identified for installation or startup. The leadership and engineering teams generally deal with schedules after the team formation event. However, in the installation and start-up teams, schedules can take precedence even before action planning. If the time span between the team formation and execution of the schedule is extremely short, the installation or start-up team may need to devote more time to schedule development and give action planning a lower priority. The presentations prepared as prework for the fact-finding task also support this task.

The structure of this exercise using the full cross-functional, cross-company group or some combination of subgroups is up to the discretion of the facilitator as long as all groups are cross company to ensure that the voice of the customer is present. It will depend on the size of the total group, the skill sets represented in the group, the quality and thoroughness of the fact-finding presentations, and the completeness of engineering designs. If fact-finding presentations include good, detailed mock schedules and the team is a small, elite group of very knowledgeable people, the team can assemble the final schedule in a few hours. It will not be possible to complete the schedule within the two-day team building if the fact-finding is poor, the group lacks critical skill representation, or the group is too large. Possibly a subgroup or steering committee will be required, together with additional time to gather data in order to complete the schedule. The facilitator needs to assess all the issues and develop a plan that maximizes the use of the team's skills and time toward the end goal of producing the final schedule. Most teams within a three- to four-hour window should be able to complete at least a preliminary plan.

In new equipment projects, it is extremely valuable to visit the supplier during *initial acceptance testing*. This is a major opportunity for the installation and start-up teams to gain first-hand information on equipment assembly, functionality, and lessons learned by the manufacturing personnel to enhance the schedule and identify potential problems. In this situation, planning and related assignments for all participants in the visit is the first priority, and the schedule becomes secondary. The installation plan development is then a separate meeting held during or after the supplier visit. As was mentioned previously in the action planning, the installation team also covers any schedule issues related to site prep unless a specific site team is established.

This task deliverable is a detailed schedule showing resources for installation or startup. The installation team may display the schedule using the network form of presentation. Showing the entire network at once is most valuable. Thus, it is common to see a wall at the installation site with a 3′ x 30′ network chart of the installation schedule with activities crossed out as they are completed. This is an excellent visual for the installation team as well as anyone else interested in the project.

PUTTING THE ORGANIZATION TOGETHER

In the MPM process, there are many different types of meetings such as the initial team formation, design reviews, status meetings, and problem solving. All meetings provide an opportunity to nurture relationships, and when conducted in a face-to-face format, represent the strongest form of communication. It is important that the meetings add value and use time efficiently. Effective meetings begin with thorough scheduling, preplanning for the facilities, agenda development, and completion of required prework.

Team Meeting Locations. The OEM and the customer are generally responsible for making all the arrangements for the leadership team formation site. This is important because it immediately involves the OEM and the customer in an active role in the team planning process and clearly establishes with the other suppliers that this process has the dual party support. The leadership team selects the site for the engineering team formation based on what is most convenient and practical. The respective installation sites are the best site for forming the installation and start-up teams.

After the initial team formation and with the concurrence of the leadership, subsequent leadership meetings take place on a rotating basis at the various participants' sites. This builds team participation since the hosting company is responsible for agenda development, travel recommendations, and the publication of meeting minutes. Sharing this responsibility builds a sense of equality in the leadership team and gives them an opportunity to learn more about each other's operations.

The status of engineering development and the site most appropriate for that time in the project drives subsequent engineering team meetings. The installation sites provide the most convenient and effective sites for holding installation and start-up team meetings with one exception: whenever an installation team plans a visit to the OEM around the time of runoff, it is convenient to hold the installation team meeting as part of that event.

Team Meeting Preplanning. A critical step in forming each team is to schedule and plan for the facilities. Typically, the OEM makes all the arrangements for the leadership and engineering teams that are held at their site; while the installation and start-up teams are best handled by the customer's project manager in coordination with the plant sites. The checklist in Figure 4.6 provides a guideline for reviewing the facility and miscellaneous supply requirements. This checklist is executed prior to each team formation meeting, and it should be given special emphasis whenever the meeting is at a new location. It is important to schedule arrangements with time enough to allow the participants to work it into their schedules. A four- to six-week lead time is best, particularly if international travel is required.

The main room should be large enough to comfortably accommodate the group planned for the team-building exercise. It should be set up in a U-shaped or conference-room style, with everyone having a chair at the main table and freedom to move about the room. All supplies and equipment—such as projectors and electronic chart boards—should be set up and tested ahead of time. If clerical support is required, a separate table can be set off in a corner with access to a computer and printer.

Once everyone agrees on the time and place, each company provides the names of their respective participants. At this point, the OEM, customer, and participating suppliers have come to some prior agreement on the use of the MPM process. Next, the OEM and customer sign and mail a joint letter of invitation. The letter includes all the travel and hotel arrangements, the generic agendas for the team in question, the dress code, and the details of any required prework. At the end of each team's formation meeting and all subsequent meetings, the next meeting time and location is determined. Thus, the only agreement necessary

Project title: _____

Team formation phase _____

Number of team participants _____

Coordinating project manager _____

#	Activity	☑
1.	Flip charts & colored markers for charts	
2.	Wall space to post charts (up to 20) and masking tape	
3.	Sufficient workspace for everyone to simultaneously make posters	
4.	Overhead transparency projector, markers, & blank sheets (Note for 3 & 4: portable computers with compatible projector are an alternate)	
5.	Electronic chart board or portable computer with compatible projector	
6.	Breakout areas (minimum 2 required. Teams greater than 15 will require additional breakout rooms.)	
7.	Room size & layout should easily accommodate all participants sitting on the outside of a U-shaped table arrangement	
8.	Copy machine readily available	
9.	Main room must be available the entire (2) days and secure at night to avoid tear-down and set-up time	
10.	Plan lunch using a breakout area for set up to avoid meeting interruptions	
11.	Breakout rooms should be available during the meeting times, but do not require securing at night since there is no setup or equipment to protect	
12.	Clerical person available on computer to enter brainstorming items, record action plans, and assist in generating meeting minutes (Preferred)	
13.	Mission statement cards (engineering, installation & start-up teams)	

Figure 4.6 Meeting facility checklist

regarding subsequent meetings is on the agenda; e-mail reminders are sent from the host containing the arrangements.

MPM Team-building Formula. The formula for building all types of teams is the same, with the exception that the leadership establishes the mission statement and goals, while the other teams receive them as a starting point. The difference is in the tools used to implement the team-building formula and the point at which the mission and goals are either developed or presented. The team-building formula consists of six steps as follows:

- Set environment—Introduction and norms
- Build linkages—Personal history
- Clarify roles—Select appropriate roles and responsibilities tool

- Generate ideas and issues—Select appropriate tool
- Mission and goals—Leadership sets mission and goals
- Action planning and scheduling—Select appropriate tool

The preceding sequence is for the leadership team. In all other teams, the mission and goals presentation occurs prior to idea generation, usually before or after the role clarification to keep it as close to the start of idea generation as practical. Table 4.3 identifies the specific tools substituted into the generic formula for each type of team. The project phase, site, and participants drive the content differences in the installation and start-up teams as well as any other work teams identified for a particular project.

Table 4.3 MPM team-building formula and tools

Activity	Tool		
	Leadership	Engineering	Install/startup
Set environment	Intro and norms	Intro and norms	Intro and norms
Build linkages	Personal history	Personal history	Personal history
Clarify roles	Organizational chart Situational matrix	Responsibility chart	RASIC
Generate ideas and issues	Brainstorming Categorization	Engineering specification review	Scope of work Fact finding
Mission and goals	Mission and goals	Leadership presentation	Leadership presentation
Action planning	Open issues list	Open issues list Categorization	Open issues list
Scheduling	Milestone chart Interface events	Gantt chart	Network diagram

Meeting Agenda. Conducting an effective meeting requires following an approved agenda (complete with timing), adhering to group norms, assigning of a facilitator for each topic, involving all participants, identifying and resolving issues, and getting a commitment to follow-up actions with accountability and timing. Effective meeting closure requires documentation of all decisions and actions, establishing a required follow-up meeting time and place, and accessing the meeting's value.

There are many sources describing content and format for various project meetings. In their book *Successful Project Management*, Gido and Clements (2006, 365–368) describe the most common status, design, and problem solving project meetings and provide generic agendas. Our focus is on the team formation meeting. The content and format is unique since it employs all the tools previously described. The team formation agenda is a good way to demonstrate the application of the tools to the various types of teams and provide readers with templates for implementing their teams.

The leadership and engineering teams are different types of teams and have unique agendas since the tools are different. However, the installation and startup are work teams, use the same tools, and employ common agendas with different content. Figures 4.7, 4.8, and 4.9 are generic agendas for the leadership, engineering, and common installation and start-up teams respectively. The preceding three chapters covering the process groups of *cooperate*, *communicate*, and *coordinate*

Leadership formation agenda

First day

- Present MPM concept
- Agreement on norms
- Develop personal history presentation
- Personal history (presented as individual to group)
- Develop organizational structure presentation
- Present organization (presented as a company to group)
- Lunch
- Complete situational management matrix
- Begin brainstorming process
- Evening social activity

Second day

- Complete brainstorming
- Categorize brainstorming data
- Develop overall mission statement
- Develop goals from above categories
- Working lunch
- Agree on mission statement
- Agree on project goals
- Develop action plans
- Communication tools (website)
- Plan next meeting (entire group)
- Assign individual to publish minutes (entire group)
- Wrap up

Figure 4.7 Leadership team formation agenda

Engineering formation agenda

First day

- Present MPM concept (presented by project manager)
- Agreement on norms
- Develop personal history presentation
- Personal history presentation (presented as individual)
- Develop responsibility chart
- Present responsibility chart (presented as a company)
- Lunch
- Present mission statement and goals (by co-chairs)
- Specification and engineering review
- Summarize open issues identified in above items
- Evening social activity

Second day

- Review leadership brainstorming items related to engineering and consolidate with engineering open issues (customer and OEM project managers present to entire group)
- Divide consolidated list into categories
- Develop actions, assign responsibility and establish timing related to items assigned to subgroup
- Working lunch
- Subgroups present above action plans for concurrence
- Agree on format to track open issues and actions
- Communication tools (website and conferencing)
- Assign individual to publish minutes (entire group)
- Plan next meeting and wrap up (entire group)

Figure 4.8 Engineering team formation agenda

describe the tools employed for each type of team for all steps in the MPM team-building formula.

Team Development Stages. There are five stages of team development: *forming, storming, norming, performing,* and *adjourning.* These stages have the following characteristics:

1. *Forming*—Inquisitive (What are we here for? What is our direction? Who are the other team members? What value is this for me? What are the constraints?)

Installation and start-up formation agenda

First day

- Present MPM concept structure (by designated proj. mgr.)
- Agreement on norms
- Personal history presentations
- RASIC charting
- Lunch
- Mission and goals (presented by co-chairs to group)
- Develop statement of work
- Site access and safety requirements
- Evening social activity

Second day

Fact finding and action planning

- OEM presentations (OEM's to entire group)
  - o   Pre-conditions
  - o   Special material, tools, people
  - o   Macro timing with special items
  - o   Requested resources, skilled trades
- Develop questions to OEM's (entire group)
- Make assignments for missing data
- Plan visit to manufacturer to observe equipment run off
- Lunch

Scheduling

- Work elements and resources (cross company sub-teams)
- Assemble preliminary plan (entire group)
- Set date to finalize the installation or start-up plan

Communication tools

- Website
- Weekly conference call

Wrap up

Figure 4.9 Installation/start-up team formation agenda

2.   *Storming*—Establishes power and influence (internal focus, testing roles and authority, increasing tension and conflict, pushing personal agendas)

3.   *Norming*—Stabilizes (accepting roles and responsibilities, strengthening linkages, increasing efficiency, growing camaraderie, increasing team focus)

4. *Performing*—Exceptional results (team synergy delivering results greater than the sum of the individual participants, high enthusiasm, high commitment, pride in team accomplishments, willingness to take on challenging goals)

5. *Adjourning*—Resistance (security concerns, loss of efficiency, sadness toward loss of relationships, desire to prolong the team)

Teams move back and forth through the first four stages depending on the individual circumstances over the course of the project. Changes in participants, for example, can result in a team going all the way back to the forming stage. Issues involving commitment, responsibilities, priorities, personalities, etc., have the potential to cause a team to slip back to the storming stage. It is the responsibility of everyone on the team to work toward strengthening relationships, building trust, demonstrating commitment, and supporting each other to help the team mature and perform. Team leaders must promote good team behaviors and take corrective action when negative behaviors occur. Social interaction beyond the normal project work provides a means to sustain and strengthen the team's personal relationships. The frequency of the leadership and engineering team meetings varies depending on the project—sometimes exceeding three months—and the meetings usually involve travel for the participants. The use of formally planned social activities outside work hours such as dinners or luncheons renews relationships and builds camaraderie. The installation and start-up teams work with each other daily, thus with the exception of the initial formation event or specific celebrations, informal socializing among the team members works best.

PART I SUMMARY

Part I covers the first three MPM Six C process groups, which are concentrated in the two-day team-building events for each of the teams identified. From a team-building perspective, their objective is threefold. First and most importantly, the teams move through the first three stages of *forming*, *storming*, and *norming* while building a solid foundation for *performing*. In a normal project without the use of the MPM approach, this can take weeks or months to accomplish, and in some cases, may never get past the forming stage. Second, from a skills perspective, the exercises use experiential learning to teach basic team dynamics and techniques required throughout the project execution. Third, the relationships and dialogue foster understanding and ensure that customer expectations remain at the forefront of the project to maximize final customer satisfaction.

From a project management perspective, the first three MPM process groups facilitate establishing a disciplined project management approach while the teams

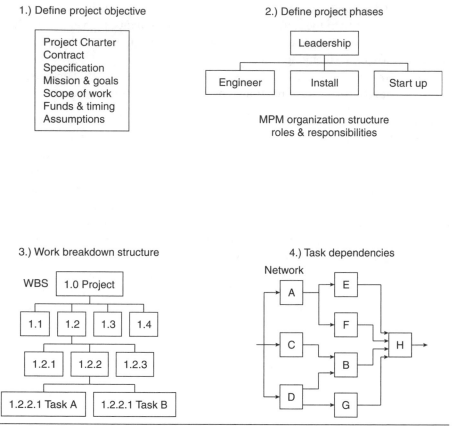

Figure 4.10a Schedule development steps 1–4

complete project initiation and planning activities. Establishing a strong discipline of project management at the beginning pays back many times over the course of the project. It consists of a definition of roles and responsibilities including the critical situational matrix, MPM organizational structure, communication plan, open issues action plans, and the baseline schedule. Figures 4.10a and 4.10b are a pictorial representation of the seven-step schedule development process illustrating the various project management deliverables achieved upon completion of the *cooperate, communicate,* and *coordinate* process groups. In step one, the *specifications* and *contract* are givens to begin the project, and are part of the charter. Another element of the charter is mission and goals, which are part of the *communicate* process group that is unique to the leadership and communicated to the other teams. All teams contribute to scope of work and assumptions as part of the

5.) Estimate/time resource

Task list			
Task	Dep.	Time	Res.
A	-	2 day	3 men
B	C, D	3 day	4 men
C	-	1 day	5 men

6.) Project interface events

Milestone chart			
#	Milestone	Date	Description
1	PO issued	1/1	Explanation 1
2	Def. content	4/1	Explanation 2
3	Order lg-ld	5/15	Explanation 3

7.) Project schedule baseline

	Project Gantt Chart							
ID	Task name	Time	Jan	Feb	Mar	Apr	May	Jun
			1234	1234	1234	1234	1234	1234
1.0	Project	12M	XXXXXXXXXXXXXXXXXXXXXXXXXXXXXXXXX					
1.1	Lead	12M	XXXXXXXXXXXXXXXXXXXXXXXXXXXXXXXXX					
1.1.2	Form lead	2D	X					

Figure 4.10b Schedule development steps 5–7

communicate process. In step two, roles and responsibilities, as well as an initial organization template, evolve from the *cooperate* process group with all teams contributing. The final five steps in schedule development all flow from the *coordinate* process group with all teams contributing to the WBS, network, task list, milestone chart, and integrated project Gantt chart. Use Figure 4.10a and Figure 4.10b as a visual tool for remembering and applying the first three Six C process groups and the project value they deliver.

PART II: MULTI-COMPANY PROJECT MANAGEMENT, CONTROL, EXECUTION, AND CLOSURE

Applying MPM Process Groups

OVERVIEW

The exercises in the preceding *cooperate, communicate,* and *coordinate* process groups prepare the teams to function effectively in cross-functional and cross-company group environments. This enables the diverse teams to collaborate and utilize consensus decision making during project execution. The relationships that are built establish a sound foundation, but the team participants need to continue nurturing their individual and company relationships throughout the balance of the project. The collaborative multi-company Six C approach fosters a commitment to the project goals. Combining commitment with the discipline of project management establishes the need to document and follow-up all actions and activities. This represents one-half of the Six C process groups and requires a lot of energy to create this environment. It takes constant vigilance and reinforcement by the project managers to ensure that the team maintains their commitment, continues to strengthen relationships, and does not forget the lessons learned, while rigorously documenting and following up all actions and activities related to the project.

Part II deals with managing the teams and project execution through the balance of the project lifecycle, encompassing the three final multi-company project management (MPM) process groups: *control, complete,* and *close.* In practice, implementation of the *control* and *complete* process groups appear as parallel processes rather than sequential groups, since part of the control group is monitoring the completion of actions and activities followed by corrective action when deviations occur. However, it is first in the sequence since the control methods should be in place before project execution begins. *Control* involves more than managing the traditional project schedule. It also involves managing all the risks and stakeholders as well, which in a multi-company project can be a daunting task. *Complete* involves the management of the teams and integration of their respective activities to ensure that the project flows smoothly. In addition, safety receives special attention due to its importance in the design and work teams. *Close* covers the traditional topics of *contract closure, evaluation, audits,* and *lessons learned,* incorporating the multi-company perspective. *Close* is an aspect of a project that is frequently short-changed, but can add surprising value. In particular, the multi-company project offers some unique opportunities that greatly enhance the value of *close,* which the section *MPM Closure Supplement* addresses.

Upon completion of the team formation event, the teams are stable, functioning in the norming stage and moving into the performing stage. They need freedom to do their jobs, which requires a leadership style characterized by support and delegation. As a result, the *control, complete,* and *close* process groups are conceptual and emphasize basic principles and tools rather than specific exercises and experiential learning. Whereas Part I is heavily weighted on team building during a two-day event, Part II emphasizes the project management discipline and team support over the balance of the project timeline. In particular, it covers several project management tools that prove valuable in MPM as well as a few unique MPM tools such as the *project phase scorecard, visual control board,* and *lessons learned integration process.* In addition, regular team agendas as well as pre- and post-project phase checklists provide practical examples to aid the reader in managing their own MPM project.

5

CONTROL

Project control requires the management of all the activities, stakeholders, and risks involved in a project. An important part of initiating any project involves the establishment of a foundation and a plan for control. Every task utilized in the cooperate, communicate, and coordinate process groups contributes to control by creating baselines and expectations or by modeling behavior and processes to support the control of project activities, stakeholders, or risks.

Activity control requires a point of reference to measure the variation followed by corrective action to compensate for the variation and to restore performance to the reference point. The mission and goals, specifications, statement of work, resolved open-issue items, and initial planning results in the creation of schedules, milestones, and interfaces for each phase of the project and establishes the project's activity baseline plan—also known as the baseline schedule and budget. This documentation contains basic assumptions, project organization, scope, timing, cost, resource requirements, etc., which is essentially all the knowledge to execute the project. Activity management uses this baseline as the reference point for regulating the time, cost, scope, and quality of the project.

Stakeholder management in a multi-company environment is more complex than a traditional project due to accessibility and organizational authority issues between the project manager and the stakeholders. The multi-company project management (MPM) team structure networks together and organizes all stakeholders. This network and organization provides an efficient way of controlling and integrating the participants to maximize results. Stakeholder management, similar to activity management, forms a baseline consisting of the norms, team structure, roles and responsibilities, and open-issue action plans to regulate the actions of the stakeholders. *Norms* define acceptable behavior, which serves as the reference point for regulating internal team relationships. The open-issue action plans are the primary tool for managing individual stakeholder involvement in the daily execution of project activities.

One tool that is beneficial in activity and stakeholder management is the one-page scorecard. This is a common tool in lean manufacturing, which has since been adapted to the MPM process. Its purpose is monitoring project performance in terms of activities and stakeholders. It does not replace any of the traditional project management tools, but rather supplements them. It can apply to any project, but the one-page format, simplicity of reporting, and overall monitoring of activities and stakeholders makes it particularly valuable in the MPM environment.

Risk management uses a tool called the *risk register* as the primary means of organizing the risk data. The *risk register* combines with the project schedule to provide a baseline or reference point for monitoring project risk. This register contains trigger points for initiating contingency plans purposed to mitigate specific risks defined in the register. This chapter consists of four sections describing project control: activity management to control project activities, stakeholder management to control project participants, scorecards to monitor activity and stakeholder status, and risk management to control project risk.

ACTIVITY MANAGEMENT

Controlling a project requires regular monitoring of the triple constraints of time, cost, and scope, together with ensuring that quality is maintained. The work packages discussed in the previous chapter contain the cost, time, and scope elements, and when assembled into the schedule network, represent the project baseline plan. The cost and time elements require tracking systems that record activity time and costs as they occur. Comparing this data to the baseline plan on a weekly, bi-monthly, or monthly basis, depending on the project needs and activity intensity, identifies deviations requiring corrective action. The critical path and earned-value techniques are analysis tools to aid in problem identification, evaluate corrective actions, develop time forecasts, and create cost forecasts. The establishment of a change control process to identify, quantify, and accept or reject any changes to the project provides control of the project scope. Existing quality management processes in place in the respective companies provide quality control of the specific project deliverables. The MPM approach focuses on the overall satisfaction of the total project and offers a few techniques to increase the level of customer and supplier satisfaction.

Critical Path. Critical path is a well-known tool used to manage schedules. It does not take into consideration any resource limitations, assumes all activities start at the earliest possible date, and assumes that one or more network paths will yield the longest duration. Thus, it establishes the project completion date. All activities on the critical path have zero float or slack. All other network paths have a positive value of float. Specific activities on the noncritical paths may have free float, which is the amount of activity delay allowed without affecting the other activities in the project. Frequently, it may be necessary to modify the initial critical path using resource leveling or constraining techniques to yield the schedule.

Critical chain is another method for managing schedules. This is a more complex method than critical path, as it adds resource constraints into the analysis. It starts with a resource-leveled critical path and assumes an as-late-as-possible start date, which minimizes work-in-process. Critical chain requires the addition of activity completion alerts and focuses on a critical resource called the *drum resource*, and manages using network buffers rather than float. The critical chain does not change over the course of the project. Application of this method requires a very skilled project manager with organizational discipline; critical chain support requires reducing multi-tasking, staggering project start times, not holding people accountable for task times but passing on completed work as soon as possible, etc.

Regardless of the method, effective schedule management requires the use of a methodology to track and react to the schedule performance. Using the same methodology in all phases and across all companies facilitates understanding, communication, and integration of schedules into the total project. Critical chain is not the preferred method to use in MPM applications, since its limited use makes it very unlikely that all companies in a multi-company project have the necessary skills or organizational discipline. Thus, for our purposes, the focus is on the traditional critical path analysis.

Using critical path simplifies project schedule management by aiding the prioritization of activities and identification of schedule impacts. Delays in a noncritical path that are within its total float do not affect project completion. Expediting an activity that is not on the critical path to achieve an early completion does not improve the project completion date. Any delay in activities on the critical path adds an equal delay to the project completion. Similarly, in a project with one unique critical path, expediting an activity on the critical path expedites project completion, provided it does not create a different critical path.

Critical path is a time-based analysis that is sensitive to any changes in the estimated time of the activities. During the course of project execution, actual activity durations above or below estimates cause the critical path to change. Each critical path analysis identifies the critical tasks and predicts the new completion date. Based on that forecast, the project team plans and implements corrective actions to keep the project time in control. Although software programs automatically generate the critical path and update it as actual times are input, it is a good idea for project participants to have a basic understanding of how the critical path is developed.

To determine the critical path, each activity must have an estimated duration and must identify the immediate predecessor activities. This information appears in spreadsheet format as shown in Table 5.1 or network diagram format as shown in Figure 5.1. The first step in determining the critical path is to conduct a forward pass, starting with the first activity in the project. This computes the early start (ES) and early finish (EF) of each activity. Each activity looks at the early finish of all its predecessors and selects the largest time (latest early finish) as its early start. An activity that has no predecessor has an ES of zero. Adding the duration to the ES time returns the EF time:

$$duration + ES = EF$$

Apply this to the spreadsheet example by starting with Activity A, which has no predecessor and thus has an early start of zero. Then add the A activity duration of 2 to get an early finish of 2. Thus, the EF for Activity A is calculated:

$$2 + 0 = 2$$

Table 5.1 Activity duration and dependency table

Activity	Duration estimate	Immediate predecessor
A	2	—
B	3	A
C	5	A
D	6	A
E	4	B
F	3	D
G	3	C,E,F

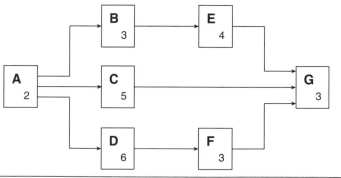

Figure 5.1 Network diagram

Activities B, C, and D have Activity A as their only predecessor, and therefore 2 is considered their early start. Continue this process for all activities. Note that Activity G has three predecessors: C, E, and F. The EF times for these activities are 7, 9, and 11 respectively. Thus, the EF for Activity F of 11 (the largest of the three) becomes the early start for Activity G. The spreadsheet with critical path in Table 5.2 highlights in black and lists the early start and finish times for the example. The network with critical path in Figure 5.2 adds these values to the original network

Table 5.2 Spreadsheet with critical path calculations

Activity	Duration estimate	Immediate predecessor	Earliest		Latest		Float or slack	Critical path
			ES	EF	LS	LF		
A	2	–	0	2	0	2	0	X
B	3	A	2	5	4	7	2	
C	5	A	2	7	6	11	4	
D	6	A	2	8	2	8	0	X
E	4	B	5	9	7	11	2	
F	3	D	8	11	8	11	0	X
G	3	C,E,F	11	14	11	14	0	X

Note: Critical path for this network is A-D-F-G

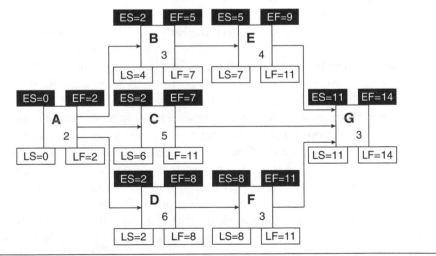

Figure 5.2 Network diagram showing critical path

diagram example in the upper right and left corners designated with a black background for each activity box.

The next step is a reverse pass beginning with the last activity in the schedule to compute the late start (LS) and late finish (LF) of each activity. Each activity looks at the LS of all its successors and selects the shortest time (earliest late start) as its late finish. Subtracting the duration from the late finish returns the late start time:

$$LF - duration = LS$$

Again referring to the example, start with Activity G, which has no successors. Thus, the late finish equals the early finish, yielding a value of 14. Subtracting the duration 3 for Activity G from 14 yields a late start of 11. Thus, the late start for Activity G is calculated:

$$14 - 3 = 11$$

Since Activity G is the only successor for Activities C, E, and F, the late finish values for C, E, and F become 11. Continue this process for all activities. Note that Activity A has three successors: B, C, and D. The LS times for B, C, and D are 4, 6, and 2 respectively. Thus, the LS for Activity D of 2 (the smallest of the three) becomes the LF for Activity A. The spreadsheet with critical path lists the LS and LF times for the example. In the network with critical path, these values appear in the lower right and left corners of each activity box.

The final step in determining the critical path is computing the float in each activity, which is the difference between the early and late start times or the early and late finish times. The next to last column in the expanded spreadsheet (Table 5.2) shows the results of this calculation, and the last column uses an X to designate any activity with zero float, which places the activity on the critical path. In this example, the critical path is A-D-F-G.

The preceding example is very simplistic, with only seven activities utilizing the most basic relationship of predecessor finish to successor start. Most project phases will contain at least 250 activities, and when integrated into the total project schedule, will contain over 1000. The predecessor-to-successor relationships also increase in complexity including start to finish, finish to finish, start to start, as well as lead or lag considerations. When the project falls behind a required completion date, the float is negative and the critical path is the one with the least (most negative) float. Activity durations, network logic, or other constraints are adjusted to get the least float back to zero and the project back on schedule. Scheduling software for managing this volume of data quickly computes the critical path and makes this technique practical and effective. It also facilitates what-if scenarios to determine the best method to get the project back on schedule. The results are only as good as the data input, so the network logic as well as the estimated and actual times must be accurate to get the correct result.

Returning to our example, assume that Activities A through D are complete with the following actual times: A=3, B=5, C=5, and D=5. The network diagram in Figure 5.3 denotes these by brackets, then displays the revisions to the forward and reverse pass calculations. The project now requires 15 days to complete and the new critical path as determined from our new table of calculations in Table 5.3 is A-B-E-G. Getting the project back on schedule requires reducing the time of one or more of the activities on the critical path. Activities A through D are complete

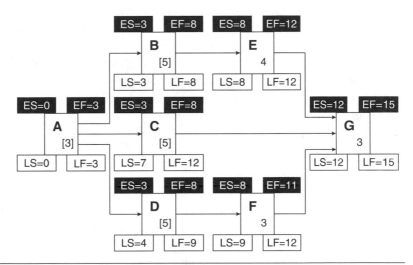

Figure 5.3 Network diagram—actual time & critical path

Table 5.3 Spreadsheet—actual time and critical path

Activity	Duration estimate	Immediate predecessor	Earliest		Latest		Float or slack	Critical path
			ES	EF	LS	LF		
A	[3]	–	0	3	0	3	0	X
B	[5]	A	3	8	3	8	0	X
C	[5]	A	3	8	7	12	4	
D	[5]	A	3	8	4	9	1	
E	4	B	8	12	8	12	0	X
F	3	D	8	11	9	12	1	
G	3	C,E,F	2	15	12	15	0	X

Note: [ ] indicates an actual value
The critical path for this project is now A-B-E-G

and no longer offer any opportunity for improvement. Reducing the time for Activity F has no value since it is not on the critical path. When looking for opportunity to recover the schedule, the nearest activities on the critical path provide the most benefit; they are the most urgent activities and generally have the greatest amount of information. Failure to consider these first will result in lost opportunities. After exhausting all opportunities with the nearest activities, the next most beneficial items to look at are the critical path activities that take the longest time to complete. It is always wise to try to recover the time within the phase in which you are working without placing that burden on other teams. For example, if engineering or manufacturing compensate for lost time by taking it out of the installation period, there is insufficient time when the installation arrives. This results in increased costs, reduced quality, and a host of other problems. This is more a case of passing the buck rather than managing the schedule.

In the given example, the two activities remaining on the critical path are E and G. Activity E is the nearest and, in this case, the longest. It is the first activity on which to concentrate for recovering the schedule. The following are some possible approaches for reducing activity duration:

1. Apply more resources to shorten activity durations
2. Assign personnel with greater expertise to perform the work within a shorter timeframe
3. Reduce the scope or requirements for an activity
4. Increase productivity using improved methods and equipment
5. Partition tasks, allowing overlap to reduce time
6. Work overtime or weekends
7. Increase productivity through new technologies

Many of these approaches have a negative impact on cost or scope as well as on quality. The project manager and the team must consider all factors when selecting the best corrective action for the project. We shall assume that the team identified an improved method of completing Activity E in three days, offsetting the additional equipment cost with labor savings. This one-day savings from the changes in Activity E on the critical path yields a one-day savings in the total project time, bringing the project back in line with the original 14-day completion. The project now has two critical paths, because both E and F are critical activities. By itself, further reductions in Activity E will not change the project completion date unless activity F is also reduced by the same amount.

The title of project manager does not necessarily give one a thorough understanding of project management methodology. In one case, I worked with a project manager from an operations background as a peer who was responsible for the site construction in support of an equipment project. He had the mistaken belief that every activity in the project must be critical in order to have a good plan. In his mind, if every activity is critical, everyone is working all the time similar to his production mentality from operations. (The flaw in this mentality in project and production environments is that it ignores the concept of constraints and bottlenecks.) My companion apparently lacked the necessary project management training and was not open to project management methodology. Therefore, he was not at all capable of controlling a project. It was a difficult relationship, because he was usually pushing the wrong priorities. Fortunately, he had a knowledgeable staff that worked around him when necessary and accomplished the job in spite of his ignorance.

Earned Value. Earned value is a tool used to analyze both cost and schedule effectiveness. It focuses on measuring the physical work performed on the project. It has varying degrees of acceptance within the project management community. In theory, earned value can track all costs such as labor, material, and equipment. In functional and matrix organizations, the traditional accounting systems typically capture and report data in a functional format. Since the WBS for each project phase is generally a product-oriented breakdown, computing the earned value requires converting functional format information into the product-oriented format. The effort to convert data from functional to product-oriented may inhibit reporting frequency, introduce time lags, and increase administrative costs that offset the benefits of using earned value. If the project manager decides to gather their own actual data to compute the earned value, it will result in two sets of costing data that never match, which can cause a considerable amount of conflict between the finance and project management organizations. Unless the accounting system provides product-oriented data, it is best to keep it simple by tracking and analyzing only labor hours and using it as a guide rather than an absolute number to predict labor costs and schedule performance. Using only the hours avoids all the conversions for different wage rates and keeps it generic. Then, the existing accounting system captures the actual labor-cost dollars as well as all the other cost elements. Earned-value methodology begins with the following three variables measured at specific points in time in the project:

- PV—*Planned value* is accumulated labor hours or dollars of each activity that is expected to be completed for a specified time period based on the project baseline. Also known as the budgeted cost for work scheduled (BCWS).
- EV—*Earned value* is the accumulated budgeted labor hours or dollars actually completed for a specific period based on the project baseline. Also known as the budgeted cost of work performed (BCWP).

- AC—*Actual cost* is the accumulated actual labor hours or dollars incurred for a specified period. Also known as the actual cost for work performed (ACWP).

Once these three variables are determined, the schedule performance index (SPI) and cost performance index (CPI) are calculated using the following formulas:

$$SPI = \frac{EV}{PV} \quad CPI = \frac{EV}{AC}$$

The SPI and CPI indexes are efficiency ratios of the schedule and cost respectively. The ratios allow use of either labor hours or labor costs in the calculations. Greater than 1.0 is good and less than 1.0 is bad. For example, a project with an SPI of 1.1 and a CPI of 0.8 is ahead of schedule but over budget. Figure 5.4 is a graphical representation of this earned value example. Note that a plot of the project baseline's cumulative budget versus time establishes the PV for the entire project. The EV and AC are

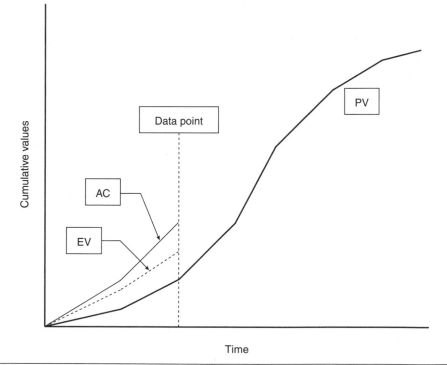

Figure 5.4 Graphical representation of earned value

calculated as the project progresses. Working unplanned overtime to get ahead of schedule is one possible cause for this condition. The SPI must be checked by verifying conclusions with the critical path. In the EV calculations, there is no distinction between critical and noncritical items. Therefore, the noncritical items that are completed ahead of schedule can give a false sense of success when the critical path items are behind schedule. The SPI should be verified by checking the critical path status. The CPI is a much more reliable indicator of labor performance.

A second example shows the computation of SPI and CPI in calculation 1 of Figure 5.5, displaying typical calculations that involve the use of earned value in forecasting. In the example, the total project budget is $4000. At a specific point in time, the PV according to the expected project baseline is $2000. The EV of the completed activities is $1400 and the actual labor cost is $1600. The SPI is 0.7 and the CPI is 0.875, putting the project behind schedule and over budget.

Forecasting. Assuming labor hours and labor costs are proportional, the CPI provides a means for computing the forecasted labor cost estimate at completion (EAC) of the project. "As early as the 15 to 20 percent completion point of any project, the cost performance efficiency factors (earned values versus actual costs) have been shown to stabilize, and the data provided can be used to predict the final range of costs for any given project" (Fleming and Koppelman 2005, 41). When forecasting using the CPI, it is assumed that past performance will continue for

Project givens: Budget = $4000, EV = $1400, PV = $2000, AC = $1600

1. Compute SPI and CPI as follows:

$$SPI = \frac{1400}{2000} = 0.7 \quad CPI = \frac{1400}{1600} = 0.875 \quad \text{(Labor efficiency)}$$

2. Assuming same efficiency for balance of project, compute EAC as follows:

$$EAC = \frac{Budget}{CPI} = \frac{4000}{.875} = \$4571 \quad (-\$571\,\text{Cost variance})$$

3. CPI needed to achieve zero variance computes as follows:

$$CPI_{new} = \frac{Budget - EV}{Budget - AC} = \frac{4000 - 1400}{4000 - 1600} = 1.08 \quad \text{(Eff. must Improve by 20 points)}$$

4. Assuming 100% efficiency for balance of project compute EAC as follows:

EAC = AC + (Budget − EV) = 1600 + (4000 − 1400) = $4200   (−$200 Cost var.)

Figure 5.5 Forecasting calculations

the balance of the project. The total budgeted labor cost is divided by the CPI to get the estimate at completion. When over-budget forecasts appear, some project managers delay their reaction and avoid facing the reality of the situation. It is important to face over-budget situations as soon as possible and implement corrective actions before things get to the point where recovery attempts may jeopardize the remaining project schedule, cost, scope, or work quality. Addressing the issue early makes it easier to find a solution.

A mistake often made by project managers when the forecast deteriorates is to either discard as bad luck the initial poor labor-cost performance, or to make excuses and then predict they will operate above 100 percent efficiency for the balance of the project to make up lost ground. Project managers who decide to make up the shortfall by operating above 100 percent must quantify how much improvement that represents over the current performance and assess the likelihood of achieving that improvement. The sample forecast calculations illustrate this point. With SPI and CPI below 1.0, the project is behind schedule and over budget. The project has earned less than planned and has spent more than it has earned. The second calculation assumes the same CPI for the entire project, yielding an EAC of $4571, which is $571 over budget. Since the project initially operated at 12 percent below 100 percent efficiency, calculation 3 reveals it must operate at 108 percent efficiency for the balance of the project to make up the shortage, which is a 20-point improvement—highly unlikely without significant changes.

Forecasting using CPI is one approach. If the reason for missing the work's completion date estimate is a special cause that has since gone away, the confidence in the original estimate returns and the estimate at completion is simply the sum of the actual cost and any remaining estimates. The remaining estimates are the difference between the budget and the earned value. Calculation 4 shows that using this approach yields an EAC of $4200, which is $200 over budget. When the EAC values are inconsistent or out of control, another useful approach is to reestimate the project from the current point to completion. The greater level of information and knowledge of the project team's capabilities, as well as a fresh look at the remaining tasks yields increased accuracy, resulting in a better forecast. It may not yield the answer the customer or boss wants to hear, but it provides a more realistic view.

These earned value techniques and related indexes normalize the data, allowing comparisons of performance across projects of varying sizes and facilitating the forecasts of future performance based on performance history. These methods are used more to analyze trends to anticipate problems. The schedules should be checked by carefully analyzing the critical path. The following approaches are possible ways to reduce the cost of activities:

1.   Substitute less expensive materials that still meet the required specifications
2.   Assign personnel with greater expertise to perform the work more quickly
3.   Reduce the scope or requirements for an activity
4.   Increase productivity through improved methods and equipment
5.   Increase productivity through new technologies
6.   Lengthen activity duration to eliminate overtime costs

Just as in reducing time, many of these approaches negatively affect time or scope as well as quality. When selecting the corrective action, the project team considers these factors to achieve the best project fit.

Activity Value Technique. If the earned value method is not used for tracking project-schedule performance, there is another technique that is crude, but simple and effective called the *activity value technique*. It is a spinoff of the earned value concept, using the number of activities completed compared to the number of activities planned to compute the schedule status index (SSI). It is most valid when the activities that make up the project are approximately the same duration (e.g., one to two weeks) and contain similar amounts of labor. Now, instead of tracking all the hours, the only thing that requires tracking is the number of completed activities. To compute the SSI at a given time, divide the number of activities completed by the number of activities planned to be complete according to the baseline plan. A schedule status index greater than 1.0 is ahead of schedule and an index less than 1.0 is behind schedule. Just as was done with the earned value SPI, the results require validation against the critical path analysis. Both SPI and SSI values that indicate corrective action require a careful analysis of the critical path in order to determine a course of action.

Figure 5.6 is a graphical representation of the activity value technique showing the earned activity value (EAV) represented by the dashed line tracking pretty close to the planned activity values (PAV) as shown by the solid black line. In this example, the SSI is fluctuating between 0.9 and 1.1 depending on the data point selected, as the EAV is shifting between below and above the PAV line.

Change Control. Change control must start with the initial quotation process. It is the responsibility of both the customer and supplier to document changes initiated by either party to ensure incorporation into the final contract and understanding by all. Nothing is more damaging to a customer and supplier relationship after reaching a contract agreement than for the customer to discover that certain deliverables were not included, or the supplier to learn that the work scope is significantly greater than expected.

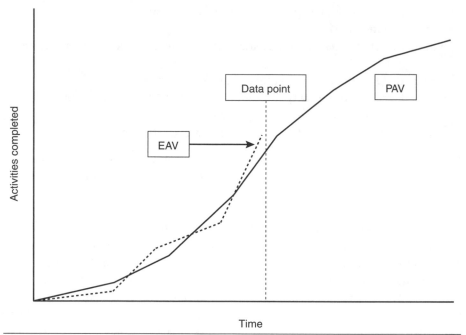

Activities completed

Time

Figure 5.6 Activity value technique graphic

In many cases, project management is not involved until after the award of the contract. Thus, it is important for the project manager to flush out and correct any misunderstandings as part of developing the project charter. The initial leadership team formation meeting provides an excellent opportunity as part of the mission and goals development to resolve these issues and ensure a common understanding by all.

Many times, companies take the position of allowing no changes, thinking that this will eliminate variation and control costs. In a large project with many unknowns, this is an extremely naive viewpoint, discourages creativity, and often results in under-the-table changes without proper reviews and approval. It is far better to recognize that changes are a part of every project and that many changes represent improvements in cost, timing, and performance that should be encouraged. Thus, implementing a clearly defined process is essential for identifying, evaluating, and approving or rejecting all changes in a timely and efficient manner.

It is important to implement a formal change control procedure as soon as possible after the project begins. Generally, the second leadership or engineering team meeting discusses the topic and approves a change control process for implementation by the team. In many cases, the customer and supplier may have standard forms they already use for tracking project changes, which can be easily adapted to the joint team process. Each company must decide who signs off on changes. This approval usually falls to the project managers up to a certain dollar amount or timing impact after which approval goes to the project sponsors. As each change control process is developed, consideration should be given to the following MPM lessons learned:

1. Documenting all changes that affect time, cost, scope, or quality— positive or negative—provides valuable information for future projects; aids in explaining the project's status; and eliminates doubt, confusion, and disagreement that is sometimes created by conflicting individual memories.

2. It is necessary to review every change in terms of all of the following elements: cost, time, scope, and quality. Changes which only benefit one of the elements, should be passed up, unless all other elements have been carefully weighed.

3. Thoroughly documenting previously identified corrective actions from timing and cost control meetings ensures the full consideration of both the triple constraints and quality.

4. Having a cross-function team review all changes prevents a single functional group from assuming that a change has little or no impact on other functional groups, and from discovering their error too late.

5. All changes should include sound business case justifications detailing the benefits, identifying any negative consequences, and quantifying any impact on time or cost.

6. Informing everyone that the process is open for anyone to initiate change encourages sub-suppliers to proffer changes. Similarly, a lack of sub-supplier empowerment inhibits ideas.

7. Everyone should be required to use the change process to make changes. Customers circumventing the process can result in changes based on personal preferences rather than on sound business cases.

8. The change process should be timely and efficient with respect to the project lifecycle. A change made early in the planning or design phase might not affect cost or time and might be easy to justify, but that same idea proposed in the manufacturing or installation phase could have major cost and time consequences, eliminating any possible justification. The change process must therefore be efficient so that delays in the adoption process do not cancel an earlier justification or obstruct the flow of ideas. Adopting changes early maximizes results and precludes rework.

Quality Control. The subject of quality is a very broad topic that is a major discipline in its own right. Quality control is a subset of the overall quality management process that focuses on the measurement of specific project variables to ensure they meet requirements and specifications. Even this subset of quality is too large to cover in this book. Thus, the purpose of this section is to briefly discuss the relationship between MPM and quality and offer insight on a few techniques that have proven valuable in controlling project quality.

In projects, quality is a given that must be achieved in order to declare success. Quality is determined by the ability to meet the deliverable specifications and overall customer satisfaction with the entire project experience. All companies in MPM must have well-established quality management processes that are consistent with globally accepted quality standards such as QS 9000. The quality management processes consist of policies and procedures that enable the project to adhere to the project specifications. Each company then integrates their quality processes with the execution of the project activities to achieve the desired quality results. Both customers and suppliers can sustain the quality of their projects by ensuring that the participating companies have quality systems in place and are certified to meet the current global standards. When it comes to deliverables, meeting their specifications and the quality systems that monitor them, MPM plays only a minor role. It does, however, make a major contribution in driving overall project customer satisfaction. Throughout the entire project lifecycle, MPM focuses on including the customer in every decision, aligning the expectations of all participants, and measuring the project results in terms of those expectations. This significantly increases customer and participant satisfaction.

A great deal of writing exists about the importance of customer satisfaction since it builds supplier reputations, drives repeat business, and is one measure of the health and viability of an enterprise. There is also value in supplier satisfaction. A satisfied supplier strives to get repeat business, is open to a customer's needs, values business to the extent where it influences prices, and willingly works with customers to help solve problems that benefit both parties. Thus, it is important for the customer as well as the supplier to strive to achieve the satisfaction of all parties in a project. The satisfaction of all participants is a focus and one of the prime benefits of MPM.

In any equipment project, there are many specifications and deliverables. The participants manage these using their established quality systems. The MPM process maintains a big-picture perspective and strives to ensure that the total system delivers equipment that when installed, performs within the customer's facility and operations environment to everyone's expectations. This requires looking at the project from a total systems viewpoint. Simulations, system runoffs, proficiency-based training, and on-the-job experience are techniques that offer great value in this approach.

Any major equipment project is highly dependent on the software design for fulfillment of the equipment's potential. If the software is not functionally tested prior to equipment installation, many problems may go undiscovered until it is too late, driving correction costs out of sight. In addition, programming completeness is extremely difficult to assess unless it is actually tested. Software simulations that test overall functionality are an effective way to determine the completeness of the software design, identify deficiencies, and make cost-effective corrections without any impact to the project. At one extreme, these simulations can be a simple electronic panel that interfaces with the new controls, providing artificial inputs and outputs. The B2C press project case study exemplifies the other extreme. It involved the purchase of four B2C press systems with a total project value in excess of $80 million. The leadership team during the brainstorming identified the software design and the associated communication network as a major risk. The customer, equipment supplier, control supplier, and drive supplier all had concerns. To mitigate the risk and to provide better project quality control, the team undertook a major simulation effort.

The customer supplied a facility and labor to set up the simulation. The equipment manufacturer provided early designs and engineering support for the simulation. To support the simulation, the controls supplier shipped control panels and network materials for the second system; and the drive supplier provided motors for the second system fitted with theoretical loads. In addition, the control and drive suppliers provided technical assistance to support the setup and actual simulation. The estimated combined labor cost was approximately $300,000, but the four participants pooled their resources and funded their individual involvement without penalty to the project. No single party could have funded or executed such an elaborate simulation. Working collaboratively, the simulation proved a major benefit to all participants. The equipment manufacturer was able to debug the system design and correct problems ahead of installation. The control and network supplier gained valuable experience with their new network product in the servo press environment, allowing them to improve their network manuals and troubleshooting techniques. The drives supplier improved their interface design with the controls and gained experience on the network, which they used on other systems. The customer gained experience on the installation techniques, control design, and network troubleshooting, which proved invaluable during the initial installation, and again during regular production. All participants benefited from the significantly improved quality of the system through a far more efficient start-up process that reduced the technical support and operating labor that would otherwise have been required. MPM made this simulation possible and everyone achieved a good return for the efforts.

A second technique that greatly improves quality is conducting a full-system runoff prior to shipping it to the customer for installation. This is no small effort since runoff costs for a $20 million system can easily exceed $1 million and can add 4–8 weeks to the delivery time of a major press system. The purchase of a single system may not warrant this approach, but when purchasing in multiples of four or more, it is cost effective. This approach allows the full functionality of the system to be tested and allows the manufacturer to make corrections and rework at their site. It also minimizes rework on future systems and significantly reduces the supplier's costs for installation and startup. The customer ends up with a proven system that allows them to focus on the integration issues of the new equipment into their facility without worrying about fixing or modifying the equipment. The proven system drives a much higher level of customer satisfaction and eliminates many cost issues related to corrections and rework that might otherwise harm the customer and supplier relationship.

Most projects take into account the delivery of the proven system at the end of a project, but MPM takes this a step further by ensuring that the system performs in the customer's facility. This requires the preparation of the customer's organization to efficiently operate and maintain the equipment. Working collaboratively, the leadership integrates proficiency-based training and on-the-job experience opportunities with the project plan to ensure that the customer's personnel have the tools and knowledge to operate and maintain the systems to their full potential. This final step in controlling quality ensures the achievement of customer expectations and determines the project's final level of success.

STAKEHOLDER MANAGEMENT

Stakeholder management is a critical factor in any project. Managing stakeholders using a traditional hierarchical structure in a multi-company environment does not work, since there is no single point of authority. Even in an internal company project, the project manager tasked with stakeholder management does not have the level of authority required to support a hierarchical approach. The website, conferences, and regular team meetings are the communication tools that keep stakeholders informed of the status, alerted to any potential problems, involved in problem resolution, and committed to project objectives. Stakeholders are best managed using a combination of influence powers and action-plan follow-up to control variation and to keep the participants in line with the project's mission and goals. In addition, stakeholder management requires an escalation process to expedite issue resolution at the appropriate level, and conflict management to maintain team efficiency.

Influence Powers. A key point on influence is that it is more the perceived degree of influence that another individual has than on the actual existence of that influence. Hersey, Blanchard, and Johnson (2008, 163–166) in *Management of Organizational Behavior: Leading Human Resources,* identify seven unique influence powers to which MPM adds *the influence power of teams.* Adding this last influence power to the original seven generates the eight types of power present in MPM:

1. *Legitimate influence power*—Possessed by those who have been officially empowered by the top authority (also known as *position power*)
2. *Expert influence power*—Possessed by those who are recognized as the expert, thereby dispensing knowledge that is accepted as fact
3. *Referent*—Held by those who possess a certain personal appeal and an ability to elicit willing commitments
4. *Reward*—Possessed by those who are able (or are in a position) to offer rewards and fulfill desires
5. *Coercive*—Held by those who are capable of dispensing penalties and affecting careers
6. *Connection*—An influence that is possessed by those who have a close professional (or sometimes somewhat personal) association with key leaders
7. *Information*—Held by those who have access to specific key information that is not available to everyone
8. *Team*—Held by those with a sense of commitment and a willingness to make sacrifices to achieve team success

MPM uses every influence type to manage the stakeholders. The leadership team by virtue of the senior executives' power and authority exercises the legitimate, reward, and coercive influence powers. The organizational chart exercise defines the combination of powers for all the companies that participate in the project. The personal history exercise reinforces the expert and referent influences by highlighting individual expertise and by building personal linkages for the participants on each team. The connection and information powers are present in the team formation process during the project manager's presentation of the mission statement and goals and again in the leadership teams' delegation process during the open-issues discussion. Finally, the entire process design focuses on building team influence to maximize its effect in driving project performance by all stakeholders.

One side benefit of MPM is that it has a dramatic effect on the influence power of the project managers in both the customer and supplier organizations. Through the leadership team, the project managers have close regular contact with the senior executives of both the customer and supplier organizations, which greatly elevates their legitimate, connection, and information influence powers, as well as the perception of their reward and coercive powers. This makes the project managers more effective and eliminates many frustrations that are encountered in non-team, multi-company project environments. Project managers often find that the other organizations give them more attention and are more responsive to their questions and suggestions. This increased influence outside their own company improves the ability to negotiate for the project and increases their connection and information powers within their own organization.

Action Plan Follow-up. Just as the schedule forms the basis for project control, the open-issues list provides the baseline for managing the various people issues. Within the open-issues list are specific actions with clearly defined accountability and completion-date commitments. Each team essentially self-manages by following up regularly to the action-plan commitments that they establish, and the leadership team provides oversight when the project managers find a need for added attention. The co-leaders for the leadership team, with the advice of their project managers, ensure that the leadership team meets its own commitments to the action plans. Maintaining and publicizing a single open-issues list for the entire project allows the leadership to model expectations and applies pressure on the leadership to walk as they talk. Publicizing the issues, avoids duplication and provides everyone with access to the same information. Visibility outside the team causes the team to be more disciplined when it comes to following up on the actions.

The leadership team must establish a regular discipline to follow-up on action plans. As part of the leadership-team formation event, team members agree to a regular sequence of meetings, which usually involves a combination of face-to-face meetings and conferencing. The face-to-face meetings are generally all-day events that justify the travel and planning, while conferences are generally a few hours in duration at most. All organized meetings are scheduled well in advance to allow executives to set aside time in their schedules. The frequency should be appropriate for the project and for the leadership's oversight responsibility; sufficient time should pass between meetings to allow for the progression of normal project activities without having to involve the leadership team in the specific activities.

A meeting is a necessary, useful, and productive event only if it is value added and timely. For example, a three-year project might start out with the premise that the leadership team should meet quarterly. Meeting particulars represent specific-dates and locations that fit selected milestones or a specific group of leadership action-plan completion dates. For example, the first meeting might coincide with a group of action plans that the leadership has committed to complete at the customer's headquarters. The second meeting might nicely coincide with an engineering review and approval milestone at the supplier's engineering site; while the third meeting might best be coordinated with the buyoff of a major component at the supplier's manufacturing site. During the engineering and manufacturing phases, scheduling meetings at sub-supplier sites around specific sub-supplier deliverables is valuable as well. This gives the sub-suppliers a chance to display their facilities and capabilities. The leadership presence at the sub-supplier sites increases the importance of the project to sub-supplier personnel and makes them feel more a part of the project. Varying the meeting location spreads travel costs, meeting costs, and planning burdens among all participants, which levels the project manager's load since they do the bulk of the planning work. The varied meeting sites give the executives an opportunity to tie in the travel with other business activities. The time between meetings might vary in the three- to five-month range. If a crisis occurs, it may become necessary to set up a special meeting with the entire team or designated subgroup to resolve the crisis. During the installation and startup, it is best to hold meetings at the installation site.

The leadership team meetings are far more than a simple project status review. They are a follow-up mechanism to the work of the leadership team in the form of the action plans, are a means to monitor and build stakeholder relationships, and are a review for ensuring that the project is in alignment with company strategies. In addition, the leadership team resolves open issues that have escalated from the other project teams, approves change requests, and discusses overall project risk management. Figure 5.7 is a generic agenda for a regular leadership meeting. Note the norms and mission and goals review at the start of each meeting by the host's key executive, which keeps the team and project focus. The agenda items represent content that is appropriate for leadership. The topics are adjusted to fit each project situation since not all topics are required for every meeting. The site tour is planned in the middle of the meeting to break up the meeting and to give everyone an opportunity to stretch their legs, as well as to allow participants to see project activity on a firsthand basis. The leadership presence in the project sends a good message as well. Since over the course of the project everyone has an opportunity to display their facilities and capabilities, the leadership team participants gain an increased awareness and understanding of each other, which further reinforces relationships. If a picture is worth a thousand words, than a site tour is worth ten thousand words. On many occasions the tours have resulted in suggestions from the visitors that have helped the existing project or host operations, and identified ideas that the visitors took back to improve their portion of the project and their own operations. On many occasions, senior executives have said that the ideas triggered from the site tour more than offset their team participant's travel costs, even when international travel was involved.

The social event is not mandatory, but provides a great opportunity to reinforce the relationships within the team. This is subject to the schedules and priorities of the team members and usually occurs the night before or immediately

Agenda review and approval	Host key executive
Review norms, mission, and goals	Host key executive
Safety topic presentation (optional)	Volunteer
Project status review	
Supplier perspective	Supplier PM
Subsupplier perspectives	Subsupplier PMs
Customer perspective	Customer PM
Lunch and site tour	Host PM
Open issue action items review	As assigned
Escalated open issues	Issue report
Change requests	Initiating PM
Risk management	Group exercise
Identify new open issues from the meeting	Host PM
Resolve, delegate, or assign new items	Group exercise
Wrap up	Host PM
Summarize new decisions and leadership actions	
Formalize agreement on next meeting date and site	
Assign responsibility and date to publish minutes	
Pre- or post-meeting social event	Host key executive
(ie: Dinner, group activity, etc. outside normal business hours)	

Figure 5.7 Leadership team regular meeting agenda

after the team meeting. A good social event ensures everyone has a good time, does not create any hardship for the participants, and avoids elaborate high-cost activities that might project a negative perception to the public. GM adopted a *zero tolerance policy* that prevented the acceptance of gifts, food, or anything of value from suppliers. GM MPM teams funded social activities by the respective participants out of their own pocket or as part of an approved company expense. The most common activity was a team dinner with meals paid by each participant. On a few occasions, I hosted team dinners at my house and followed it with a game of pool. Other activities such as picnics, attending sporting events, wine tasting, or playing golf are also popular.

Although many companies cover several of the leadership team topics in their internal project status review meetings, the multi-company nature of the leadership team gives these presentations and the resulting discussions a new dimension. It prevents individuals from presenting selected facts from a single perspective to drive a desired decision. Instead, a decision requires the presentation and evaluation of all perspectives before becoming final. For the project manager, this may seem like a loss of power, but it is more than offset by the other gains in influence power discussed previously. The decisions are also better, leading to improved project performance. This approach is a huge benefit to the key executives responsible for making critical project decisions, since it provides them with a multicompany perspective on the issue. It results in a more thorough investigation and analysis by the presenters, opens up possible solutions unrecognized in a single company environment, and builds buy in to the final decision from all parties. The high-level multi-company buy in factor simplifies the project manager's implementation of the decision.

The leadership team meetings are very important events, and disciplined attendance by the key executives is critical to the continued success of the process. An isolated absence by a key executive due to a major business or personal problem is manageable, but a repetitive absence undermines the effectiveness of the team process. Asking a key executive to dedicate one day every three months on a project that is significant to the company's strategic plan is reasonable (see *Strategic Project* in Chapter 1). In fact, the focused day is probably more efficient and higher in quality than the normal intermittent attention the project receives over three months without the team approach.

The engineering team meetings are easy to establish since most design processes have engineering events scheduled over the course of the project. It simply remains to structure these events as a team meeting-type process. Operating together as a team generally improves the results of the design reviews without placing any burden of additional meetings on the participants. The engineering agenda follows a format similar to the leadership team. Figure 5.8 is an example of a typical engineering team agenda. The meetings are opened with a review of engineering norms and the project mission and goals. This is particularly effective if the sponsor from the hosting company kicks off the meeting and reviews the mission and goals. This sponsor would generally begin the meeting, depart to let the team conduct its meeting, and return at the end for a report. The open-issues action planning is a major topic in every meeting, which includes the follow-up of previous actions and creation of actions with accountability and dates for any new issues. The meetings are scheduled at the site most appropriate for supporting the design topics in the agenda. Other necessary items to perform are the appropriate upfront planning for each meeting, documenting the results with minutes, and updating the open-issues list on the website.

The participants on the installation and start-up team work together daily during the execution of their respective phase of the project, and they accomplish action-plan follow-up as part of their daily activities. Thus, the only requirement for a special meeting outside the team formation event occurs if there is a need for follow-up between the team formation and the beginning of the project phase activities. There is usually a project status review meeting involving key members of the install or start-up team and other site and engineering representatives, primarily to coordinate activities for the next few weeks and to update all partici-

Agenda review and approval	Host key executive
Review norms, mission, and goals	Host key executive
Safety topic presentation (optional)	Volunteer
Project design review	
Subsupplier design status	Subsupplier PMs
Subsupplier submission approval	Supplier lead engineering
Design submissions and status	Supplier PM
Customer approval of submissions	Customer lead engineering
Customer design perspective	Customer PM
Lunch and site tour	Host PM
Open issue action items review	As assigned
Engineering change requests	Initiating PM
Identify new open issues from the meeting	Host PM
Resolve delegate or assign new items	Group exercise
Wrap up	Host PM
Summarize new decisions and engineering actions	
Formalize agreement on next meeting date and site	
Assign responsibility and date to publish minutes	
Pre- or post-meeting social event	Host PM
(ie: Dinner, group activity, etc. outside normal business hours)	

Figure 5.8 Engineering team regular meeting agenda

pants on the status of the project. This is an informational meeting, since it involves many diverse groups and frequently includes on-site and teleconferenced personnel.

Escalation. In most projects, unexpected issues arise that fall outside the ability and authority of a particular team. These issues require direction or decisions from upper management. Oftentimes the process for getting resolution on such an issue is unclear, particularly in multi-company environments. Each project manager receives direction from the appropriate leader, and when this direction does not match, the project managers find themselves in a stalemate that has serious ramifications regarding project performance. MPM eliminates this impasse by bringing the decision makers together to establish a common direction and to arrive at a single decision for the project issue. The leadership team must make sure that the issues they decide to tackle are appropriate. Too often, the other teams determine that an item belongs to the leadership because it is expedient and allows the individual team to pass the buck to the leadership. In other situations, teams fail to escalate an item that if left unresolved, may hurt project performance. Finally, there are occasions when the timeliness of a decision can drive the need to make decisions that do not fit in the leadership team's regular meeting schedule. To overcome these obstacles, the leadership team must establish criteria to guide both the teams and the project managers in the escalation process.

The project managers are the main communication link between all the teams, and so they are the logical individuals to carry the escalation issues to the leadership to determine the timeliness of a particular decision. The basic premise of the MPM process is this: *The people closest and most knowledgeable to an issue make the best decisions.* When teams lack the authority or business perspective needed to make the decision, issues often escalate. One approach to dealing with escalated issues is to require the team to recommend a minimum of three possible solutions, listing the pros and cons of each. This way, the team has thoroughly discussed both the issue and the possible corrective actions. If the leadership can live with the three options and feels that the team has the appropriate perspective, leadership delegates the authority back to the team for that decision. If not, the leadership will have to make the decision, but they still have the benefit of the team's input. If the team takes the easy way out and escalates without the options, leadership can refer it back to the team for appropriate discussion. It is a good idea to have the project managers serve as the gatekeepers for escalation issues and task them with requiring the necessary discussion before escalating. In a similar manner, the project managers must identify issues that the teams are not addressing in a timely fashion. Many times, it is simply a matter of leadership setting a deadline for the team to resolve the issue. A crisis that cannot wait for a meeting requires the establishment of a communication protocol between the key executives and project managers to deal with those issues. Planning arrangements ahead of time regarding how and when to set up the communication expedites the issue when the need arises.

Conflict Management. Conflict is a natural part of any project. It occurs at all levels with varying intensity over the entire project lifecycle. The critical issue in conflict is not that it exists, but the manner of management. In fact, a project without conflict is probably not achieving its potential, because the limited discussion of issues does not expose all the possibilities. Some conflict is good in that it fosters discussion and creativity, leading to innovation that improves performance. The existence of good conflict is the result of varied experiences, knowledge, perspectives, and process approaches. Some conflict is destructive and must be eliminated or managed proactively to mitigate its destructive effects. Personality clashes, commercial issues, individual and company responsibilities, stress reactions created by project constraints, and differing objectives are the drivers of bad conflict. Conflict management begins in the initial team formation by defining acceptable behavior with the team norms, building personal linkages through the personal history exercise, clarifying organizational and individual relationships with the roles and responsibility exercises, and establishing a common set of objectives via the project mission and goals. In addition, the group and subgroup exercises model collaborative techniques to optimize the blending of experiences, knowledge, perspectives, and process approaches to achieve consensus results. Conflict management is everyone's responsibility, but initiation of corrective action typically falls on the shoulders of the project manager.

In most internal company projects, project managers use all their influence to acquire the best talent for their project. This is usually a subjective evaluation of personnel based on their credentials, years of experience, prior successes, and personality fit. When identifying potential team members, diversity should receive proper weight to avoid building completely homogeneous teams. Proper diversity creates good conflict that fosters innovation. In MPM, there is little or no opportunity to influence team-member selection from an overall standpoint, since each project manager selects a team prior to the team formation event. The diversity grows with multi-company projects since each company has their own culture, procedures, and processes. International projects push the diversity issue much farther with the wide range of cultures and personal beliefs represented in global teams. This diversity is a real strength of MPM when managed properly.

There are five basic approaches to managing conflict: force, accept, avoid, compromise, and collaborate. *Force* is simply imposing one's will on another. Implementation is less effective due to lack of commitment, and it creates bad feelings that stand in the way of resolving future conflicts. This approach is a last-resort approach, and those who employ it should be sure they can live with the consequences. *Accept* involves giving in with little or no discussion and agreeing to the other's viewpoint. This is also known as smoothing. This sacrifices individual thought in the mistaken belief that it helps to maintain team relationships. Working through the conflict and not glossing over it strengthens team relationships. *Accept* is just the other side of *force*, but minimizes the bad feelings. Both *force* and *accept* have the potential to take a project in the wrong direction, and both lack the commitment for success. *Avoid*, also called *withdraw*, involves ignoring the conflict, intentionally acting to separate from the conflict, or creatively going around the issue. If the issue is minor and has no impact on the project or team, this may be an expedient solution. Minor issues left festering, however, can grow into a major conflict. *Compromise*, often referred to as a win-win solution, involves each party giving up a little to reach an agreement. In reality, since everyone gives up something and no one achieves their goal, this is a lose-lose situation. A buyer and seller negotiation that is resolved by each giving up a little to meet in the middle typifies this style. The final *collaborate* approach, which combines PMI's collaborating and confronting techniques, is a true win-win solution, and the one most used in the MPM process. *Collaborate* requires all parties to work together to achieve the best possible solution for the project regardless of individual biases going into the problem solving process. It requires objectivity and data to support the final resolution and optimizes the commitment of all participants to the final solution. A *collaborate* solution can run the gamut of possibilities: total acceptance of one party's position, a combination of multiple-party positions, or a new solution. It is data driven, focuses on what is best for the project, and has the full understanding and commitment of the team.

Figure 5.9 is a generic graphical display of each type of conflict resolution mode plotted against the most common project value and team value that it delivers. *Force* and *accept* deliver negative value due to the potential wrong direction, lack of commitment, and bad feelings generated, with *force* being the worst. *Avoid* essentially has no value. *Compromise* and *collaborate* deliver positive value to the project and team, with *collaborate* producing the highest value. Note the second scale on the horizontal axis, which shows the relative team effort required for the various conflict resolution modes. Each conflict method requires increasing team effort starting with *force*, which requires the least and ending with *collaborate*,

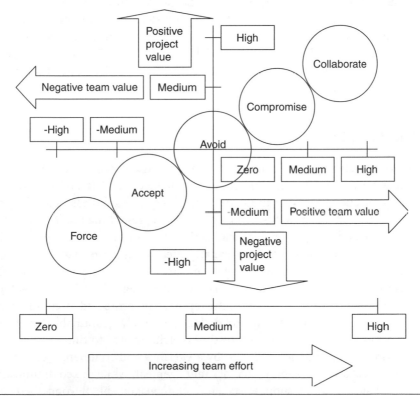

Figure 5.9 Conflict approaches vs project and team value

which requires the most. *Collaborate* is definitely the method of choice in handling conflict since it delivers the greatest results, but it also requires the greatest team effort. *Collaborate* is simply a problem-solving approach. There are many good problem solving models from which to choose and lots of information describing their use. A few of the more popular models are:

- Six Sigma DMAIC (define, measure, analyze, implement, control)
- Lean manufacturing PDCA (plan, do, check, act)
- IT system development lifecycle (SDLC) (define, analysis, design, development, test, implement)
- Total quality management (understand, select opportunity, analyze, generate alternatives, select alternative, plan, implement, check results)

Most companies are familiar with problem solving and may have either their own version or one of the models listed previously; which model depends on the given situation and the companies involved. Regardless of the model selected, the important points are that everyone understands and is comfortable with the process, and everyone commits to following the process discipline in an objective data-driven manner. Using an accepted step-by-step problem solving approach helps to take personalities and feelings out of the equation, which aids in maintaining objectivity and improves the collaborative results. The problem solving approach focuses on achieving the best solution rather than compromising to satisfy individual interests.

SCORECARD

In lean manufacturing operations, scorecards are a useful tool for identifying and tracking a key set of metrics to measure performance. The basis of the scorecard is that organizations focus on those areas in which they are measured. The principle is to agree on a common set of metrics that represent the major elements of the enterprise and apply them across all activities to meet a performance goal or to drive continuous improvement. Regularly measuring performance to the goal and making corrections during execution ensures success. The MPM leadership team established goals as part of the initial team building, which is a natural foundation upon which to build a scorecard report. The scorecard is confined to a single page, with all elements expressed clearly in easily quantifiable terms. The scorecard has four core sections addressing metrics related to timing, cost, communication, and open issues, followed by a variance and comments section. The timing and cost sections support activity management, while the communication and open-issues sections support stakeholder management. Beyond these four sections, the project manager may modify or add sections to match the leadership goals and align them with the project phase or site requirements. For example, the installation and start-up phases typically add safety metrics while the engineering phase may add change control metrics. A single scorecard can apply to the entire project since the four core sections are common to all phases. However, for best results, each phase or site maintains a scorecard to better target team requirements while increasing team accountability and motivation.

Table 5.4 is an example of a typical scorecard for the installation phase of a press project. The project manager added safety metrics to the core metrics to reflect the importance of employee safety in the installation phase. Each metric requires a goal from which to track variation and formulate corrective actions. Safety performance tracks recordable accidents, lost time, and near misses. Earned value is the ideal tool to use in reporting time and cost performance via the SPI and CPI indexes discussed previously. These ratios provide an excellent means for comparing projects without disclosing cost or labor-hour data directly. For those who do not want to use earned value, the earned-activity technique or milestone variance (complete versus planned) is an alternate method for schedule reporting. The variance in actual labor hours to planned labor hours or total budget variances can be used as alternate measures for cost performance. Communication tracks conformance to the communication plan developed earlier, and the open issues tracks the issues and status of the corrective actions identified in the team meetings.

The scorecard is updated on a weekly basis and reviewed monthly with the leadership team. The one-page summary provides a weekly snapshot for the teams to monitor their performance. Reporting the most recent four weeks provides trend data. The example incorporates a status designation for each section to aid the leadership in scanning reports to identify areas of concern. Using green, yellow, and red colors on the circle, as well as triangle and X status symbols makes sections that require attention stand out from across a room. These metrics measure the project's progress and reveal trends at a macro level, aiding management in focusing their attention and asking the right questions. For the example shown, the cost performance index is less than 1.0 and the status of cost is a triangle, which indicates corrective actions are in process. Looking at the variance explanation at the bottom, a reduced crew size is helping to recover losses created earlier in the project. This approach is viable even though it is causing some schedule slippage since the project is ahead of schedule. Under the heading *Comments and concerns*, the rate of new issues is slowing and they are holding the open issues to less than 10. Whenever any metric indicates a problem, the responsible team analyzes the project detail to identify the cause of slippage and develop corrective actions.

Table 5.4 Sample installation phase scorecard

Install start: 6/2/2008 Data as of: 10/19/08	Goal	Current four-week trend				Project cumm to date
		Week #17	Week #18	Week #19	Week #20	
Safety	●					
Near misses	0	0	1	0	0	2
Recordables	0	0	0	0	0	1
Lost time days	0	0	0	0	0	0
Timing	●					
Earned value SPI	1.0	1.2	1.18	1.16	1.14	1.14
Cost	▲					
Earned value CPI	1.0	0.9	0.91	0.92	0.93	0.93
Communications	●					
Meetings/conference planned		1	2	1	1	25
Meetings/conference held		1	2	1	1	24
Variance	0	0	0	0	0	1
Open issues	●					
Opened		3	2	1	1	100
Closed		0	3	2	1	91
In process	<10	10	9	8	8	8
Older than 4 weeks	0	0	0	1	0	0
Current week variance explanation	Continuing to work smaller crew to recover labor cost but getting some slippage in schedule as anticipated.					
Comments and concerns	Overall project is going well. Rate of new issues are slowing and expect open issues to be under 5 in two weeks					
Status code	● On target					
	▲ Corrective action implemented					
	X Corrective action required					

RISK MANAGEMENT

Controlling risk involves keeping a watchful eye on potential risks to the project and being able to react quickly when the risks materialize. Risk is controlled using a process called *risk management,* which identifies, assesses, plans responses with trigger points, and monitors risk. Risk management is more of an art than a science and starts before project initiation. Risk management starts with the identification and assessment of opportunities and threats as part of the SWOT (strengths, weaknesses, opportunities, and threats) analysis used to develop the company strategies. Risk management continues as part of the project portfolio development that selects the project portfolio used to implement the company strategies. The definition and selection of a strategic project as described in Chapter 1 requires a more detailed project-specific assessment of risks in order to determine if MPM is appropriate. The risk identification and assessments from the strategy development, project portfolio-selection process, and strategic project analysis should provide plenty of background data to begin the individual project's risk management.

Risk Strategies. Project management literature identifies four basic risk response strategies: *avoidance, acceptance, transference*, and *mitigation*. The MPM approach, by virtue of its principles of project ownership and team organization, offers a unique opportunity to implement a fifth risk strategy referred to as *partnering*. Table 5.5 defines the five risk strategies.

In MPM, risk management occurs initially during the team formation in the leadership brainstorming, engineering team specification review, installation and start-up fact-finding, and the subsequent schedule development activities. The engineering, installation, and start-up teams address most of their perceived risks as they develop their schedules. They use a combination of *avoidance, partnering*, and *acceptance* strategies by selecting a set of activities that avoids the risk, collaborating with plans to reduce the impact, or planning for the risk by including a factor to cover the cost and schedule losses in their estimates. During project

Table 5.5 Risk strategy definitions

Risk strategy	Definition
Avoidance	Selecting a different course of action resulting in the risk disappearing or having no impact on the project
Acceptance	Planning for the risk by building in additional time and cost factors comprehending the probability and impact of the risk
Transference	Shifting the risk to another party such as securing insurance against a possible loss or establishing a fixed cost contract with someone else to do the work associated with the risk
Mitigation	Facing the risk and developing contingency plans which are triggered by a defined set of conditions to minimize project impact
Partnering	Form of risk mitigation that involves sharing and collaborating on the risk to develop plans to minimize the impact on all participants

execution, risk impacts appear in the form of cost or schedule losses, which the teams address through corrective actions using a partnering risk strategy. Major risks identified by the teams that are outside their control must escalate to the leadership team. Thus, the leadership has the greatest responsibility for managing project risks.

Risk management is a prime responsibility of the leadership team. Their view of the overall project from a multi-company perspective, knowledge of the company strategies and priorities, understanding of industry and market conditions, and access to items escalated from the other teams makes them the ideal risk management group. This view, knowledge, understanding, and access, enables the leadership team to identify the project risks. To support this responsibility, the previously discussed leadership agenda lists risk management as a regular topic in all leadership meetings. In most leadership teams, the topic of risk is an informal discussion with each company, identifying risks from their perspective followed by a qualitative assessment of the probability and impact. Next, each risk receives a priority rating. Finally, the team selects strategies for dealing with the highest priority risks. Use of the transference risk strategy is rare, since the leadership team treats the risk to any one company as a risk to all. The main exception to this would be the possibility of insurance to cover certain risks such as liability, fire, etc.

Partnering is a viable risk strategy whenever multiple companies are facing the same risk, although the resulting impact on each company is different. The opposite of transference and a form of mitigation, *partnering* involves multiple companies collaborating with each other to create corrective actions to minimize or eliminate the risk impact to all companies. MPM makes this approach possible, maximizes the effectiveness, and uses it as a central strategy in risk management. In the automotive industry, joint ventures are a prime example of companies partnering to reduce risk. Another example is in any industry where companies undertake joint research. In the earlier section on quality control, the B2C press project case study utilizing the controls and network simulation to control quality is a perfect example of *partnering* to implement corrective actions, reducing the risk impact to all participants. In the case study, no one company had the resources, hardware, or knowledge to implement the simulation, but together, it was feasible and highly successful. The multi-company ownership of risk in the partnering strategy combined with effectiveness of MPM in collaborating with all knowledge and resources is extremely powerful.

The other risk strategies—*avoidance, acceptance,* and *mitigation*—are very viable and employed by the leadership team. The methods, level of detail, use of qualitative versus quantitative assessment, risk response strategies, etc. are at the discretion of the respective leadership team. They must decide what is appropriate for their project, industry, and company to support their risk tolerances and resources. The critical element is that risk management, which covers risk identification, assessment, response planning, and monitoring, is a regular part of every leadership meeting.

Risk Register. There is a great deal of literature regarding risk management and it is important to avoid spending too much time on it at the expense of other project responsibilities. This is particularly true of risk assessment that can become very sophisticated, time consuming, and resource intensive when trying to quantify probabilities and cost impacts. However, ignoring risk would leave the success of the project to chance. One formal tool that appears in most risk literature and is a best practice reported by the Project Management Institute is the *risk register*, also referred to as the *risk matrix*. This tool is simply a spreadsheet summarizing all aspects of risk management that functions as a baseline or reference for making decisions as risks begin to appear. It details all the contingency plans developed ahead of time to mitigate specific risks and identifies trigger points used to initiate the contingency actions. This documentation can be very useful in structuring and maintaining continuity of the risk management discussions at the project review meetings. It can also be a valuable starting point for future risk management, and can provide lessons learned for all parties involved in the project. The risk register or matrix shown in Table 5.6 is an example of a partial listing of risks to build a small manufacturing facility. In this example, risk assessment was qualitative, simply identifying probability and impact as low, medium, or high. A quantitative assessment would show the probability as a percentage and the impact as a dollar cost. It would also develop a dollar cost for the contingency plan.

Table 5.6 Risk register sample

Risk	Consequence	Probability (L, M, H)	Severity (L, M, H)	Action trigger	Responsibility	Response plan
Permit delayed	Delay construction	M	H	Permit status slipping	PM	Reduce rennovation time
Public relations problems	Delay construction and site approval	L	H	Negative local news/editorials	Marketing specialist	Address negative opinions
Production equipment problems	Production delays	H	H	Machine does not meet spec	Manufacturing engineer	Equipment run off at source prior to shipment
Price increases on building materials	Exceed budget	H	M	10% Increase in building economic activity	Purchasing manager	Early fixed price purchase of building materials

## 6

COMPLETE

After forming teams, establishing baseplans, and putting controls in place, the *complete* phase of the Six C process begins. This involves completing the project's work activities from the schedules and the teams' open-issue action plans. The first part of this chapter discusses team management philosophy including safety, leadership, decision-making, character traits, and the concept of project balance. The second part covers the integration of project management, teamwork, and safety into each phase of project execution along with tools and suggestions to aid in project execution. By their nature, the integration discussions by project phase and the related tools are specific to new equipment installations. Although these are generic to any new equipment installation, readers must interpolate these for their own project applications.

MULTI-COMPANY TEAM MANAGEMENT

Team management and project management are on opposite sides of the same coin. A very simplistic view is that team management focuses on the people, and project management focuses on the activities. There is a lot of overlap, but it is necessary to fully utilize both to realize maximum project results. The focus of this section is on the five most critical team management aspects in any multi-company project: *safety*, *leadership*, *decision-making*, *character traits*, and *balance*.

Safety. In project execution, safety must always be the number one priority. This is particularly important during large equipment installations or construction projects, which have the potential to cause serious—sometimes fatal—accidents. Every activity involves a plan for safety. It requires the right attitudes, proactive leadership, observation of safe methods, safety plans, safety audits, safety performance measurements, corrective actions, team safety awareness, and a willingness of team members to look out for each other. The elements of a solid safety performance are also the elements found in good project management. A good way to assess an in-progress project is to first assess the overall safety. If the overall safety is poor or lacking in any of the above elements, it is likely that the same elements are deficient in the project management plan. Safety information is not confidential or proprietary, and is therefore readily available in mandatory public safety reports, onsite observance of safe work practices, and interviews of project participants.

Safety begins with leadership. In the initial team formation, leadership must establish safety as the number one priority and then back it up through their words, actions, and decisions. It must be a prominent part of the project mission and goals. They must ensure that the teams adapt a *safety first* attitude and implement awareness activities to keep it in front of all participants. For the installation and start-up teams, the use of daily toolbox meetings (with safety as a regular topic) helps to build awareness—if held before any work begins. The leadership and engineering teams can reinforce this concept and set a good example by holding a short safety talk at the start of each team meeting. That is the purpose of the safety topic item listed early in the recommended agendas for the regular leadership and engineering meetings of the previous chapter. The engineering team has a major role in safety through their responsibility to design safety into every aspect of the new equipment. The work breakdown structure in the installation and start-up phases must consider safety when developing all work packages The teams build safety considerations into the schedule by introducing task dependencies or scheduling tasks on alternate shifts to prevent safety conflicts due to performing tasks in the same area or at the same time. Other considerations include ensuring proper tool and equipment applications and planning mobile equipment movements. The site must ensure that everyone has proper personal protective equipment for each task, restrict site access to only authorized personnel, and provide a safety orientation for all new project personnel.

Safety is even more critical in the multi-company project management (MPM) process since team members from different companies and potentially different countries will have varying ideas about safety. An accepted assembly practice in Japan or Germany during manufacture might be unacceptable at the U.S. site during installation. The procedure could be completely safe in the Japan or Germany environment while posing a major safety hazard in the United States due to different supporting procedures. Miscommunication or misunderstandings regarding safety procedures can have serious consequences, but extensive communication among all participants can mitigate the issue. The great thing about safety is that it is in everyone's best interest—from the company president to the project worker—regardless of job, company, or country.

Many companies fail to take a proactive approach to safety. Instead, they wait for an accident to occur, then analyze the cause and take corrective action. Developing a WBS built on solid safety principles and procedures is the first step in a proactive approach. Another proactive technique that proves beneficial is the tracking and follow-up of near misses. A near miss is anything that goes wrong that has a potential for injury yet causes none. Analysis and corrective action of the near miss eliminates the potential for the injury in the future.

Returning to leadership's responsibility to set the example: On several occasions, project sites were shut down for periods of one to three weeks when either near misses or accidents indicated a weakness in the safety plan. Project personnel used the time to analyze the situation, then planned and implemented corrective actions before resuming work. This occurred on both outside contract and internal GM and the UAW installations. Although some sub-suppliers and contractors balked at this drastic measure, the MPM co-leaders always supported this position. Surprisingly in every case, both safety and project performance improved dramatically without serious impacts to the project's completion. This fact supports the belief in the close linkage between safety performance and project management performance.

Using the above safety philosophy in all MPM teams from 1994 to 2004 generated over 3 million hours of work and with the support of plant sites, suppliers, and GM staff achieved the following safety performance:

- Safety incident rate was 28 percent below national average
- Zero lost time on all but two projects
- Zero lost time for the last three years (2002–2004)

Situational Leadership. In the MPM environment, it is important for the key executives and project managers to share a common vision regarding the leadership style used to manage the multiple teams responsible for the various project phases. Using a common approach eliminates problems and confusion that arise when co-leaders attempt to manage using conflicting methods. A great deal of information is available concerning various leadership styles for managing teams. Team leadership styles have the following characteristics:

- Leadership is flexible and changes to fit the situation
- Leadership requires the right balance in multiple styles
- Relationships vary in influence depending on the task
- Consensus decisions are not always predominate
- Leaders match style/discipline to the readiness/objective
- Team leaders determine and make adjustments

I am a proponent of the Hersey Blanchard Situational Leadership model for managing individuals and I believe it applies to team management as well. The Hersey Blanchard situational leadership model follows the premise that leadership styles must change to fit employee readiness in terms of their competence based on job experience and skills, and commitment based on willingness and desire. It identifies four quadrants of leadership styles: *directing, coaching, supporting*, and *delegating* (Hersey, Blanchard, Johnson 2008, 142).

Situational leadership is more a continuum of four styles applied to individuals based on their readiness. Situational leadership has been around for over four decades, has gained wide acceptance, and is relatively easy to understand. A project manager applying situational leadership to a team would potentially require a different style for each individual. The application of a variety of styles simultaneously required within the team environment makes situational leadership complex, but best describes the project management environment. The same logic applies when managing teams. MPM leadership uses this logic for issues from the various teams. They must avoid the one-size-fits-all mentality and assess the individual team's readiness to take on a given assignment.

The team's maturity in terms of their development stage is a good indicator of their readiness. If you recall, the team development stages in Chapter 4 identified five stages of team development: *forming, storming, norming, performing*, and *closing*. The first four stages of team development match closely with the four main leadership styles of the Hersey Blanchard situational leadership model (ibid., 269). Table 6.1 displays the four leadership styles with the corresponding individual readiness, relationship modes, and team readiness. Characteristics of the forming mode are enthusiasm and new opportunities mixed with uncertainty. This creates

Table 6.1 Hersey Blanchard situational leadership model

Leadership style	Individual readiness	Relationship mode	Team readiness
Directing	Low competence Questionable commitment	Low	Forming
Coaching	Growing competence Low commitment	High	Storming
Supporting	High competence Variable commitment	High	Norming
Delegating	High competence High commitment	Low	Performing

a level of confusion with questionable commitment. Team competency is very low in the initial stage. As the team moves into storming competency grows, but disillusionment resulting from the struggle for position, awareness of the challenge, and a what-is-in-it-for-me attitude keeps commitment low. By the norming stage, team competency grows to *highly competent* and commitment builds, usually varying between *medium* and *high*. In the performing stage, teams are highly competent and committed. The relationship mode applies both to the individual relationships when managing people within a team, and the interteam relationships between the leadership team and the other teams for which it is responsible. Consider the following team management examples:

- You are assembling a new MPM installation team, and the leadership team chooses you as the person to help them through the first few days. You gather the team in a room, give them the written specifications and design drawings, then tell them the installation must be finished in four weeks. You leave telling them you will be back in two weeks to check their progress. Everyone loses because the new team feels helpless and overwhelmed. They have more questions than answers and do not know where to start. They feel as though the challenge is impossible, and blame leadership for not doing their part. The installation does not meet schedule.

- You have an experienced installation team that is functioning in the performing stage and you tell them they must cut two weeks out of the current installation schedule due to a crisis elsewhere. You list all the tasks that will require modification and identify the resource reassignments. You then follow up with a detailed set of instructions on how to carry out each task. They complete the work, but not as you expected. The team feels insulted and discouraged. Creativity is lost, and team morale and motivation decreases.

- Swap your actions from the two situations above, and things improve. Leave detailed instructions and a checklist for *the new team*, and they will thank you for it. Give *the performing team* the quick chat, explaining the issue to their satisfaction, while simply making yourself available to answer any questions—this team will probably exceed your expectations.

From the above examples, the importance of having a detailed plan to manage the initial team formation event is very evident. This explains the need for the extensive details, checklists, and sample agendas provided for the initial team building of each phase of the project. However, once the teams are performing, it is better for the leadership team to function in a delegating role. As mentioned previously, depending on the circumstances, the teams will move back and forth through the four stages, which requires the leadership team to adjust their style according to the stage a team is in for a given time and issue. The real key to this process is conscientiously taking the time to assess the team's readiness before proceeding. An inaccurate assessment will yield less than desirable results.

As indicated in Chapter 5, the MPM structure with the leadership team greatly enhances the project managers' legitimate, connection, and information influence powers. The connection powers are most effective in the forming and storming phases, while information power is of the greatest value in the norming and performing stages. The legitimate powers bridge the gap with primary value in the storming and norming phases. This makes the situational leadership model an ideal fit for MPM. For over two decades, I have found situational leadership to be very effective for managing individuals and teams in project and operations environments, and I highly recommend it for multi-company projects.

Decision-making. Considering all the discussion concerning consensus, readers may be confused by the observation that pure consensus decisions are not always the predominate mode. The collaborative mode of conflict resolution described in Chapter 5 exemplifies consensus, which delivers the highest-quality decision. However, it also takes the greatest amount of time and team effort. Consensus is a disciplined problem solving approach that yields a mutually understandable, explainable, and supportable decision. Some teams want to make every decision by consensus. Although producing an ideal result, this results in extended meetings and discussions that consume the valuable time of all participants in an effort to reach consensus on every little item. The team process bogs down, lacks agility, participants stress due to neglecting their other duties, and team effectiveness suffers. There is always a point on the scale of diminishing returns where the time invested to reach the consensus fails to outweigh the benefits of the consensus decision. The team does not reach consensus through compromise or unanimous vote, and consensus is not the result of all participants getting their way. In one team, some participants never agreed to a solution unless it was their way. In this case, the attempt to achieve a consensus solution involved endless hours of discussion, yet failed to produce results since consensus was not possible on those terms. The consensus or collaborative approach should be reserved for those decisions that have the greatest impact on the project or that involve large quantities of people. The project's mission statement and goals developed by the leadership team, the milestone dates established by the engineering team, and the detailed schedules developed by each team are examples of high-impact decisions involving large quantities of people.

There are six decision-making approaches most common in MPM as shown in Table 6.2; the table lists the six approaches along with their typical applications. Consensus decisions have synergy, creating results greater than the sum of the

Table 6.2 Team decision-making approaches

Team decision	Application
Consensus	Decisions with high impact on the project
	Decisions involving large numbers of people
	Requires the most time and team effort
	Everyone understands the decision
	Everyone can support the decision
Subgroup with buy in	Expedite the consensus decisions when time is short
	Slightly lower creativity and commitment
Subgroup with information	Subgroup contains all knowledge and expertise
	Subgroup implements the decision
	Decision has little impact on other actions
Expert leader	Time is of the essence
	Crisis with no prior planning
Planning	Decisions made in anticipation of an event
	Baseline project plans
	Contingency plans as part of risk management
Voting	Consensus is not possible in time allowed
	Everyone is knowledgeable of the topic
	Everybody understands the others' perspectives
	The majority can implement the decision
	There is a plan to address the minority

parts. In the mid-1980s my plant staff participated in team training that involved a wilderness exercise. They divided the staff into three groups and each group had to make a series of survival decisions in response to specific wilderness conditions using a consensus process. The staff viewed the plant's master mechanic as the recognized expert in wilderness survival due to his annual hunting trips and stories of his exploits. The master mechanic was in my group. Along with the rest of the group, the master mechanic also believed himself to be the expert. As such, the entire group simply accepted his decision for every condition without question, and so we finished the assignment early. The other two groups had no expert, and so they spent a great deal of time making their decisions. The facilitator ranked each decision based on recognized authorities in wilderness survival and totaled the results for each of the three groups. The results were astonishing. The two groups with no experts scored about the same, receiving approximately eight points on a 1 to 10 scale. My group (with the expert) scored a five, essentially failing the exercise. The expertise represented in my group far exceeded that in the other two, but by using consensus against the single expert, they far exceeded my group's performance. This exercise only measured the quality of the decision. In real life, commitment would be an even greater factor, and there is no doubt in my mind that the commitment to the decisions was far greater in the other two groups who had collaborated on the answers.

Another approach to decision-making is utilizing subgroups to reach a consensus decision and seeking buy in from the full group. The open-issues action planning is an example of this approach. Dividing the team into groups allows for the simultaneous discussion of multiple topics, and the smaller group speeds up consensus. The tradeoff is some loss of creativity and perhaps some level of commitment from those not in the subgroup. Involving everyone in subgroup activities with the need to get buy in from the others helps to build a sense of reciprocal commitment to the other groups that minimizes any decrease in commitment from not being in that particular subgroup. A variation of the subgroup approach to decisions is completely delegating a decision to a subgroup, requiring only that the subgroup inform the team of their decision. This approach works best when the subgroup contains all the people with the knowledge and expertise on the issue, only they are involved in implementing the decision, and it has little effect on any other activities within the project.

Another decision-making approach is designating one person to make a decision. This approach fits well in emergencies when time is of the essence, and someone within the team is the recognized expert and trusted by the team. Picture yourself a member of a 10-person crew on a fishing trawler in the Atlantic Ocean. The engine compartment floods due to an unknown leak. At the rate of flooding, the trawler will sink in 30 minutes. This is not the time to hold a problem-solving meeting seeking a collaborative solution to the leak. Ideally, the experienced captain provides clear authoritative direction and the team responds efficiently and without question, with full commitment. The captain may even employ subgroups with designated experts as leaders to expedite the action. For example, chief engineer to lead damage control, chief radio operator to send out distress calls, and first mate to lead the lifeboat crew preparing to abandon ship. Projects encounter crises as well and need similar authoritative action. Effective teams presented with a crisis respond extremely well to the authoritative approach. A significant difference between this approach and the traditional authoritarian leader is that the leader changes within the team based on the individual best qualified to lead in a given situation. The expert leader does not provide synergy but does expedite decisions. The team participants understand the need for immediate action and set aside any reservations they have in the interest of the team. The crisis elevates the team's energy and strengthens their working relationships and their commitment to the project's success. However, using the expert leader authoritative approach too frequently, employing it on inappropriate issues, or designating incapable leaders or leaders unable to attract faith from their team often results in the team slipping back into the norming or storming phase with a loss of performance.

Project management minimizes crises by always looking ahead to anticipate potential problems and using the risk management strategies described in Chapter 5 to avoid, transfer, mitigate, or partner. One way to reduce risk is by developing *contingency plans*. A *contingency plan* is just a set of decisions made in advance of a particular event. It may also require some prework. Making the decisions prior to the event allows the team to work through the collaborative process and reach a high-quality decision in case there is not time enough to do so when the event occurs. What appears as an authoritative approach by the captain in the sinking trawler example may very well be a detailed contingency plan that the crew developed ahead of time to handle such a situation. In fact, the three subgroups—communication, engineering, and lifeboat—probably did some prework in the form of drills to increase their proficiency in anticipation of such a crisis. Thus, contingency planning is a form of team anticipative decision-making. In retrospect, the entire baseline project schedule generated by the team is really a series of team decisions made in advance using a collaborative process to optimize results. Planning is therefore another form of team decision-making that provides the time needed to reach a consensus decision as part of normal project execution or to react to crises identified in the risk register.

The final method of team decision-making is voting. It can be a simple majority vote, two-thirds majority, three-fourths majority, etc. This applies when a consensus is not possible within the time constraint, everyone is knowledgeable on the topic and understands each other's viewpoints, and implementation does not require the active minority involvement. There should also be a plan to address the minority who disagree with the outcome (Scholtes, Joiner, and Streibel 2003, 3–26).

Character Traits. During project execution, individuals within a team will assume different character traits or roles depending on the task, personality, and team relationships. Some of these roles are beneficial to the team process while others inhibit team progress. There are eight basic character traits that support a positive team environment and eight traits that are harmful to the team environment. The list is not inclusive, but represents the roles most common in multi-company project teams. Many times the same individual assumes multiple roles, both positive and negative, during the course of a single meeting. Positive character traits increase team communication and improve team performance though encouragement, understanding, and knowledge. Negative traits decrease team communication by discouraging, blocking, or misdirecting the flow of information, which is critical to team effectiveness. Project managers and the team must be aware of these traits and work to reinforce the positive characteristics while discouraging the negative. Project managers should be skilled in all the positive traits in order to perform or coach others who are fulfilling those positive roles. The following eight positive character traits are for the most part self-explanatory. However, the accompanying text should aid readers in identifying and understanding the various positive traits and offer a few ideas to maintain balance in these traits within the team environment:

1. *Organizer*—Organization ability is a key trait for project managers. They organize activities, plan agendas, keep the team on topic, and help facilitate team discussions. Some people are natural organizers and enjoy the involvement and satisfaction they get from this work. Project managers must utilize these natural organizers to free up their own time by allowing these natural organizers to fill in for them and coach others in meeting the team's needs. Utilizing team members in this capacity helps to develop these skills for future advancement to project manager, develops backup personnel for a project manager's unexpected absence, and increases the organizer's ownership in the team.

2. *Recorder*—Almost every group has a person that is a recorder. This person usually carries a laptop computer, is extremely proficient in typing, and is generally well versed in all forms of written communication. This is the perfect person to help document meetings. It is important that the individual does not use the recording function to avoid participating, or that they do not become overburdened to the point that it inhibits participation. As was done in the brainstorming sessions, the individuals perform this function on a rotation and only record decisions, issues, and action plans utilizing a group memory approach to avoid these situations. Group memory is simply recording decisions and action plans in front of the group for concurrence as the meeting progresses; this keeps the meeting minutes concise and ensures concurrence.

3. *Timekeeper*—This person watches the clock and prods the team when the meeting is falling behind in the agenda. They are usually very sensitive to breaks and lunch. There are times when a precise schedule of breaks, lunch, and other prescheduled events needs be lower in priority than the issue on the table. Oftentimes the timekeeper is sensitive to these situations, but the project manager may have to override the timekeeper by politely suggesting that the group give an issue a higher priority.

4. *Inquirer*—The inquirer is always seeking information and data. This keeps team discussions more objective and less emotional. They are good at asking the right questions and getting to the heart of an

issue. This trait should be encouraged, and those who put down the inquiring mind for asking pertinent (albeit many) questions should be discouraged from doing so.

5. *Expert*—Most diverse teams have multiple and varied subject matter experts. These experts provide critical information to the team. It is important to verify the credentials and experience of any expert who is offering expert opinion. Even expert opinions should not be blindly accepted by team members without a full discussion and buy in from the entire team (as my group did in the wilderness exercise).

6. *Analyst*—The analyst's forte is numbers, formulas, statistics, forecasts, and spreadsheets. This is a valuable resource for gathering and interpreting of information and data to aid others in understanding the issues. The analyst is a critical asset during problem solving and decision-making affairs.

7. *Achiever*—The achiever is highly motivated in goal achievement—both personal and professional. This person derives great satisfaction in reaching measurable goals and always strives to do more. Achievers are quick to volunteer and often push the team to reach higher goals. They tend to be overly optimistic and impatient with those that do not share their enthusiasm. They are best utilized to help the team set stretch goals. It is important that their impatience does not discourage the achievement of team consensus.

8. *Peacemaker*—Peacemakers are skilled in interpersonal relations and strive to minimize conflict. They enjoy encouraging people and giving positive feedback. Their weakness is their tendency to shy away from conflict of any sort, preferring to ignore or smooth over any conflicts. Some conflict, however, helps to stimulate thinking and creativity, and is therefore productive. The peacemaker's interpersonal relationship skills and positive encouragement can be used in the compromise and collaborative modes. They should be kept out of the *avoid* and *accepting* modes of conflict resolution.

The cartoonist Patrick Hardin illustrates eight negative character traits in Figures 6.1 through 6.8 to provide a humorous visualization of these traits. The accompanying text provides descriptive information and offers some suggestions for minimizing their impact on the team:

1. *Riddler*—Have you ever been in a meeting and not been able to figure out the point the speaker was making? If so, you have probably encountered the riddler trait. No one understands the riddler's discussion points or identifies with the perspective. As Figure 6.1

Figure 6.1 Riddler

indicates, the riddler is a big question mark. They are predisposed to disorganization and are out of tune with the rest of the group. Without discouraging participation, it is sometimes helpful for the facilitator or organizer to ask a clarifying question or offer a statement regarding the point of discussion or value to the group to get the team on track. This trait can also indicate a lack of preparation for the discussion topic on the riddler's behalf. Establishing preparation as a norm and providing proper material ahead of time can circumvent this problem.

2. *Devil's advocate*—It is common for someone to start promoting an opposite viewpoint even though they do not take ownership of it. In the proper situation, this can provide value by fostering more discussion. However, in many cases this is a means of disguising their disagreement with the topic and creating dissenting opinions. As the horns and trident in Figure 6.2 imply, this trait describes the devil's advocate. In a team environment, this goes against the principles of honesty and trust. Without an honest statement of position from participants, confusion occurs in the discussion and it is difficult to assess the group's level of consensus. The recorder can begin to offset this trait by asking participants to state their position on issues and seeking a consensus.

3. *Filibuster*—The filibuster consumes large amounts of time, adds little value, and prevents others from contributing to the conversation. This individual has difficulty getting to the point, tends to introduce war stories, and steers the discussion into tangent territory. Figure 6.3 represents the filibuster as a long-winded speaker at a podium. Try utiliz-

Figure 6.2 Devil's advocate

ing a combination of agenda topic timing along with the timekeeper trait and the norm of full participation to improve efficiency of the discussion. For example, before beginning a topic that might foster a filibuster, discuss with the team the importance of everyone participating and the time constraints of the topic within the agenda. Ask the team to set a time limit on individual discussions and suggest playing a

Figure 6.3 Filibuster

game of hot potato. Ask someone to volunteer as the game timekeeper and provide a tennis-sized red ball that is lightweight but easily thrown across the room without causing any damage (such as a Nerf ball). The timekeeper's role is to toss the red ball to anyone that is within 15–30 seconds of the discussion time limit. The speaker must wrap it up and toss the ball back to the timekeeper. Using this on repeated occasions builds discussion habits for the group, makes the timing issue fun, and usually develops some lighthearted joking without ever taking direct issue with the filibuster.

4. *Hermit*—The quiet person in the corner that contributes little to the discussion and is difficult to read due to stoic body language is probably the hermit. As the cartoon illustrates in Figure 6.4, the hermit tries to hide or become invisible to avoid participation whenever possible. This is harmful to the team because it represents a resource loss due to the hermit's lack of contribution that limits team achievement. Similar to the previous approach using the hot potato game, discussing the value of everyone participating can be beneficial, followed by a game of cold potato. The facilitator starts the game of cold potato by tossing a tennis-sized blue ball that is lightweight but easily thrown across the room without causing any damage to anyone in the group to respond to a discussion question. When finished, the speaker tosses the ball to someone else that has not spoken. The last person to speak

Figure 6.4 Hermit

tosses the ball back to the facilitator. If more discussion is appropriate, the process begins again. This has the same benefits as hot potato. If both the filibuster and hermit traits are in the same group, the two games can be combined into one, hot potato–cold potato, and things really get interesting. If the team also contains the inquirer trait, this is very beneficial in helping to draw out the ideas and participation of the hermit.

5. *Critic*—Criticizing every idea and everyone is the modus operandi of the critic. Often the individual does this to increase his or her own standing or demonstrate superior knowledge of a subject at the expense of others. The, "Yes, but . . ." prima donna attitude in the cartoon of Figure 6.5 epitomizes this character trait. Factual data provided by the expert that is based on knowledge and experience can help to diffuse the critic. In addition, team norms regarding participation, respect, and avoiding criticism enforced by the entire team can provide an objective way to minimize the negative effects of the critic without getting into personalities.

6. *Naysayer*—This character trait is a close cousin to the critic, opposing every idea or suggestion. This person feels any challenge is too great and sees negativity in everything. Figure 6.6 characterizes the naysayer as a protestor with an *N* representing a negative attitude. Other names are *pessimist* or a *glass-half-empty person*. Naysayers are destructive when attempting to establish team stretch goals or when developing

Figure 6.5 Critic

Figure 6.6 Naysayer

action plans. The team norms, risk management process, and analyst traits can counteract the negative effects. The naysayer's one value is in helping to identify risk as part of the risk management process, provided they offer specific examples and data to support their pessimistic position.

7. *Procrastinator*—Everyone knows someone that is a great procrastinator, and most everyone has exhibited this trait at one time or another. As the cartoon in Figure 6.7 implies, the procrastinator moves at a snail's pace, always putting everything off until the last minute and beyond. The procrastinator generally has good intentions, is convinc-

Figure 6.7 Procrastinator

ing in his commitment, but never finds the time. This is particularly harmful in the team process due to the extensive level of activity inter-dependence. Failure to complete an activity according to plan can have a domino effect on the project. The procrastinator should receive only short-term assignments or assignments with a series of interim dates or checkpoints to allow regular checkups on their progress. Failure to complete a task will therefore have only a minor impact on the project, allowing for a quick recovery. The traits of the achiever can be chan-neled to seek results and demand action to keep the procrastinator on track and meeting commitments.

8. *Gladiator*—The gladiator or antagonist represented by Figure 6.8 has a rather negative outlook on life, believing that people are against him and seeing conspiracy behind every door. The gladiator has a strong dominating personality, has a win-lose mentality, loves conflict, and uses forcing as the primary mode in conflict. Although the gladiator is the first person you would choose for your side when going into battle, it is a very destructive trait in the team environment. Reassigning into a traditional functional organization with a lot of structure is probably the best fit. However, in multi-company teams this is generally not an option since multiple companies are involved and each make their own assignments. Gladiators should have assignments that minimize

Figure 6.8 Gladiator

interaction or should be isolated to a specific portion of the project. This minimizes the personality trait impact on the overall project. If there is a particular individual that has a good relationship with the gladiator and possesses strong peacemaker traits, pairing them for assignments can be an effective combination, since each offsets the other's weakness.

People exhibiting negative roles can be frustrating and difficult. It helps to visualize the cartoon when faced with people in these roles. It is the same principle as visualizing an audience wearing funny hats to reduce the fear of public speaking. The visualization can ease frustration and may increase the effectiveness of the working relationship with the negative individual. Positive traits within the team can offset the negative traits. Table 6.3 aligns the positive roles with the respective negative roles that they are most useful in mitigating. The blending of these various personality traits establishes the team's personality and significantly influences the team's overall effectiveness. The team norms established in the initial team formation meeting are a major tool that regulates team behavior and provides an objective way to address negative traits without introducing personal opinion or judgment.

Table 6.3 Positive and negative team roles

Positive roles	Negative roles	Positive role mitigation effect on negative role
Organizer	Riddler	Clarifies and summarizes comments
Recorder	Devil's advocate	Seeks position and consensus of participants
Timekeeper	Filibuster	Keeps discussion within time limits
Inquirer	Hermit	Seeks information and input from all participants
Expert	Critic	Offers valid data based on knowledge or experience
Analyst	Naysayer	Analyzes data to dispute negative viewpoints
Achiever	Procrastinator	Seeks results and demands action
Peacemaker	Gladiator	Strives for peace and harmony

Project Balance. A project manager is a key part of any project and must possess a wide array of skills. In one leadership team after reviewing all the roles and responsibilities, someone commented that a project manager needed to be Superman. In our next meeting, one of the participants brought in a picture of the project manager dressed as Superman. This characterization is a common view. In actuality, the most important attribute is not a superpower, but exceptional balance.

A more accurate characterization of a project manager is that of a juggler, as shown in Figure 6.9. The three balls he is juggling represent time, cost, and scope. The cup and saucer on the juggler's head represent project quality and technical concerns, while the ball on which he is balancing are the people issues. A project manager does not require superpowers if there is good team support, but the project manager still must exercise balance in almost every action. In fact, too much skill in any area may cause the project manager to lose the balance that was necessary for a given situation—a common problem that occurs when a highly technical and competent person becomes project manager. Instead of delegating or working with the team in solving technical issues, the project manager jumps in and does it, losing team synergy and often arriving at the wrong solution.

In one situation, the project manager was great at building relationships and keeping the peace, but could not handle confrontation and stepping up to difficult issues. When things got very stressful, his focus on relationships and keeping the peace caused him to sacrifice the project schedule at a critical point in the project. It was necessary to replace him in order to maintain the project deliverables. In another situation, the project manager was highly knowledgeable in project management and very demanding toward project deliverables, but utterly lacking in people skills. This required intervention on several occasions to keep the teams functioning. It was necessary to be very selective in the projects and role he played to minimize the adverse consequences of his inferior people skills.

Projects require balance throughout their lifecycle. Beginning with the initial selection of projects, companies must ensure that the project portfolio has the proper balance of risk, resource requirements, and strategic fit in terms of

Figure 6.9 Project manager as a juggler

sustaining current business and growing future business. In MPM, there needs to be a good balance of advantages and opportunities for all participating companies. The mission statement and goals, situational matrix, and roles and responsibilities reflect this balance. The situational leadership model in team management involves balancing the team readiness with the appropriate leadership involvement. During schedule planning and project execution, risk management provides a means to balance all risk factors. In a similar fashion, the triple constraints of time, cost, and scope must be in balance over the project lifecycle to achieve success. In the character traits of teams, the positive traits offset the negative traits to maintain team balance. These examples and many more encountered over a typical project lifecycle confirm the importance of maintaining balance in your projects.

PROJECT INTEGRATION AND EXECUTION

The WBS work packages clearly spell out the specific project activities and methods. While executing each activity, it is important to ensure integration with other activities and phases within the project. This section deals with the integration of project management, teamwork, and safety during project activity completion in the engineering, install, and start-up project phases. This is not required in the manufacturing phase or any other operations-designated phase, since it is already a fully integrated process within the context of the operations environment and linked to the project via the interface events or milestones. Since MPM adds significant value to the engineering phase by facilitating the definition and implementation of commonality and the alignment of system design with users, this section covers these topics as well. In addition, this section covers checklists and visual control boards, which are vital tools in the Six C's *complete* phase.

Checklists. Everyone uses checklists in their daily lives, such as a to-do list on their PDA or phone, a grocery list, troubleshooting a computer problem, or instructions for assembling a child's toy. Since they are so common in everyday life, they are often an underrated tool. The purpose of a checklist is to avoid an item or task slipping from one's memory, or perhaps to document the completion of a task. In some cases, a checklist dictates a certain sequence of tasks. Historical information, previous experiences, and standard templates help to create checklists. Checklists are not a substitute for the schedule and action plan tools discussed previously, but rather a supplement that allows for the highlighting of specific items.

If the project manager uses the checklist for personal benefit to ensure completeness without referencing it in the future, the text checklists can be used without modification. The meeting facility checklist introduced in Chapter 4 is an example of a checklist that a project manager might use and lose after completion (see Figure 6.10). Only the blank template remains as is for use by the next person and for a reference to incorporate lessons learned into the process. Using the checklist for project documentation requires the addition of a signature and date. The date should reflect the date the checklist was completed, and the signature should be from the person who completed the checklist. This establishes credibility and facilitates follow-up when referencing the checklist later. Some organizations add a second-level signature for approval or acceptance, but I recommend keeping it simple by avoiding the extra signatures. Second-level signatures add bureaucracy and display a lack of trust. It also represents a form of after-the-fact duplicate inspection that is not value added. Many companies use checklists as a

Project title _____

Team formation phase _____

Number of team participants _____

Coordinating project manager _____

#	Activity	✔
1.	Flip charts & colored markers for charts	
2.	Wall space to post charts (up to 20) and masking tape	
3.	Sufficient workspace for everyone to simultaneously make posters	
4.	Overhead transparency projector, markers, & blank sheets (Note 3 to 4: portable computers with compatible projector are an alternate)	
5.	Electronic chart board or portable computer with compatible projector	
6.	Breakout areas (minimum 2 required. Teams greater than 15 will require additional breakout rooms)	
7.	Room size & layout should easily accommodate all participants sitting on the outside of a U-shaped table arrangement	
8.	Copy machine readily available	
9.	Main room must be available the entire (2) days and secure at night to avoid tear down and set up time	
10.	Plan lunch using a breakout area for set up to avoid meeting interruptions	
11.	Breakout rooms should be available during the meeting times, but do not require securing at night since there is no setup or equipment to protect	
12.	Clerical person available on computer to enter brainstorming, record action plans, and assist in generating meeting minutes (Preferred)	
13.	Mission statement cards (engineering, installation & start-up teams)	

Figure 6.10 Meeting facility checklist

form of process quality control. This context requires the addition of a form identification and revision level to the signature and completion date requirements.
The form identification and revision level follow a format dictated by the company
that creates the checklist. The checklists in this text are in their simplest form; they
allow readers to add signatures, a completion date, form identification, and revision level requirements based on intended use and specific situation.

Although teams frequently use checklists for specific activities within their
responsibility as appropriate, our prime focus is on preparation checklists and
deliverables checklists, which are the two basic types of checklists used in MPM.
A preparation checklist identifies those predecessors that are required before
beginning a project phase, and a deliverables checklist defines the interim project
deliverables that are required between project phases. Each phase provides checklists that facilitate integration with the other phases; this is in conjunction with
other scheduling and stakeholder management tools. MPM checklists verify key
interface issues and ensure that nothing falls through the cracks. The checklists
provided in this section are thought-starters and should be used as a baseline from
which to build checklists for each specific project situation.

The preparation checklist is for a particular project phase or activity. It ensures
all preparations are complete before starting implementation of the phase, which
avoids false starts or inefficiency in the initial execution of the project phase. Since
this checklist is completed prior to team formation, the project managers, working
as a subset of the leadership team, create the initial template of the preparation
checklist. The preparation checklist is primarily an assessment of the overall organizational readiness to begin a specific phase. The preleadership formation checklist introduced in Chapter 1 is an example of a preparation checklist for the
leadership phase that checks organizational readiness. Its purpose is to avoid any
problems in the critical formation stage (see Figure 6.11).

In general, any project phase that has successor activities linked from another
project phase requires a deliverables checklist. These deliverables between phases
are actually interim deliverables to the total project. This synchronizes expectations of the deliverables and helps to ensure that the project phases interface
smoothly with each other. Figure 6.12 is an example of the design deliverables that
the engineering phase provides to the installation phase in an equipment acquisition project. Whenever possible, participants are involved from the successor
project phase in the development of the deliverables checklist. In addition, if the
predecessor phase is operational, the MPM project team takes the lead in initiating
the task to create the phase-to-phase deliverables checklist. As a secondary benefit
in MPM, the deliverables checklist provides a sense of accomplishment to the
teams through completion of the interim deliverables when the final deliverables
of a completed project are months or years away in the timeline. As a company

Project title _____

Customer _____ **Supplier** _____

Key executive _____ **Key executive** _____

Project manager _____ **Project manager** _____

#	Activity	✔
1.	Establish strategic value of project to your company and secure support from your key executive	
2.	Schedule meeting between initiating company and the other customer or supplier key executives	
3.	Present merits & requirements of MPM and determine strategic value to partnering organization	
4.	Secure agreement between customer and supplier to implement the MPM approach	
5.	Agree on leadership team participants	
6.	Agree on place, date, and duration for leadership formation meeting	
7.	Verify meeting facility and equipment (checklist Chapter 4)	
8.	Arrange refreshments, lunch	
9.	Finalize leadership agenda (template Chapter 4)	
10.	Prepare and send invitations signed jointly from both customer and supplier	
11.	Customer and supplier assign agenda topics to participants	
12.	Review available materials on agenda topics from text and other sources as appropriate with assigned topic leaders	
13.	Review final presentation content	

Figure 6.11 Preleadership formation checklist

executes subsequent MPM projects, the checklist templates are updated with lessons learned to improve project execution.

Engineering Phase. The company engineering groups complete a lot of engineering prior to formation of the engineering team, no matter how early the team is established. The customer engineers have a specific view of what the equipment should look like by virtue of their development of the engineering specifications and similar systems they have previously purchased. The suppliers have another view by virtue of their proposal development and any similar systems they have engineered in the past. Thus, everyone has a vision of the new system based on

Project title _____

Equipment identification _____

Site locations _____

Project manager _____ **Date** _____

#	Activity	☑
1.	Power requirements Machine voltage, amperage, phase, special computer power, and special grounding requirements	
2.	Schematics and one line diagrams	
3.	Air requirements Minimum supply pressure, maximum consumption demand CFM Inlet pipe size, and air dryer requirements	
4.	Cooling water requirements Cooling water flow rate GPM, water pressure drop across exchanger Maximum water inlet temperature, HP heat dissipated, water inlet and outlet sizes	
5.	Ventilation Chemical composition of fumes/smoke, # of point sources requiring ventilation, maximum annual production volume	
6.	Process waste Type of fluid, MSDS sheets, max discharge volume and flow rate, and outlet pipe size	
7.	Oil & lube Type of fluid, MSDS sheets, maximum discharge volume in case of spills	
8.	Foundation requirements: • Location, size, elevations • Special base plate drawings • Tolerances for elevation, flatness, position • Slope of floor for drains • Scrap hole location and size • Special pits for equipment • OEM minimum recommended pit size	
9.	Static/dynamic loads for foundation requirements: • Quantity of supports • Static load on each support • Dynamic inertia load on each pier • Dynamic reaction loads on each pier	

Figure 6.12 Design deliverables checklist

their experiences, and all visions are different. Soon after forming the engineering team, it is important that they blend their visions into one.

From the suppliers viewpoint it is important to maintain commonality in their designs to drive efficiency, serviceability, and reliability in the systems they produce. Of course, the suppliers base their perspective of commonality on the systems they have designed in the past. They have also built relationships with their sub-suppliers and gained experience in the use of their systems. The suppliers use lessons learned in prior projects to eliminate specific components deemed ineffective and focus on those yielding the greatest value.

The customer generally looks at commonality first from the strategic purpose of the new equipment, which involves manufacturing capability and flexibility to meet market demands. The following are three generic levels of commonality applied to most manufacturing equipment:

- *Identical*—Contains the same software, hardware, and drawings. This applies to systems of the same size, configuration, and level of technology purchased from a single supplier.
- *Functionally identical*—Refers to equipment capable of using a variety of tools to make different parts without the need for modifications. This applies to equipment of the same size, configuration, and function, but could incorporate new technology or be from any number of different suppliers.
- *Tooling interchangeable*—Some tooling modifications may be required to move tooling between systems. This applies to equipment of the same size and function.

In addition to viewing commonality from a strategic perspective, customers frequently view it from an operations perspective. Here, the customer is concerned about reliability, availability of spare parts, and workforce training needs for operation and maintenance of the equipment.

The importance of commonality and related design decisions on both the customer and supplier is particularly crucial when a single customer is purchasing systems in quantity for multiple locations. In the mid 1980s, General Motors embarked on a major modernization of their stamping equipment, which involved the purchase of approximately 100 transfer press systems in four basic sizes from a variety of suppliers located in Germany, Japan, and the United States. The quantity of systems in the relatively short timeframe required multiple suppliers for a given system size, eliminating the ability to achieve identical systems—the highest level of commonality. In addition, divisional interests dictating special configurations of the systems and allowing each plant to dictate different brands of controls to fit their existing workforce experience further sacrificed the level of commonality. The systems were very expensive and failed to achieve many cost and performance goals related to commonality that were inherent in such a quantity purchase for both the customer and suppliers. System startups were slow with a minimal transfer of lessons learned between systems and plants. After turning the systems over to production, the plants used their own discretion to make further revisions that detracted from the functional and tool interchangeability of the original systems. As a result, by 1994, after the largest press modernization program ever undertaken by an automotive company, GM's press equipment productivity was among the lowest in the automotive industry as reported by the *1994 Harbour Report*.

In 1995 GM reorganized all the stamping operations into a single division for the first time in its history. The new division embraced the importance of commonality and began a second modernization effort of stamping. System purchases had the goal of being identical. The significantly reduced spending rates matched supplier and GM resource availability. Money was allocated to purchase new systems and to refurbish and commonize existing systems. By 2003, the modernization program covered 60 percent of all stamping processes. Combined with the organizational focus on stamping and the efforts of all personnel in the plants, GM achieved first place in equipment productivity as reported by *2003 Harbour Report*.

One of the first priorities for the engineering team is to determine the level of commonality required in terms of design, manufacturing, maintenance, and operation. Maintaining commonality offers the following benefits:

- Improves initial system design efficiency
- Increases reliability
- Expands flexibility in manufacturing operations, including the ability to carry a reduced spare-part inventory (tool swapping, part interchangeability)
- Compresses learning curves and training time (in-plant maintenance staff, mechanical technician support)
- Enables spreading improvements
- Reduces risk (offsetting a part, tool, line, or plant failure with another identical part, line, or tool)
- Offers lifetime cost benefits through improved quality control, reduced training requirements, interchangeability of personnel, etc.

The project managers and engineers collaborate during the design development as well as throughout the life of the project to achieve the desired level of commonality. This may require deciding against the implementation of new technologies or new ideas that may be more cost effective upon initial investment in order to achieve performance and cost efficiencies over the equipment lifecycle. Both the customer and supplier need to be very sensitive to the other's concern.

For example, the customer may specify a particular Drive X for use in the new system due to extensive use and experience their personnel have with this brand of drive. Its selection reduces training requirements, spare parts, service support contacts, etc. for the life of the equipment. However, Drive Y proposed by the supplier meets the supplier's special needs in terms of performance, size, interface with other supplier systems, initial cost effectiveness, the supplier's engineering and servicing experience, etc. The use of Drive Y may well have been the result of years of research and development or extensive experience with actual applications in the field. In making the final decision for commonality, the supplier must understand the impact of Drive Y on the customer's operating cost, and the customer must understand the cost consequences of Drive X on the supplier's initial system cost. Both parties must determine whether it is best to train the operations personnel in Drive Y, or the supplier's engineering and service personnel in Drive X. Both must understand the level of risk introduced into the overall project by the selection of a different drive. On the positive side, the introduction of a second drive for the supplier or customer potentially increases competition that could reduce initial drive costs for the supplier or drive servicing costs for the customer and could provide protection from both drive supply and service interruptions.

The introduction of new technology should be based on a solid business case with consideration for the impact it has on the system's definition of commonality and project risk from both the supplier's and customer's perspective. Any new technology or device naturally attracts the interest of engineers anxious to apply new ideas in their designs. Engineers must use caution not to introduce change without a thorough business case. Too often, engineers have taken something that works well and have changed it to fit their preferences, display their own individuality, or achieve some minor advantage without the prerequisite business case to support the change.

It is the project manager's responsibility to maintain commonality and control change on the equipment until the completion of and signing off on the Final Acceptance Testing (FAT). During the project, all changes are subject to the project-change control-process discussed previously. The project-change control-process documents all changes, providing managers with a tool to maintain commonality. Its clear contractual language keeps project costs in line, and it has an added bonus of documenting changes from lessons learned that can be incorporated into future projects. Leadership must also play a key role in the initial decisions. They must follow up to ensure that the common direction established by engineering is supported by their organizations and that they have buy in. After project completion, leadership needs to ensure that the operations organization has a disciplined change control process to maintain commonality, and that the only changes implemented during the life of the equipment are the changes that a good business case supports.

Aligning the design with the true end user at the earliest part of the design phase can drive significant efficiency in the project, higher-quality results with less rework, and higher levels of customer satisfaction. In an equipment project, two tools to facilitate this alignment are the functional specification and the Task Based Risk Assessment (TABRA). The purpose of the functional specification is to focus on developing the details of the man and machine interface. This is performed upfront and involves the operators and maintenance end users together with the supplier's and customer's design and specification engineers, and defines the various control interface screens to meet the needs of the users and the capabilities of the designers. This exercise can provide great value to the designers by expanding their knowledge of the system from the user's perspective, allowing designers to deliver superior results in the eyes of the users with minimal effort, and yielding a man and machine interface that is user friendly and effective.

The second tool useful for aligning the design with the end user is the TABRA. This tool is the result of GM and the UAW's efforts to improve the level of safety for new equipment designs. Engineering plays a major role in equipment safety by virtue of their impact on equipment operations and the configurations required to maintain the equipment. For example, on a large system there are main energy lockouts for electric, air, hydraulics, etc., as well as various auxiliary lockout devices. Depending on the specific task undertaken to maintain or operate the equipment, the lockout design configuration dictates lockout content and sequence to accomplish the task in the safest manner. By planning this ahead of time, the design incorporates the proper lockout devices, locates them ideally to facilitate tasks, and matches them to the customer's safety procedures. In similar fashion, the design incorporates maintenance tasks such as component lubricating, filter changes, etc., with optimum safety and efficiency. This TABRA is accomplished by assembling a team made up of the design engineers, experienced operators and maintenance personnel, and appropriate safety experts to systematically review all the tasks involved in operating and maintaining the system. They evaluate all the safety risks associated with each task in terms of frequency and severity to prioritize the risks. Finally, the team develops action plans, design approaches, manufacturing aids, protective equipment, and procedures to minimize or eliminate the safety risks identified. The final product is a much safer machine with many built in safety features, which aligns the equipment design with the final user needs.

The final design is the primary output of engineering; manufacturing uses this design to build the system, and the installation team uses it to plan their activities. In addition, engineering must supply basic information for the installation phase to support site preparations and enable the installation team to ensure readiness to begin the installation. The previous design deliverables checklist is an example of engineering deliverables to the combined installation and site prep phase for a typical transfer press project. This template provides a baseline for preparing a design deliverables checklist that is appropriate for each situation.

Visual Control Board. Visualization of work progress significantly aids in communication from the installation team to site personnel and management. A great tool to aid in this visualization is the visual control board. The visual control board applies to both installation and startup. Thus, as the project moves from installation to startup, the responsibility for maintaining the board moves to the start-up team and the information details shift in focus to meet the needs of the start-up team. The visual control board is simply a large display board typically 4' x 8' located in a prominent location on the construction site with information of general interest concerning the project. At a minimum, this board can be simply a 4' x 8' sheet of plywood, pegboard, cardboard, etc., that facilitates posting information. This can be set on an easel, or mounted on a building column or on the equipment. It is best located in an area that does not interfere with the project and provides space for a small group to assemble safely to make presentations or hold discussions. Ideally, it becomes the focal point for conducting the daily toolbox meetings.

The information is usually a combination of handwritten and computer generated notes and charts. It is best to keep it simple with the most frequently changing information, such as daily safety performance and daily workplace information, handwritten or noted on a standard chart. More stable information, such as project overview and contact numbers, is in the form of computer-generated charts. The information is categorized on the board by the following six sections:

Safety	Project overview	Schedules
Contact list	Issues	Launch status

Figure 6.13 is a recommendation of the type of content to display on the board for each of the above categories. The information listed in bold print represents the minimum requirements, while that shown in parentheses is optional. The data on this board keeps the site personnel and management up-to-date on the project status and displays how the project is progressing. In the initial assembly portion of construction, it is easy to see progress. However, visualization of progress in the balance of the installation and startup, which represents over 50 percent of the timeline, is very difficult; the board is particularly valuable for making this type of effort and progress visible. The information requirements on the visual control board ensure a disciplined approach from the team in planning their work and tracking their progress, which must be done in order to keep the board current.

Project title

Safety	**Project overview**
Green cross	**Mission statement and goals**
Accident report	**Scorecard**
(Safe operating procedure)	**Layout**
(Lockout requirements)	**Key supplier list**
(OSHA reporting information)	(Work scope)
(Monitored power information)	(Pictures)
(Plant tracking requirements)	(Project network chart)
(Safety talks and audits)	

Schedule	**Contact list**
Daily work plans	**Key plant personnel**
Two-week look ahead	**Engineering support**
Macro project schedule	(Supplier service support)
(Critical path plan)	
(Earned value)	
(Activity value)	
(Week end work plan)	
(OEM shipping schedule)	

Issues	**Launch status**
Punch list	**Training plan**
Punch list status	**Spare parts status**
(Supplier problems)	(Buy-off criteria)
(Lessons learned)	(Program launch data)

Bold type represents required information

Type in paranthesis represents optional requirements

Figure 6.13 Site visual control board

The following are some visual control board tips from lessons learned on previous projects:

1.   There should be no special information made for the board. The board should contain the information from the original form used by the team. The board is simply a central place to display the information.

2.   People responsible for a piece of information should keep the board information updated. Maintenance of the board should not be a major administrative task.

3.   Project personnel should seize every opportunity to use the board in communication and presentations with plant personnel and management so they become accustomed to using data from the board to answer their questions.

4.   The board is a focal point for daily and weekly team floor meetings to build awareness. The team's ideas should add information to the board to increase ownership.

5.   The board should not be placed inside a trailer or conference room. It should be kept on the job site in an open space, preferably with no chairs or tables.

6.   Presentations and meetings should be in a stand-up format, keeping the interaction concise and to the point.

7.   Archiving the control-board data as it changes to document the project's history will provide data that will improve subsequent installations.

8.   All the information updates from the visual control board should be transferred to the project's website weekly. This communicates project status to personnel that are not on the project site.

Installation Phase. Approximately two months prior to the start of installation, the project managers from each company in the MPM process begin preparing preliminary information for the installation team fact-finding (see *Fact-Finding* in Chapter 3). This information includes macro scheduling data, recommended milestone dates, and a preliminary work breakdown structure of manageable work packages and traceable tasks. A company that follows a good project management discipline has plenty of data, WBS templates, and lessons learned to help in the preparation of this preliminary information. The team formation event occurs two weeks prior to installation and officially kicks off the installation phase following the prescribed team-building protocol. During this event, the team finalizes the work packages, integrates the various macro schedules, and establishes the project baseline plan for installation. The team formation event provides an excellent opportunity to accomplish many of the items appearing on the preinstallation checklist. To verify all key interface issues, the preinstallation checklist in Figure 6.14 is completed between the team formation event and the actual start of installation.

During the installation, the team utilizes the preshift meetings at the toolbox to review safety and communicate daily WBS tasks to all team members. Technical support personnel from the joint engineering team provide guidance and assistance to the team in the assembly process by providing timely clarification and detailed technical direction to expedite the installation process. The installation project manager conducts weekly progress meetings with the project team at the

Project title _____

Installation lead company _____

Install site _____ **Project manager** _____

#	Activity	✔
1.	Meet, secure contact info, and installation responsibilities from the following customer personnel *Project manager*　　　　　　*Safety supervisor* *Engineering personnel*　　　　*Construction personnel* *Installation supervisor/contractor*	
2.	Create a RASIC chart and contact list	
3.	Review all parking, site access, and safety requirements	
4.	Review job site and establish on site work area	
5.	Review scope and detail specific work requirements for all companies in installation	
6.	Review mission and goals and resolve any open issues assigned to installation	
7.	Detail site requirements	
8.	Detail special tools and responsibility for providing tools	
9.	Establish shift hours and starting times for weekdays and weekends with customer	
10.	Establish installation routine: meetings, daily log, site board, punch list, checklist, etc.	
11.	Review layouts, machine location, and general equipment info build and testing	
12.	Review site preparations and verify completeness by installation start date with customer	
13.	Review packaging, truck loading plans, and agree on truck sequencing/timing	
14.	Establish unload area, special equipment, and work site staging area requirements	
15.	Agree on plant internal equipment move logistics/ timing	
16.	Review a preliminary installation schedule with personnel requirements	
17.	With the input and agreement of all parties update the installation schedule and distribute to all participants	
18.	Establish scheduled communication links (conf call, e-mail, etc.) with all participants	
19.	Distribute all info gathered from above checklist to affected personnel within supplier and customer	

Figure 6.14 Preinstallation checklist

installation site to monitor progress and performance of the project. The schedule is posted and updated at this meeting. If status is behind schedule, a recovery plan is developed and implemented. Upon completion of the install, there must be an acceptance review prior to allowing the equipment to be red-tagged in preparation of *power on*.

The most critical element in a successful installation is plant involvement and resource commitments. The plant needs to assign a full-time project manager to lead the facility preparations, equipment installation, and startup. The project manager's main role is to be the focal point for the project through which everyone communicates and coordinates their activities. Ideally, this project manager is a seasoned employee with many years of experience at the plant site, is highly respected with a history of getting jobs done, and is a good communicator and planner with effective people skills. A project manager must also be knowledgeable in use of project management methodology or receive project management training prior to the assignment. A strong technical background is desirable but not required. All plants have people with these credentials within the organization, but they are reluctant to free these people from their everyday jobs to support the project, because it represents a real sacrifice and may hinder the rest of the operation. Plants need to understand the long-term benefits of this sacrifice. Not only will the installation be more effective, timelier, and at a lower cost, but the launch will be far more successful for the plants. A strong project manager will ensure consideration of plant interests, avoid disruptions between the project and the plant, ensure training and preparation of plant personnel, and become a knowledgeable resource for the plant's long-term equipment operations.

Each project is unique based on the scope of work, people skill sets, and individual personalities. The team-building event provides a common framework for the plant project manager, ensuring the dissemination of information to all teams, establishing effective working relationships, and creating the baseline plan for project execution.

As always, the team develops an installation completion checklist to ensure all deliverables are complete to support the subsequent project start-up phase. They involve the start-up personnel in creation of the checklist. Figure 6.15 is an example of an installation deliverables checklist for a press project.

Start-up Phase. The start-up phase involves powering up the equipment, checking all input and output terminations, performing mechanical adjustments, and demonstrating the performance of the equipment for buyoff. Like installation, startup is a work team. Therefore, the process is identical to the installation phase with the exception that the participants and topics change to fit startup. The installation consists primarily of mechanical activities, while the bulk of the

Project title _____

Installation site _____ **Project manager** _____

#	Activity	✔
1.	Mechanical installation of equipment is complete	
2.	Electrical installation of equipment is complete	
3.	Live incoming power is connected to control panel(s) disconnect	
4.	Safety devices (fencing, handrail, light curtains, doors, floor mats, etc.) installed and approved	
5.	All flooring around equipment is complete, including trench covers	
6.	All gearboxes and reservoirs (hydraulic, washer, lubrication, etc.) filled	
7.	All required utilities (air, water, gas, etc.) connected & tested	
8.	Mechanical integration to adjacent equipment completed	
9.	Electrical integration to adjacent equipment completed	
10.	Equipment is grouted—if required	
11.	Equipment is clean (including surrounding floor area)	
12.	Touch up painting (as needed) completed	
13.	All inspections and/or approvals are complete for equipment startup and/or operation	
14.	Test materials are on site for debug of equipment	
15.	Proven tool(s) are on site for equipment debug	
16.	Pallets and/or dunnage for part stacking and equipment for handling stacked parts are available	
17.	Production materials are on site	
18.	Experienced/trained operators are available for equipment debug	
19.	Skilled trade personnel are available for equipment debug and/or adjustment	

Figure 6.15 Installation deliverables checklist

start-up activities involve electrical, alignment, and fine-tuning. The change in required skill sets drives a change in participants.

As with installation, the fact-finding information is prepared two months prior to startup. The start-up team formation event is conducted two weeks prior to startup, and the prestart-up checklist shown in Figure 6.16 takes place between the team formation and startup. The team formation covers many of the items on the prestart-up checklist. The safety issue intensifies the need for integrated coordination of all start-up activities. Start up is very complex and generally involves technicians from several different sources to start up the various component systems. In order to ensure safety while efficiently employing the various technicians

Project title _____ **Start up site** _____

Supplier project manager _____ **Site project manager** _____

#	Activity	✔
1.	Insure installation deliverables checklist has been completed	
2.	Meet, secure contact info, and start-up responsibilities from the following customer personnel _Project manager_ _Engineering personnel_ _Start up supervisor/contractor_ _Construction personnel_ _Key maintenance personnel_ _Safety supervisor_ _Key production and quality personnel_ _Key training personnel_ _Parts and service ordering personnel_	
3.	Update RASIC chart and contact list	
4.	Review scope and detail specific work requirements for companies participating in startup	
5.	If leadership team is in place, review mission, goals, and resolve any open issues assigned to startup	
6.	Detail site requirements for startup	
7.	Detail any spare parts and identify responsibility for providing the parts with customer	
8.	Establish shift hours and starting times for weekdays and weekends with customer	
9.	Review a preliminary start-up schedule	
10.	Agree on personnel and productive material requirements along with responsibility for providing each	
11.	Update the start-up schedule and distribute to all participants	
12.	Review open punch list items from installation and action plans to correct with customer	
13.	Review Final Acceptance Testing requirements and insure concurrence with customer	
14.	Define and reach agreement on customer training needs	
15.	Define and reach agreement on customer on site support needed from suppliers during ramp up	
16.	Establish scheduled communication links site suppliers	
17.	Distribute info gathered to all affected personnel	

Figure 6.16 Pre start-up checklist

in starting components of the system, a very detailed plan is required. Utilizing the full 24-hour timeframe of each day expedites the start-up process. MPM's multi-company resources and coordinated scheduling facilitates the three-shift startup by providing engineers and technicians to support the normal maintenance personnel during startup. Task assignments by shift match the skill levels of the personnel to the task requirements. The final plan not only has sequence dependencies for starting specific components, but also contains dependencies to reflect items that cannot occur within the same time frame due to safety concerns. Taking advantage of the three-shift operation allows for the scheduling of items that are in safety conflict on different shifts.

During this step, the focus is finding and correcting installation errors. Component infant mortality issues begin to appear and it is important to have a supply of spare parts for equipment commissioning readily available. The customer and supplier need to have carefully planned for this many months earlier. If not previously involved in installation, plant production and skilled personnel who will eventually be running and maintaining the equipment should become involved in the process. It is important that these plant personnel have received the appropriate prerequisite training so they can take maximum advantage of the opportunity.

Safety awareness and planning is extremely crucial at this stage. Without going into all the detail of the start-up schedule, the following tips will promote safety during startup if incorporated into the planning:

- Develop a well-defined *power on* entry procedure to ensure the proper lockout of all energized areas before any work begins in the exposed area. This includes locking out the main power supply at the substation prior to *power on*. After meeting all safety requirements, lock out the main control panel, and then remove the lock from the substation. Finally, assign responsibility for control of press power to the start-up teams.
- Turn on electric power to the equipment following a detailed power on procedure (received from the equipment supplier). For complicated equipment, there should be a sequence of disconnects, circuit breakers, and fuses to switch on or install. Following this sequence, there are specific power checks and other device checks that occur after switching on each device or group of devices.
- Verify that the posted lockout procedures reduce the equipment to a zero power state.
- Conduct a *power on* acceptance review prior to allowing the equipment to be debugged and FAT to begin.

- Confirm the level of necessary personal protective equipment for each task.
- Following the I/O check, conduct a walk-through prior to starting the machine adjustment.
- At the start of each machine adjustment, check equipment for proper guarding, close and secure gates or doors, and check the integrity of safety fencing. Notify everyone working in the area regarding which range of motion and function is being verified.

Machine adjust begins with a thorough walk-through and visual inspection of the equipment and surrounding areas. The first priority of the walk-through inspection is safety. The second priority is to verify that nothing is prohibiting first-time movement such as shipping straps, packaging material, etc. Check for freedom of movements on each device, looking specifically for interference or clearance issues. Check and correct housekeeping issues. Remove extra parts and hardware from any devices where movement is expected. Check for loose or missing hardware, cables, or components and tighten or replace as required. Using the supplier-provided information and system drawings, measure the movement and compare with the data at hand. Any discrepancies are investigated and corrected as needed. Once the dimensional checks are finished, manually cycle the movement to check for binds, adjust for smoothness, tune drives, etc.

Once machine adjustment is complete, the final step involves verifying that the equipment performs to the specifications. Establishing testing procedures for buyoff using the joint engineering team early in the project provides insight into machine performance deliverables and helps to define the project scope. The buyoff testing involves a lot of participation from the engineering team to ensure consistency in the interpretation of requirements and test results. Engineering involvement in the buyoff is a huge benefit to both the customer and supplier in terms of the experiential learning and the opportunity for the engineers to incorporate the lessons learned in future projects or equipment improvement efforts. Operations personnel involvement is critical as well. They require sufficient lead times to ensure that all materials and tooling are available for the buyoff. As the final user, they operate the equipment with the coaching of the engineering personnel to build confidence in their ability to operate the systems to the equipment's specifications and validate the project deliverables.

CLOSE

Close is the final group in the Six C process, and the group frequently given the least attention. This lack of attention is due to the following closure characteristics: risk and costs are very low, stakeholder influence is minimal, paperwork is laborious, and opportunity value is not recognized. The start of new projects, personnel reassignments, and organization focus shifting to the next project or ramping-up new systems further aggravates the situation. *Closure*—as defined in this context—is not a single point in time but rather a series of actions within the Six C's *close* process group, carried out over time and requiring planning and resources.

Project termination occurs for a variety of reasons. Authors Gray and Larson in their book *Project Management: The Managerial Process* (2005, 471–3) identify five basic categories of project closure: *normal, perpetual, failed, premature*, and *changing priorities*. New equipment projects are particularly susceptible to becoming perpetual projects. If the user organization is not involved upfront or lacks the proper training, the users might lack confidence in their ability to operate the equipment or fear accepting responsibility for the new equipment. In addition, the organization receiving new equipment grows used to the extensive resources in the start-up phase and is reluctant to accept responsibility for the new system even when properly trained. Consequently, they continually find the need for more improvements to the system and hold the supplier responsible for making these improvements before they will finalize the buyoff. This essentially turns this into a never-ending project. This approach creates added costs, ties up valuable engineering resources from both the customer and supplier, and prevents full realization of the project benefits. This situation can be avoided by defining the project goals and deliverables upfront, controlling project scope as described in Chapter 5 using a well-defined change control process, and involving site operations personnel in the installation and startup as described in Chapter 6. In addition, executing the project-to-user linkage discussed in the *Project-to-User Linkage* section later in this chapter also helps to mitigate the situation. In general, following the multi-company project management (MPM) process in conjunction with early user involvement prevents projects from becoming endless.

There is no guarantee of project success, since by their very definition they are unique and contain unknowns. However, following MPM with its disciplined project management approach and incorporating the full support and involvement of all stakeholders helps to prevent failure in most cases except for major catastrophes, which are totally outside the control of the project organization.

Factors outside the control of the project may also drive premature and changing priority project closures. It is the project leadership team's responsibility to anticipate these situations far enough in advance to minimize negative effects on the project participants while at the same time maximize the project results. A severe shift in a company's economic condition or market forecast is a typical situation that can result in the premature closure or termination of an equipment project. The leadership team's senior executives provide the early warning of pending changes in priority. Immediate access to senior executives increases the response to these types of situations. Using MPM also provides an advantage through the team's ability to collaborate on ways to avoid termination by scaling back the scope or by retiming their spending to meet either the company's cash flow or other financial objectives that drove the initial change in priorities. These approaches as well as others can often adjust the fit of the project within the new priorities to achieve a normal closure.

The balance of this chapter assumes a normal project closure. Project closure is more than closing contracts and finalizing related documentation. It also involves project and team evaluations, lessons learned, reassigning resources, and celebrating the results. While contract closure only happens once at the end of the project, it is best to perform the following steps at the completion of each phase of the project:

- Perform an update
- Perform a project evaluation
- Reassign resources as necessary
- Verify the accuracy of records
- Review lessons learned
- Celebrate the results

Each phase of a project has its own team identity and, with the exception of contract closure, it makes sense to perform all other aspects of *close* as a wrap-up to each phase while the team is still in place and resources are still available, experiences are still fresh in everyone's mind, and recognition is timely.

By virtue of the multi-company environment and team structures, MPM puts its own twist on the traditional project management closure topics. In addition, MPM offers additional perspectives that supplement the closure activities and add value to the project. This chapter covers the traditional closure topics of *contracts, evaluation, audits,* and *lessons learned* followed by the MPM value-added topics of *project-to-user linkage, celebration,* and *beyond the project.*

TRADITIONAL CLOSURE

Contract Closure. Contract closure is a necessary step in any project, which consists primarily of an administrative set of tasks best performed within the traditional organizational framework. The basic tasks of project closure include customer delivery acceptance, closing accounts and work orders in the respective company systems, and paying all bills. The contract closure ensures the receipt of all deliverables by the customer and the receipt of all payments by the supplier as specified in the contract. This closure requires appropriate documentation from the supplier indicating final payment to all sub-suppliers and from the customer detailing the acceptance of deliverables along with an agreement between the customer and supplier regarding the warranty. The supplier is responsible for getting documentation from their suppliers and for making sure that those suppliers secure documentation from any other suppliers in the supply chain. The purpose of the documentation is to ensure that all deliverables are complete, all bills are paid, and all dates for the contracted warranty periods are established. Typically, the customer as the final owner of the project requires direct suppliers to provide all documentation including that of the sub-suppliers in the supply chain as a condition of final payment. All the real physical value of the project resides at the customer in the form of the installed equipment. Thus, any supplier within the supply chain can only leverage the physical equipment to secure unpaid bills. This documentation protects the customer from the possibility of anyone placing liens on the equipment, which could come from a supplier's or sub-supplier's nonpayment.

The customer must verify all deliverables. The supplier then requests a *formal acceptance document* signed by the customer as their proof of project completion. Formal acceptance for projects with multiple systems is generally required for each system. One would expect that after all the work and effort expended to deliver the project, this final step would be almost automatic. Care should be taken to ensure the hard-earned customer and supplier satisfaction built to this point is not lost due to disagreements or failure to resolve relatively minor issues. Generally, the major deliverables and all tasks in the project schedule are not an issue. The issues usually arise around unresolved items from the open-issues list or peripheral deliverables. In an equipment project, the peripheral deliverables are such things as service manuals, *as built* drawings, accurate spare parts lists, spare parts, training, etc. These are all issues that can be easily resolved by simply planning ahead to complete the peripheral items in a timely manner and applying a discipline that systematically resolves open issues as soon as possible. The leadership team plays a role in this process by looking ahead to ensure that these requirements are being built into the timelines by the appropriate teams, and that the teams are appropriately addressing the open issues.

Evaluation. Project evaluation has two dimensions. The first dimension involves evaluating the project in terms of its goals to determine the degree to which the project achieved the satisfaction of both the customer and supplier. This evaluation provides valuable data used to develop future projects and evaluate suppliers. The second dimension of evaluation relates to the project management and team process used to manage the project, which is an evaluation of the MPM process. This process evaluation leads to the incorporation of process improvements into MPM that benefits all future projects and customer and supplier relationships. The leadership performs both project and process evaluations since they are the only group with a view of the total project. They draw input from the other teams or participants in the process of formulating their assessment. Ideally, they perform evaluations after each project work phase is completed. However, in many equipment projects the close timing and interaction between installation and startup often end up as a single evaluation for each system delivered.

The final project evaluation is a full leadership team exercise usually scheduled during the last leadership team meeting for the project. One of the leadership participants acts as the facilitator—usually the customer's or supplier's key executive. Prior to the last meeting the designated facilitator e-mails a request to all participants informing them that there will be an evaluation at the next team meeting and proposing the use of a *circle-triangle-X* rating system for the goals as shown:

● Goal achieved or exceeded
▲ Major portion achieved; some improvement needed
✗ Goal missed

The evaluation is conducted as a team exercise with everyone offering their opinions and discussing the logic for their evaluation. The idea is to reach a consensus rating for each goal. The open discussion is critical for everyone to share perspectives on goal performance. Input from all the participants, forms the basis for the performance rating. The philosophy is *all for one and one for all*. For example, meeting the budget is often a cost goal for projects. In some projects, a scope increase could cause the customer to go over budget, or an engineering problem might cause the supplier to exceed the budget. If one participant goes over the budget while others meet the budget, the project team did not meet the budget overall, and the goal is *triangle* or *X*, depending on how far over budget that one participant was. Project phase evaluations follow the same pattern as described above except they occur during the project at the next leadership meeting following the completion of a specific phase. Most customers have some internal form of supplier evaluation, and suppliers have specific customer satisfaction forms for their internal use. After the final project evaluation exercise, it is a good idea for the customer and supplier to complete these forms while the entire project is fresh in everyone's mind. Reviewing these internal company forms in the leadership team meeting immediately following the project evaluation builds trust and understanding among the participants.

Figure 7.1 is an example of a completed project evaluation form for a very successful progressive press project that either met or exceeded every goal. Figure 7.2 is an example of a multi-system, multi-site project with combined evaluations that occurred after the completion of each set of installation and start-up phases. Note that the separation between the first and last systems was two years. This project encountered a design problem, and the best efforts of the supplier's design engineers and customer's approval engineers failed to anticipate the problem. The initial runoff at the supplier prior to shipment went without a hitch. The problem appeared after installation of the first system when certain components failed prematurely in production. As a result, the first phase rating was very bad with four goals *X*, three goals *triangle*, and two goals *circle*. However, as subsequent phases were completed, the ratings improved until in the last phase, only the *meet budget* item was *X* and all others were *circle*. The late discovery of the design problem had a severe impact resulting in the budget loss. Design modification and the retesting of the third system at the supplier further exacerbated the budget issue. The systems at Pontiac and Marion required retrofitting on site, which was very costly as well. As a result, the supplier was not able to recover sufficient costs to meet the original budget and the team had to report that goal as *X*.

The MPM process portion of the rating uses a survey. Figure 7.3 is a completed form for reference. It is best to develop a common survey to evaluate all projects for comparison and for tracking continuous improvement. The top portion is a simple assessment of the process in terms of seven parameters with related comments, and the bottom portion is a list of improvements. The participants simply put an *X* in the appropriate box for each of the seven parameters and included any comments and process suggestions they felt appropriate. The project manager from the company initiating the MPM conducts the survey and distributes it to all leadership participants for completion and return prior to the last leadership meeting.

Progressive Press Mission Statement

Provide globally common progressive press systems that meet or exceed GM, vendor and teams' expectations. Success will be achieved by using advanced cost effective technology, strategic teams, and communication that fosters mutual trust.

Goals	Rating
Safety	
1. Zero lost time	●
Timing	
2. Create and manage a schedule to meet target dates	●
Cost	
3. Avoid scope and price changes	●
Leadership	
4. Utilize teams in leadership, engineering, & installation	●
Engineering	
5. Meet performance benchmarks	●
Communication	
6. Utilize effective/targeted communication systems and procedures	●
Training	
7. Provide timely and cost effective training	●

Key:

● Met or exceeded goal   ▲ Improvements needed   **X** Goal missed

Figure 7.1 Final project evaluation

Upon receipt of the surveys, the project manager, while maintaining anonymity, summarizes the numerical results by adding the Xs for each box across all the surveys, entering the total in the appropriate box on a summary sheet. This step repeats for all boxes on the survey. The project manager then lists all comments and improvement recommendations for review and discussion at the last leadership meeting. Frequently the same project will have similar comments and recommendations since each person is submitting the survey without consultation with other team members. All comments should be included, regardless of duplication. Multiple items add more weight to a given comment or suggestion. In some cases, the participants from a single company may elect to submit a single survey response representing their consensus on the parameters with their consolidated comments and suggestions. Typically, the combined comments and suggestions are one to two pages in length.

Tryout Cell Mission Statement

GM and SCHULER working together shall implement leading technology tryout cell systems to reduce die construction lead time and cost.

Project phase evaluations

Goals	Marion 3/9/01	Pontiac 9/4/01	Mansfield 5/8/02	Grand Rapids 7/23/03
Project management				
1. Meet project milestones	X	X	▲	●
2. Develop installation plan for each site using teamwork to achieve shortest time	X	▲	●	●
3. Provide timely training to the right people	X	●	●	●
4. Meet specifications	▲	▲	●	●
5. Meet budgeted cost	X	X	X	X
6. Minimize changes and risk	▲	▲	●	●
Safety				
1. Provide safety training to increase self-awareness	▲	●	●	●
2. Design equipment to prevent all harm	●	●	●	●
3. Achieve zero lost time accidents during project implementation	●	●	●	●

● Met or exceeded goal   ▲ Improvements needed   X Goal missed

Figure 7.2 Evaluation by project phases

Figure 7.4 is the summarized MPM process survey for the tryout cell project discussed previously in the multi-phase evaluations. Note that the summary report uses the same survey form to summarize the results. The most valuable information is in the second part of the survey, which asks for process improvements on future projects. The comments and improvement suggestions listed in the summary are only a partial listing from the tryout cell project due to space limitations. The suggestions regarding minutes, video conferences, online database, installation team participants, project expectations, and plant management involvement represent the partial input of a single project. This information gathered over the past decade drove MPM process improvements resulting in the

MPM Process Survey

Project Name: <u>Tryout Cell Systems</u>

1)   Did the MPM process improve the following:

		Help +2	+1	No 0	-1	Hurt -2
A.	Performance & technical specifications		X			
B.	Roles & responsibilities	X				
C.	Communication requirements		X			
D.	Initial timing requirements			X		
E.	Supplying a better product		X			
F.	Recognizing risk/potential problems	X				
G.	Maintaining or adjusting schedules	X				

Comments:

   a.   Realizing the interdependence of the businesses, the leadership team and team process helps create an environment to work together and make the right project decisions

   b.   Throughout the entire process, there was strong commitment to the process by participants

   c.   Initial timing was clearly detailed in the purchase agreement prior to start of MPM

_____

_____

_____

_____

_____

2)   Please comment on how the MPM process can be improved on future projects:

   a.   Video conferences save cost and make more frequent meetings possible

   b.   Involve plant management in the leadership team earlier than start of installation

_____

_____

_____

_____

Figure 7.3 Tryout cell process survey form

MPM Process Survey

Project Name: <u>Tryout Cell Systems</u>

1)   Did the MPM process improve the following:

		Help		No		Hurt
		+2	+1	0	-1	-2
A.	Performance & technical specifications	1	2	3		
B.	Roles & responsibilities	4	2			
C.	Communication requirements	2	4			
D.	Initial timing requirements	1	2	3		
E.	Supplying a better product	2	1	3		
F.	Recognizing risk/potential problems	2	2	2		
G.	Maintaining or adjusting schedules	3	3			

Comments:

a.   It is a good instrument for making decisions during the project

b.   Realizing the interdependence of the businesses, the leadership team and team process helps create an environment to work together and make the right project decisions

c.   Throughout the entire process, there was strong commitment to the process by participants

d.   Measurement against goals as each phase was completed was very beneficial in making continuous improvement over the course of the project

2)   Please comment on how the MPM process can be improved on future projects:

a.   As already done, use a projector in the meeting and write minutes simultaneously for everyone to approve

b.   Video conferences save cost and make more frequent meetings possible

c.   Project data should be tracked in one on line database, allowing each team member to get an overview at any time

d.   When installation teams are formed it is critical that the participants are the same as those that will be on site full time for the installation

e.   Project management expectations particularly related to installation and startup need to be clarified by all participants early on

f.   Involve plant management in the leadership team earlier than start of installation

_____

_____

_____

Figure 7.4 Tryout cell process survey summary

robust flexible process of today. Each company uses this survey to improve their future efforts as they deem appropriate.

Audits. Project audits are a common method used by organizations to assess the performance of projects and ensure conformance to company policy and procedures. Audits are a means for companies to fulfill their fiduciary responsibilities to their stockholders by ensuring the company's adherence to proper procedures. Unlike the project evaluations discussed previously, individuals with no involvement in the project perform the audits. These individuals may be a third party employed by a specific audit company or, in the case of internal audits, a special group within the company tasked with audit responsibility. In many cases, the audits take a very narrow functional view focusing on a particular aspect such as financial controls and fail to look at the entire project management process. Progressive companies take the broader viewpoint and often consider the total project management process, but fail to assess the teamwork and relationship aspects of the project. Since audits access sensitive company records that are often related to financial issues, out of necessity, each company conducts them from a single company perspective even in a multi-company project.

Project audits conducted during project execution provide the most accurate assessment of the project since data is real time, personnel are more accessible, and procedure observation occurs during actual execution. Auditing a project in progress provides an opportunity to correct any discrepancies as opposed to a post-project audit, which provides no chance to correct errors. However, the audits can place a heavy burden on the project organization as it responds to the various audit requests for information and often introduces a new level of anxiety into the project team. In my experience, an audit of the press modernization program encompassing several projects involved as many as four fulltime auditors for a period of six to eight weeks to cover the full scope of project management and financial procedures. The organization initiating the audit must balance the demands of the audit with the available project resources to determine whether to conduct the audit during execution or after the project or program is complete.

Companies that are going to conduct a project audit involving MPM should consider auditing the entire project management process including aspects of teamwork and relationships, which MPM refers to as a *Six C audit.* A Six C audit is the evaluation of a project in terms of its conformance to both team and project management principles. It consists of evaluating each MPM phase of a project against the six process groups of *cooperate, communicate, coordinate, control, complete,* and *close.* After identifying the project phases, a matrix is constructed with the MPM phases listed across the top and the process groups listed on the left. Table 7.1 is a sample matrix constructed assuming a project with four MPM phases consisting of *lead, engineer, install,* and *startup.* The elements are listed that

Table 7.1 Six C audit matrix

Six C	Project phases			
Process groups	**Lead**	**Engineer**	**Install**	**Startup**
Cooperate	Norms Personal history Team process Organizational charts Situational matrix Project team identification Conflict resolution	Norms Personal history Team process Responsibility chart Project team identification Conflict resolution	Norms Personal history Team process RASIC Project team identification Conflict resolution	Norms Personal history Team process RASIC Project team identification Conflict resolution
Communicate	Mission and goals Website Scope agreement Brainstorming Communication plan Status meetings	Mission and goals Website Spec/engineer review Open issues list Communication plan Status meetings	Mission and goals Website Statement of work Fact-finding Visual control board Daily lineup meetings	Mission and goals Website Statement of work Fact-finding Visual control board Daily lineup meetings
Coordinate	Open issues/action plan Macro project plan Project milestones Risk management Verify plan integration	Open issues/action plan Engineer and manufacture schedule Purch and contract plan Manpower plan Customer document requirements Customer engineer approves requirements Risk analysis	Install punch list/issues Install schedule Logistics plan Manpower plan Site interface requirements Risk analysis	Start-up punch list/issues Start-up schedule Launch support plan Manpower plan Customer training plan Customer buyoff requirements Risk analysis

Table 7.1 Six C audit matrix - con't

Six C Process groups	Project phases			
	Lead	**Engineer**	**Install**	**Startup**
Complete	Manage stakeholders Information distribution Safety Situational leadership	Direct and manage engineer. Information distribution Safety Definition of common User alignment Checklists	Direct and manage install Information distribution Safety User involvement Checklists Visual control board	Direct and manage install Information distribution Safety User involvement Checklists Visual control board
Close	Evaluate goals Assess team process Lessons learned Contract closure Recognition awards Checklists Beyond the project	Engineer assessment Lessons learned Finalize all documentation Recognition awards	Install assessment Lessons learned All punchlists closed Recognition awards	Training completed Start-up assessment Lessons learned All punchlists closed Recognition awards Project-to-user-linkage

make up each Six C process group and MPM project phase combination within the matrix. The project phases that use operational methods of management use the operational audit procedures already in place. Through interviews with participants, observance of project execution, and review of documentation, the auditors analyze the project against each element in the matrix to identify conformance or opportunities for improvement. Once the analysis is complete, the audit team identifies components that are missing and areas for improvement. Applying the assessment across multiple projects within the same company drives standardization and implementation of best practices.

Lessons Learned. Lessons learned can add significant value for improving future projects as well as the entire company enterprise. To maximize value, MPM recommends conducting a lessons learned session for each phase of the project involving all the key participants for the phase in question. In many cases, companies elect not to conduct a lessons learned activity. Instead, they refer future project participants to history, which has documented prior projects as a means of identifying lessons for future projects. The documentation can be overwhelming, and unless there is something specific to investigate, it yields very little insight. Progressive organizations maintain a lessons learned data file consisting of a lessons learned listing from specific projects organized by project source. In the ideal situation, the database offers additional sort capabilities by topic, project phase, etc. The problem with this improved approach is that it does not take the final step of implementing the corrective action necessary to integrate the lessons into the project process or company enterprise. Instead of asking participants on the next project to integrate lessons from past projects into a new project at a time when the risk, planning, and engineering activities are at their highest, lessons should be built into the standard project and engineering systems as soon as they are identified. This allows the individuals who are most knowledgeable in the lessons to perform the integration at a time when the project demands are declining. The person who actually experienced the lessons is also more committed to building this into the standard procedures. This eliminates misinterpretation of the lessons, avoids multiple teams generating parallel corrections, and documents the process in support of continuous improvement. Of course, this assumes that each company follows lean principles with established standardized processes and procedures combined with a continuous improvement methodology enforced by discipline. In a typical equipment project, lessons learned are assigned into four basic categories and are supported with appropriate documentation. The four categories are *equipment specific, general equipment, project process related,* and *team process related.* Table 7.2 lists these categories along with the documentation and its owner.

Each company must determine the appropriate set of categories along with documentation and owners. If there is a Project Management Office (PMO), it is

Table 7.2 Possible categories for lessons learned

Owner	Category	Documentation
Lead engineer	Equipment-type specific	Specific project spec.
Functional manager	General equipment issue	General equip. spec.
Project manager	Project process related	PM manual
Organizational development	Team process related	Team process guide

the natural owner for project- and team-related process issues. Another approach further defines equipment specific and general categories by functional groups and assigns them to the functional managers. Regardless of the structure, the important point is to have a defined process for integrating continuous improvement ideas into the standardized procedures.

The flowchart in Figure 7.5 is one possible method for integrating both the lessons learned and the audit recommendations into the company procedures. Equipment-type specific lessons learned go into the project specification, and the new document is saved as the modified version of the project specification for use on future projects. This is the responsibility of the lead engineers. Appropriate functional managers review general equipment lessons learned for incorporation into the general engineering specification. Process-related lessons learned and audit recommendations add to the Project Management (PM) manual or the team process guide after approval by the appropriate staff. In some cases such as MPM, project management and team processes are represented in one manual. It is the responsibility of the project manager to present these to the staff for concurrence, and the owners listed previously incorporate the changes.

The following is an actual example of using the above lessons learned process. A requirement in the general equipment specification for all equipment was *no lead paint*. This may seem like an unnecessary specification since paints in the United States have been lead-free since 1978 thanks to the Consumer Product Safety Commission. However, in one project involving equipment purchased from a Japanese supplier, the installation team discovered lead paint on certain equipment components during the installation. They stopped the installation and performed abatement of the lead hazard at considerable cost to the supplier and loss of time in the installation. An investigation found that the paint came from one of the Japanese sub-suppliers. This lesson was folded into the general specification with the requirement that MSDS sheets specifying the chemical content be provided directly from the paint supplier validating that the paint does not contain any lead. Four years later, lead paint appeared on another project from a German supplier, even though the MSDS sheets from the U.S. headquartered paint supplier confirmed that the paint was lead-free; again, a major cost impact on the supplier

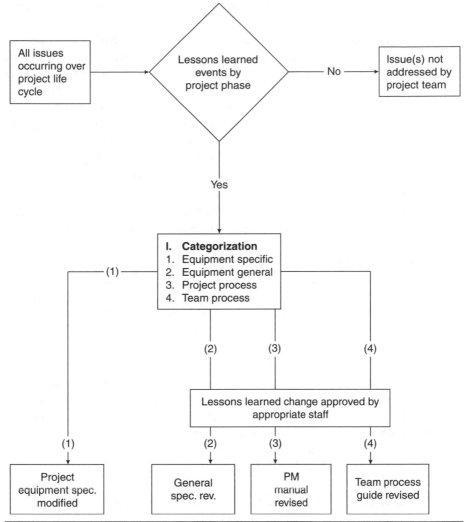

Figure 7.5 Lessons learned integration process

and time impact on installation. As a result, a simple test that detects lead paint is now incorporated into the general specifications, and the test is included in the buyoff engineer's quality check tasks at the manufacturer's site. This lead paint issue never appeared in any other project; a project manager reviewing project history might never have identified the problem or may have found only the first solution that as of yet, had not been fool-proofed. A project manager reviewing the lessons learned may not have realized the significance of the fool-proofed testing solution. Building this lesson into the documentation addresses this issue without the project manager ever having to worry about it other than following the documented procedures.

The generation of the lessons learned is best done by having each project phase team set aside specific time to collectively identify and discuss the lessons learned. The session needs to be nonthreatening with a high level of trust. Asking the team to conduct the exercise keeps everyone more at ease and yields better results. Teams must explain the lessons in objective terms without involving personalities or trying to place blame. It is important to list the good and the bad. In many cases, the things that went wrong do not provide definitive solutions for what to do correctly. The positive experiences are more valuable because they clearly spell out actions to repeat the positive performance. The positive experiences reinforce the importance of the established processes and procedures, which supports the discipline and culture that will sustain them in the future. The multi-company perspective of the team provides valuable insight into the lessons learned and results in creative approaches for correcting issues.

In summary, the lessons learned on each project improves the performance of future projects and of the company enterprise. Rather than maintaining a large database of lessons learned, this approach identifies opportunities by conducting a lessons learned event after each phase and integrates the resulting opportunities as quickly as possible into the appropriate documentation for use on future projects. It is the project manager's responsibility to conduct the lessons learned sessions. By following this approach, the people most familiar with the situation take the necessary action to incorporate the change into future projects rather than count on a new engineer who may struggle to interpret and apply the lessons learned from someone else's project. Conducting lessons learned with each phase ensures the timely incorporation of changes rather than waiting for the end of the current project or initiation of a future project.

MPM CLOSURE SUPPLEMENT

Project-to-user Linkage. Contracts define the point of project closure and handoff to the customer. In reality, the handoff for most projects is not a point in time, but a transition from delivery to full production. The users of the project are the focus during this transition. The users are those individuals within the customer's organization who regularly use or maintain the equipment. This transition period, referred to as the *project-to-user linkage,* has a dramatic effect on project acceptance and long-term customer satisfaction.

Linking the equipment installation team with the manufacturing site team can create great synergy. The equipment manufacturer and manufacturing site leaders must be aware of the benefits each can derive from such a linkage. The equipment supplier gains valuable information and assistance related to site issues and resources from site user team representatives involved in the installation. The site manufacturing personnel know local procedures about site access, health and safety requirements, etc., which can be invaluable in reducing lost time for the installation team. This higher level of cooperation helps when installation needs impact current manufacturing operations. It also facilitates the resolution of unexpected installation problems when everyone's collective knowledge and resources are required. In many cases, local construction trades perform the installation. In such situations, the manufacturing personnel fill a knowledge gap about basic manufacturing equipment that may be lacking in the outside construction trades. This all translates into a more efficient and cost-effective installation. Involving users early builds equipment ownership. This ownership causes the manufacturing personnel to actively seek knowledge of the equipment, improve their skills in operating the equipment, and become more committed to proper maintenance. As a result, the equipment startup and buyoff process is more efficient and has higher acceptance, thus minimizing the demand for equipment suppliers and achieving the buyoff in the shortest time possible. Improving success in these areas is significant since the installation, startup, and buyoff can make the difference between a highly successful project and a big financial loss for the equipment supplier. Overall, the project-to-user linkage drives a higher level of customer satisfaction, a potential for repeat business, and fewer warranty problems.

The project-to-user linkage has similar benefits for the manufacturing site as well. A site leader's failure to understand the significance of these benefits along with a reluctance to invest resources today to reap future success are the major obstacles that stand in the way of establishing a cooperative project-to-user linkage. The project-to-user linkage has even greater significance for the manufacturing site since results last for the life of the equipment for the ongoing manufacturing operation. Getting involved with the installation at the outset avoids disruptions to current manufacturing operations by ensuring the existence of proper allowances in the installation team's plan and that the plan conforms to the site's procedures and standards. Oftentimes, the customer is supplying the installation labor either from internal resources or outside contractors, so an efficient installation goes immediately to the operation's bottom line. Even if the supplier is funding the install, a faster completion aids the operating site since it begins generating the improvements previously expected by the project. The start-up and buyoff activities generally require more support from the manufacturing source. Thus, improved efficiency here saves site costs and shortens equipment delivery time as well. Achievement of full production usually occurs some time after the equipment buyoff since it represents the performance of the entire manufacturing enterprise. Maintaining the project-to-user linkage during the ramp-up ensures that the site can secure the help it needs to reach the goals.

The biggest challenge for any site with a large equipment project is integrating the completed project into the manufacturing operation as quickly and as smoothly as possible. The critical factor to success is the workforce. The manufacturing team needs the necessary support environment, proper training, and desire to succeed; the project-to-user linkage facilitates the acquisition of these elements. Early involvement in the installation enables the manufacturing team to define the special equipment, tools, and skills they require. Early involvement provides free on-the-job training for the team representatives and helps to define a more structured training program for the entire team. As the team gains ownership through their involvement, they become more committed and confident in the equipment, increasing their desire to succeed.

Most manufacturing operations are trying to either implement a team process or improve on the one they have to increase the effectiveness of their operations. A disciplined project following an MPM process provides an excellent model from which to initiate or upgrade the manufacturing team process. The norms of effective project and manufacturing teams are the same. Project teams focus heavily on activity planning to meet project deadlines while manufacturing teams plan to meet production schedules, maintenance requirements, and process improvements. Both teams need first-rate workplace organization and visual controls. The project needs an effective change control process, and manufacturing must have a structured continuous improvement process. Both teams set their goals in the areas of safety, quality, productivity, and customer satisfaction. Team members working in the right project environment see many opportunities to transfer what they learn and experience to their production teams.

The leadership team is responsible for directing the project-to-user linkage since it requires the commitment of senior management from both the supplier and customer to succeed. In the beginning, the linkage is lead by the supplier and heavily manned by installation personnel with small support from the site. Over time, the amount of resources and leadership shifts until in the end, the manufacturing site is leading the process as part of its continuous improvement process and the supplier is providing support on request. The point in time at which majority leadership shifts from supplier to customer is typically the official contract closure. After contract closure, the supplier provides support to complete the project-to-user linkage to ensure maximum customer satisfaction. Whether you are the supplier or the manufacturing site, the pre- and post-contract closure activities associated with the project-to-user linkage are critical to maximizing project success.

Celebration. The rewards and recognition systems are unique to each company's culture and procedures. In celebrating team accomplishments, it is important to avoid conflict with existing company rewards systems. Thus, it is best to avoid specific monetary gifts or individual awards. In many cases praise from superiors and acknowledgement of accomplishments from peers can be a greater motivator and even more satisfying than any small monetary reward. Involving the families in the recognition is also a consideration, since in many cases team commitments require some sacrifice or adjustment on the part of the team member's families. Family involvement builds additional support for future team projects and expands the level of recognition from fellow workers to the family as well. Team recognition is an important element—not only as a good way to thank the teams for their efforts—but also as a means of fostering a positive atmosphere to support future team efforts.

Recognition works best when it is simple and applied equally to all teams. Serving coffee and cake, holding a cookout, a pizza party, or serving a catered meal are effective recognition methods. Family events such as picnics or a group day at an amusement park can be very effective events. The leadership should participate in the event to acknowledge the accomplishments of the teams, perhaps by acting in a serving capacity or by cooking on the grill. Use the recognition event to publicize team accomplishments and link those benefits in terms of the value, both to the individual and to the organization. For example, most new equipment projects provide an organization with additional capacity and capabilities, greater flexibility, or better quality. This drives both increased competitiveness and market share, and can open new markets for the organization. These increases yield an increase in job security, improve working conditions, and expand employment opportunities for individuals. The recognition is best if scheduled when each project phase is completed. Leadership attends each recognition celebration. Previously, we discussed the negative aspects of teams in the *adjourning* stage. A properly planned and executed celebration event helps the team through this stage by building a positive expectation for the event, providing a sense of closure on the project, establishing positive memories, and offering an emotional release for all participants.

When planning a recognition event, it is helpful to hold to the philosophy that no team ever fails. Every team provides valuable project learning opportunities—even if the learning is nothing more than discovering what does not work or eliminating an issue that inhibits performance. When teams in the MPM structure fail to meet expectations, responsibility falls on the leadership team. The leadership team must determine if their goals were realistic and reevaluate the support and resources provided to the teams.

As we have done throughout this book, the checklist shown in Figure 7.6 provides a template for project managers to ensure all issues involved in a typical project closure are covered. The list can be modified to fit closure requirements for specific project phases. In a similar fashion, Figure 7.7 is a typical agenda for a leadership closure meeting. This is modifiable and can fit an engineering closure meeting. Typically, installation and start-up teams hold specific lessons learned

Project title _____

Customer _____ **Supplier** _____

Key executive _____ **Key executive** _____

Project manager _____ **Project manager** _____

#	Activity	✔
1.	Ensure all project phase teams have completed all tasks, summarized achievements, developed lessons learned, and received recognition	
2.	Quantify and summarize all results in final report to leadership	
3.	Ensure reported results relate directly to the initial goals established by the leadership team	
4.	Measure customer satisfaction using standard company reporting forms	
5.	Request all participants generate a lessons learned list	
6.	Agree on place, date, and duration for leadership close out meeting	
7.	Create and distribute MPM process evaluation surveys to all leadership personnel	
8.	Collect MPM surveys from all participants	
9.	Summarize MPM evaluations with anonymity and prepare presentation for leadership	
10.	Verify meeting facility/network and equipment	
11.	Make appropriate plans for leadership celebration timed with close out	
12.	Finalize close out agenda with participants covering following items at a minimum: • Lessons learned review and discussion • Customer satisfaction forms • Future follow up and opportunities	
13.	Conduct leadership close out meeting and project celebration	
14.	Publish minutes of close out meeting detailing follow up actions and potential business opportunities	
15.	Each company integrates the lessons learned into their processes and procedures as appropriate	

Figure 7.6 Leadership team closeout checklist

meetings and the celebration events take the place of closure meetings for those project phases.

In the leadership closure meeting, the lessons learned activity has great value for both the customer and supplier. However, from the supplier's perspective, the opportunity the closure meeting presents to the supplier for future business can

Agenda
Leadership Project Closeout
Location: Customer Site TBD

Welcome and review of norms	Customer key executive
Review project goals and deliverables	Co lead key executive
Project evaluation	Customer PM
Identify and detail follow up actions	Supplier PM
Review customer satisfaction ratings	Project managers
Lessons learned review and discussion	As assigned

       Customer lessons learned
       Equipment supplier lessons learned
       Sub supplier lessons learned
       Discussion of key lessons

Review and discuss MPM survey summary	Assigned PM
Discussion of future opportunities	As assigned

       Customer perspective
       Supplier perspective
       Sub supplier perspective

Wrap Up	Host key executive

       Verify all issues have been closed
       Distribute MPM survey summary
       Assign and set date to distribute minutes

Project closure celebration event

Figure 7.7 Leadership closeout agenda

overshadow the lessons learned. In most customer and supplier meetings, the supplier gives a sales pitch about something they are going to do and its potential value to the customer. The closure meeting is a far more important selling opportunity for the supplier since they can emphasize actual accomplishments and the value they provided to the customer in real quantifiable terms. This gives the supplier's presentation greater credibility and is more significant to the customer. The supplier has direct access to the customer's senior management, thus providing the ideal opportunity for the supplier to learn more about the customer's future needs and offer new ideas or suggestions to spark future projects. From the customer's perspective, they have a corresponding opportunity to influence the supplier's senior management in capacity planning or product development, which is most beneficial for the customer.

Beyond the Project. As you near the end of a successful MPM project and work through the related closure activities, it is important to look beyond the project with both short- and long-term views. In the short term, the prime issue is the reassignment of resources. As indicated previously, the adjourning team stage represents resistance due to security concerns and the desire to prolong the team. Proper reassignment planning and selection helps to minimize the duration and resistance intensity in the adjourning stage. To the extent possible, each individual is involved in the selection of new assignments, taking into account both their skills and desires. Team members should be encouraged to work with the receiving manager to help build a good relationship with the receiving manager while gaining background on the new project. The current project manager can help the relationship by carefully defining the individual's availability needed to complete closure activities of the current project and securing agreement from the receiving manager. The project manager must ensure coverage of the lessons learned and of the post-contract closure portion of the project-to-user linkage. As each team member gains insight and becomes comfortable with their next assignment, resistance will dissipate.

The other side of this reassignment involves helping the user organization to accept the reassignment. This is often the most difficult part to achieve and easiest to accomplish if the departing engineer or technician understands that they must step down and transfer the necessary knowledge and confidence to the user organization. The project managers from both the customer and supplier organizations can aid the users in two ways: First, by identifying and involving the support personnel from the organizations that will be supporting the users during the life of the equipment, users will gain confidence in the normal support structure, shifting their dependence from project personnel; Second, project managers need to select personnel in the closing stage of the project who are effective teachers and who enjoy transferring knowledge to others.

While the project managers are working through the reassignment of their team personnel, the senior managers on the leadership team need to follow a similar approach when planning the reassignment of the project managers. Just as was done with the team members, this reassignment involves the individual and considers the skills and desires of the individual. It also details a realistic transition plan. From the user side, the key enabler is the presence of a site project manager who leads the equipment ramp-up after contract closure. This site manager is the logical individual to transfer their leadership responsibilities to, both for the customer's and for the supplier's project managers.

The long-term view is the responsibility of the customer's and supplier's senior executives on the leadership team. First, looking at the lifespan of the specific equipment involved in the current project, what are the possible interactions of benefit to both the customer and supplier that might ensure sustained success of the project results? Second, looking at the success of the current MPM relationship, can leveraging this relationship improve other projects in which they are involved? Finally, the executives have a chance to collaborate when developing future opportunities that would prove beneficial to both organizations. In collaborating on future opportunities, the executives should think outside the box and beyond projects into any business area in which their collaboration could yield a competitive advantage. Since MPM yields significant results in projects, why not apply it to other strategic business issues to gain significant results?

A main premise of this book is that the customer and supplier relationship spans both project and operations phases of the equipment lifecycle with a significant impact on competitiveness. The application of the MPM process, combining teamwork and project management with the customer and supplier relationship, details the steps needed to take full advantage of this relationship in order to maximize project success. The process description presented in Chapters 1 through 7 includes many checklists and sample agendas to aid in implementing the process. This process detail with the supporting checklists and agendas combined with the survey results and MPM project examples identify and validate the power of MPM in the project portion of an equipment lifecycle. Therefore, the remaining three chapters of this book are devoted to applying MPM to the operations side of the equipment lifecycle.

PART III: MULTI-COMPANY PROJECT MANAGEMENT APPLIED TO OPERATIONS

An Integrated Approach

OVERVIEW

The multi-company project management (MPM) process began with the idea of combining project management with the lean and teamwork principles from the operations environment while employing the services of both the customer and the supplier to achieve higher success in projects. Given the successes of this approach, a logical next step is to take the idea full circle back to operations to gain the benefits of customer and supplier collaboration and project management methodologies in operations performance. However, operations represent an existing activity that has organizational structures and process already in place, and has an ongoing characteristic. On the other hand, MPM utilizes a temporary organization structure that has a finite end. Therefore, this must be a consideration when MPM is a component of an operation. Another consideration is the effect MPM has on the operations activity after it is complete; this requires modifying the original MPM process to fit operations.

Looking at the operations side of the equipment lifecycle reveals many common interests between the customer and supplier. This includes such things as service support, technical support, refresher training, spare part inventories, annual inspections, planned maintenance events, software upgrades, extended warranties, new technology upgrades, and many others. There are many configurations for building multi-company relationships around these interests. There is more than one workable approach since much depends on the opportunity each interest represents in terms of value, both to the customer and to the supplier. The topic of continuous improvement is an umbrella that covers virtually all the common interests of the customer and supplier relationship. Thus, one approach for building customer and supplier relationships around operations is to apply the MPM process to continuous improvement in the operations environment.

Continuous improvement is like a collection of mini projects designed to improve quality and productivity. Different from project management practices, continuous improvement is a process where an existing team organization carries out the mini improvement projects while at the same time, executes the ongoing activity of the enterprise. In reality, many of the principles and techniques of project management are more appropriate than the operations procedures when implementing continuous improvements. Thus, continuous improvement is an excellent venue for the application of MPM within the operations environment.

In any project, the prime deliverable is the operational product while in operations improvement, the focus is on the results achieved by the total enterprise. Thus, applying the MPM process to operations instead of projects is more complex due to the integration with lean principles, quality using Six Sigma, and improvement events. The MPM modifications require a new definition of *strategic project*, a timeline based on days and weeks rather than on months and years, and controls to sustain results as well as to achieve them.

Part III uses an actual case study as the framework for explaining the modifications to MPM and the application to continuous improvement in the operations environment. It consists of three parts: First, Chapter 8, *MPM Modifications Overview,* describes the blending of MPM and operation concepts, resulting in a changed MPM process and a revised definition of *strategic project* in terms of the improvement process. Then Chapter 9, *Improvement Initiation,* covers the topics of organization, initiation, measurement, and planning as it relates to improvements. This is similar to MPM Part I with the addition of measurement—one of the MPM modifications. The final chapter, *Improvement Results and MPM Conclusion,* consists of event requirements, event completion, closure, and MPM conclusion, which parallel the MPM Part II topics of control, execution, and closure, along with a few concluding remarks regarding MPM.

8

MPM MODIFICATIONS OVERVIEW

In multi-company project management (MPM) the multi-company teams build the customer and supplier relationship. The strategic value of the project motivates the participants, and the project management methodology drives the completion of project activities. MPM easily adapts to retail, finance, information technology, or any other business project environment. It covers the timeframe from the initial project contract to project startup at the customer's site. One can visualize the process as a triangle—the three following processes represent the three corners of the triangle: a strategic project, project methodologies, and a multi-company organization. In a similar fashion, we can depict a continuous improvement process as a triangle consisting of quality using Six Sigma, lean principles using the metric of overall equipment effectiveness (OEE), and improvement events. The result of applying MPM to operations improvement is the combined process shown in Figure 8.1, which is an overlay of the MPM and continuous improvement triangles. It incorporates the techniques and methods of the Six Sigma DMAIC framework and the lean manufacturing metric of OEE applied to specific improvement events to create a project-style equipment enhancement process for improved performance. The use of the OEE metric makes this application more manufacturing specific. Thus, the detailed checklists and agendas may have limited applications outside the manufacturing environment. However, the concepts employed should provide insight into developing other MPM improvement applications.

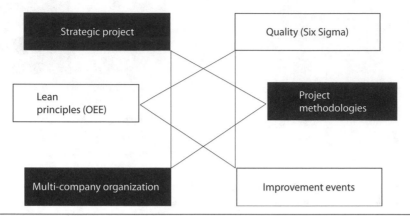

Figure 8.1 Overlay MPM and operations processes

BENEFITS

My first experience applying the MPM process in an operations environment was an internal customer and supplier relationship within GM involving six AA transfer press systems. As background, in the mid-1990s GM consolidated all its stamping operations into a single division and initiated the first new equipment project of the division, which involved the purchase of six AA transfer press systems. These were the largest transfer press systems ever purchased by GM. They installed the systems in pairs in two new contiguous facilities and in one refurbished plant. All three facilities employed new labor agreements that dramatically reduced skilled and non-skilled classifications, expanded operator responsibilities, required new operating methods, and necessitated extensive retraining of the entire workforce. Staffing of the new contiguous sites was lean; the staff often lacked experience in stamping and many assumed multiple roles. The tooling for the contiguous sites originally ran in conventional press systems and required extensive modification to fit into the new systems, while the tooling for the refurbished facility was the first ever designed for the new systems. The AA transfer press systems were strategic since they were the only systems capable of producing the large one-piece body sides, and were positioned to support the contiguous stamping facilities, which were critical to new-product programs. The project for the acquisition of these six systems occurred over a four-year period and followed the normal project management process within the division. The project encountered major cost, timing, and performance problems, and thus became the prime motivation for finding an improved project management approach, which ultimately lead to the development of the MPM process.

By 2002, AA system performance was far below expectations to the point that Rick Wagner, GM's CEO, sent a letter to Joe Spielman, vice president and general manager of the metal fabricating division, requesting that these systems receive more attention and be considered a higher priority issue. In addition to the six systems in production, four more were due to be online within the next few years. Given the success of the MPM process in the project environment and the strategic importance of the AA systems, the manufacturing engineering department within the GM Metal Fabricating Division (acting as the supplier), approached the manufacturing department (as the customer) with the MPM process as an internal improvement project process for the AA transfer systems. The die design department was included as a critical supplier as well to ensure tooling representation on the leadership team. After forming the leadership team, the leadership established an engineering team and plant improvement teams similar to the engineering and installation teams in MPM.

The improvement process applied over a 16-month interval across three locations and six systems yielded a 20 percent increase in throughput measured in pieces per hour based on the principles of overall equipment effectiveness. To put a 20 percent increase in perspective, consider the following numbers: A 20 percent improvement in net productivity across just five systems is the equivalent of having another system. Ten years ago, these systems and related facilities cost over $40 million each. In addition, the direct and indirect labor cost (including wages with benefits) associated with the operation of six systems conservatively runs over $10 million annually. Thus, a 20 percent improvement is the equivalent of having an additional $40 million in capital and $2 million savings in annual labor costs. There are many other benefits as well. The tight linkage between stamping and assembly plants that follow the just-in-time philosophy means reduced assembly plant disruptions, reduced pressure on the process, improved quality, and free time for routine maintenance to sustain equipment performance.

Although this was an interdepartment rather than a true customer and supplier improvement project, it validated the benefits of the MPM process applied to operations improvement. A core element of the combined process was the use of specific improvement events to formulate and implement the improvements, followed up with planned actions to resolve open issues between events. It proved the validity of applying MPM several years after the initial installation. It reinforced how important it was that the improvements be strategic, since the leadership and plant's interest shifted as the improvements removed the systems as a critical constraint and the systems reverted to the normal continuous improvement processes within the plants.

This experience identified the following critical values that MPM brings to the operations improvement process:

- Drives an increased focus on high-impact improvements
- Compliments existing systems and teams

- Involves and links all stakeholders
- Provides leadership for high-level decisions
- Establishes clear priorities and timetables
- Assigns required resources and provides access to equipment
- Consolidates customer and equipment supplier experiences and knowledge
- Applies team and project management methodologies
- Utilizes lean tools and techniques

CASE STUDY

Automatic Feed Company, a supplier of blanking equipment to the automotive industry, participated in several projects referenced earlier that employed the MPM process. Subsequently, I facilitated the establishment of Automatic Feed's own MPM process, tailored to their company needs. After the success of their MPM process, Automatic Feed Company made a proposal to expand MPM into their operations improvement. The lessons learned by Automatic Feed Company through their participation over the years with their customers on a variety of improvement efforts and my experiences on internal GM improvement teams formed the foundation for the development of the improvement process.

As background, they were facing a very competitive industry; capital for any type of added or replacement capacity was severely limited. They expected the focus over the years ahead to shift heavily toward improvement with minimal investment. The low customer demand would increase the availability of personnel within equipment supplier operations, driving suppliers to find opportunities to utilize their resources. Most customers employ some form of team process and improvement process within their operations. However, oftentimes they are improperly linked, lack discipline in their methodology, and lack the necessary support from the engineering and leadership teams. Consequently, the typical improvement process results in small incremental changes and it is common for the actual performance of the equipment to fall short of the engineered capacity by as much as 40 percent.

The approach employed the same pattern previously used for integrating the MPM process into Automatic Feed Company's project process with a workshop to design the process followed by a pilot implementation to validate and fine-tune the process results. Initially, key personnel from Automatic Feed Company worked with me in a one-day workshop to formulate the modified MPM process-template. The following personnel helped design the process:

| Dean Baker | Tim Barry | Kim Beck | Ian Blease |
| Todd Hernandez | Jon Knepley | Jeff Stover | Marlowe Witt |

The preceding personnel represented the disciplines of leadership, sales, engineering, and project management. They developed the team structure by defining team types, membership, deliverables, and linkages. They detailed the tools from engineering, improvements, teams, and project management for the application and created an agenda for leadership team formation.

Automatic Feed Company's primary business is supplying coil feed and related equipment to the automotive industry. One application of their coil feed equipment is in blanking operations. This blanking operation decoils the coil steel into a flat sheet of steel, which is then cut into pieces with a specific outline and holes cut out as required—also known as blanks. Typically, the process includes stacking the blanks for transport. Figure 8.2 is an isometric of a typical blanking system. In the drawing, flow is from lower right to upper left. The front of line process consists of uncoiling the steel, pinch rolls to feed the sheet into a washer and leveler, a deep loop thread table, and roll feed to load a precise amount of steel into the press. The press holds a die used to stamp out a specific blank configuration. The end of line system moves each blank from the press via a run-out conveyor and overhead magnetic stacker system that stacks the blanks on transfer carts that change automatically to allow offline packaging a full stack of blanks in readiness for shipment to the customer. These systems require a facility with high bays, overhead cranes to handle the dies and coil steel (which often weigh as much as 25 tons), and a scrap disposal system to remove any offal generated during blanking. In addition to the manufacturing space required for the systems (40' x 150' each), the facility must have space for storing coil steel and the dies required to stamp different blanks. There must also be sufficient space to allow for the staging of finish blank stacks for shipment to the customer, as well as space for normal operating needs like material movement, die change, maintenance, etc. The initial investment in new facilities and equipment for a two-blanker operation runs in excess of $25 million. Two-shift operations of the equipment—including all support personnel and management—require approximately $4 million in annual labor cost with benefits.

Automatic Feed Company secured the agreement of Kasle Metal Processing to participate in the pilot as the customer. Kasle Metal Processing is an ideal choice since it consists of only two blanking systems and the study addresses 100 percent of their key productive equipment, making it strategic to plant management. In addition, Kasle Metal Processing was pursuing new business opportunities that would require more capacity. This added capacity, however, did not justify another whole system. Automatic Feed Company originally supplied all of Kasle's blanking equipment and therefore had full technical knowledge of the equipment. They saw

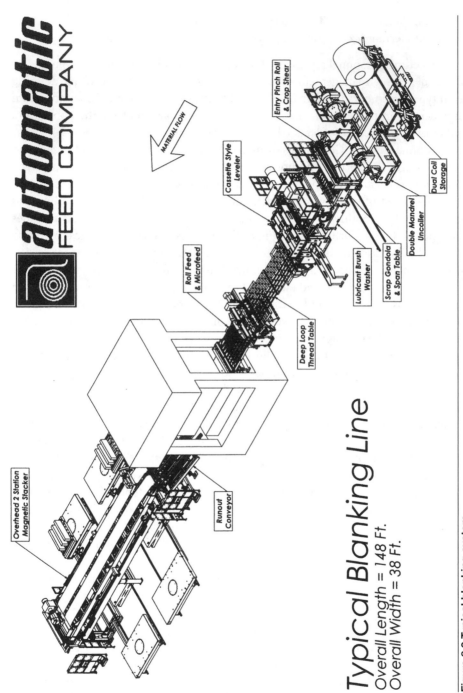

Typical Blanking Line
Overall Length = 148 Ft.
Overall Width = 38 Ft.

Figure 8.2 Typical blanking system

this process as an opportunity to build relationships and expand support to their customers. The balance of this book presents the final process that evolved from this case study—applying MPM in an operations improvement environment.

IMPROVEMENT VISION

The vision is an MPM improvement project targeted for applications in high investment manufacturing systems with strategic value to the companies involved that delivers a double-digit annual performance improvement while remaining highly flexible so it easily adapts to any organization's existing team and improvement processes, regardless of their maturity level. The intent is to apply the process to specific equipment within a manufacturing operation to achieve significant improvement while investing as little as possible and training key personnel within the organization to make them self-sufficient enough to repeat the process on other equipment. MPM is limited to equipment that has strategic value, since leadership involvement is a key ingredient. Leadership involvement is possible only if they see significant value to the overall organization in the process.

This MPM improvement process is ill suited for the replacement of ongoing continuous improvement processes within the operating plant. Rather an MPM improvement process is a special case of an improvement project that meets the test of being strategic and enhances continuous improvement efforts. The vision is for the improvement results to yield improvement percentages in the double-digits within a short amount of time (three to nine months) and with minimal costs. This improvement should also eliminate the equipment as a constraint in the operations process. Once it is no longer a constraint, it ceases to be strategically significant, and the focus shifts to other constraint operations. Thus, this improvement process appears more like a project with a beginning and end rather than an ongoing improvement process. Of course, the customer may elect to apply MPM to other constraint operations, but the supplier participants and customer improvement-team participants will be different, requiring a reformulation of the entire process.

It is important to view the MPM improvement project as a compliment to whatever improvement processes are already in place. An organization will not readily admit that they do not have an improvement process. Anyone trying to make improvements is a valuable resource who needs to buy in to the proposed improvement process. It is important to sustain any process improvements to add to the overall results. Referring to MPM as an enhancement means there is no admission to the absence of an improvement process, no rejection of current improvement efforts, and the existing improvement process remains in place after the enhancement is complete.

The MPM improvement enhancement is like a project or group of projects layered on top of the existing improvement processes. Each project has specific improvement objectives and a specified beginning and end. Thus, the leadership team has a defined lifespan. Therefore, do not view the leadership team as the improvement process but rather as a supporting element of a specific overall MPM improvement effort. Note that even though the leadership team disappears, the relationships continue to have an effect on the improvement results. In addition, many of the techniques and tools employed in this MPM improvement enhancement project can also add value to any additional continuous improvement efforts that the customer may undertake in the future.

A core ingredient of the improvement process is the cross-functional plant floor teams. This is completely under the control of the operations management and reflects the plant's culture, organizational structure, and management philosophies. These teams take years to evolve. The creation and maintenance of these teams is beyond the scope of any improvement project any outside supplier can provide. The MPM enhanced improvement only recommends some personnel and responsibility changes to influence the team evolution.

The status of the plant floor teams can dramatically affect the improvement results. Nonexistent, immature, or ineffective plant floor teams require a hierarchal structure in order to meet their responsibilities. Improvement results will be slower, smaller, and more difficult to sustain. In these situations, a careful analysis of risks and rewards is made before proceeding, which may result in withdrawal until the plant organization is more compatible with the MPM process. Changing the plant organization requires a completely different approach and skill set from those offered in MPM. The key point is the MPM improvement enhancement works with the existing operations and floor organizations, but the final results depend heavily on the maturity of the plant floor team.

Since the enhanced improvement project is simply a modification to the MPM process, it is named Multi-company Project Management Modified, or MPM^2. The project design allows implementation by either the equipment supplier or the equipment user, and this text fits either perspective.

MPM^2 incorporates the principles of teams, project management, and customer-supplier collaboration with lean and Six Sigma tools and techniques to create an implementation plan and execution that achieves double-digit improvement in overall equipment effectiveness. It incorporates the Six Sigma improvement methodology of define, measure, analyze, improve, and control (DMAIC) while focusing on the following four opportunities for improving equipment: availability, performance, quality, and upgrades.

PROCESS DESCRIPTION

Continually striving to reduce variation by operating to a predetermined set of process parameters using standardized operating procedures is one philosophy used to manage and improve manufacturing operations. With this philosophy, it is important to avoid any arbitrary variation from the parameters or procedures, even in the interest of continuous improvement. Improvement is best performed by changing the parameters or procedures in a controlled manner. It is important that everyone understands the objectives and that everyone is involved in the improvement. It is also essential to document the improvements—along with the new parameters and revised operating procedures—and to communicate the results. All too often companies make well-meaning changes in a haphazard fashion without any planning or control. This introduces more variation into the process, decreasing rather than improving performance. In many cases, companies fail to sustain performance improvements due to their failure to communicate and standardize the improvements across the involved equipment and shifts.

MPM^2 overcomes these deficiencies by providing a controlled environment in which to implement improvement and by sustaining the results. This includes adding a step to ensure the establishment of appropriate controls. A major strength of the MPM^2 process is that it is not a new process, but rather an integration of thoroughly proven, broadly recognized management concepts: teamwork and project management represented in the MPM process together with Six Sigma and overall equipment effectiveness. In order to understand the modifications necessary for MPM to blend with operations, a basic understanding of the Six Sigma methodology and OEE is required.

Six Sigma. Six Sigma is a widely accepted methodology used in many industries to achieve continuous improvement. It drives a short timeline for improvement, uses measurements and data to identify the right tasks, and incorporates controls that focus on sustainment. It follows a project-style mentality and employs a leader referred to as a *black belt* in a role that is very similar to the project manager. Thus, MPM is an excellent fit for adapting to the Six Sigma process in operations for maximizing results using a multi-company approach.

In 1986, Bill Smith, a senior engineer assigned to Motorola's communication division, introduced the Six Sigma concept as a method for improving quality within the manufacturing environment. After concept adoption, it became a central strategy used throughout the Motorola organization to deliver high-quality products (McCarty 2004). Since then, the concept has gained acceptance on a global basis across many industries, and its application has expanded beyond the traditional manufacturing environments into all forms of process improvements. The Motorola website (http://www.motorola.com/content.jsp?globalObjectId=3069-5787) offers a series of six-minute lessons concerning the use of Six Sigma. The heart of the Six Sigma concept is the use of a specific improvement framework known by the acronym DMAIC. It is a series of actions designed to improve process performance and reduce variation, which consist of the following five steps:

> *Define*—Develop a clear statement of work and overall project scope with measurable goals that relates to the desired bottom-line results
> *Measure*—Gather specific data on process performance
> *Analyze*—Determine the cause and brainstorm for corrective actions
> *Improve*—Plan and implement corrective actions; then verify results
> *Control*—Ensure the sustainability of the improvements by implementing documentation, monitoring, and accountability measures

By design, the DMAIC framework is implemented as specific projects using floor-teams in a controlled manner. Thus, it aligns well with the MPM² philosophy of integrating project management methodologies and teamwork. The broad variety of industries utilizing the widely accepted and successful DMAIC framework for over twenty years makes it a natural candidate to mate with MPM². With the exception of measurement, the following MPM Six C process groups correlate to the DMAIC processes:

- *Communicate*—Define
- *Coordinate*—Analyze
- *Complete*—Improve
- *Control*—Control

Incorporating DMAIC's strong emphasis on measuring the current situation before the improvements and again after the implementation, along with establishing controls to sustain improvements strengthens MPM² to make it more effective in the operations environment.

Overall Equipment Effectiveness. The MPM² process created through the integration of teamwork, project management, and DMAIC requires a set of metrics that support the integrated processes. Leadership and floor personnel must understand the metrics and use them to keep their focus on the improvement opportunities, assist in the prioritization of tasks, and ensure bottom-line results. The OEE metric meets these requirements. Seiichi Nakajima at Nippon Denso developed this metric for use with Total Productive Maintenance (TPM) in the late 1960s. The recognition and use of the OEE metric has grown globally in a variety of industries. Throughout the world lean manufacturing, total productive maintenance, and other continuous improvement efforts accept this as a key metric. OEE is actually the product of three metrics, which represent the equipment's availability, performance, and first-time quality. Availability is defined as equipment uptime; performance is related to the speed of the equipment, and first-time quality is defined as the type of quality that exists in new parts just off a manufacturing process; free from defects and meeting all specifications. In the following discussion, ideal refers to the utopian situation in which the equipment runs 100 percent of the time at its designed speed, producing parts of perfect quality. To maintain a strong focus on improvement, this guide uses the term *opportunity gap*, which is simply the OEE value subtracted from 100 percent. The following formulas define these three metrics, the resulting OEE, and the opportunity gap:

$$Availability = \frac{actual\ run\ time}{schedule\ run\ time} = uptime$$

$$Performance = \frac{actual\ pieces\ per\ hour}{ideal\ pieces\ per\ hour} = speed$$

$$Quality = \frac{first\ time\ quality\ pieces}{actual\ pieces} = quality$$

$$OEE = availability \times performance \times quality = \frac{first\ time\ quality\ pieces}{ideal\ pieces}$$

$$OpportunityGap = 100\% - OEE$$

Note that when the various units cancel each other out in the OEE equation above, it returns the first-time quality pieces divided by the ideal pieces for the scheduled period. Thus, it is possible to determine the OEE quickly without actually computing the component metrics. The opportunity assessment to be discussed later uses this shortcut.

To understand OEE, it is a good idea to level expectations. An OEE of 85 percent is a *world-class* level. At first glance, this may seem low. However, consider what the three component metrics would need to be to achieve 85 percent. For example, over a three-month period, an operation might have an uptime of 90 percent, operate on average at 94 percent of the equipment's maximum designed speed, and produce parts with a 10 parts per million defect rate. This yields an OEE of 84.6 percent. When you view the OEE using the component metrics, it brings the 85 percent into perspective in terms of what is required to achieve world-class levels. It is easy to see how the use of the OEE metric along with its component metrics helps to set the most beneficial priorities and target the most rewarding improvement efforts.

While 85 percent OEE is world class, it is common for successful manufacturing operations to be in the OEE range of 60 percent to 70 percent. Figure 8.3 is a graphical representation comparing OEEs at 60 percent and 85 percent. In the world-class OEE, the quality losses are so small they are almost nonexistent on the

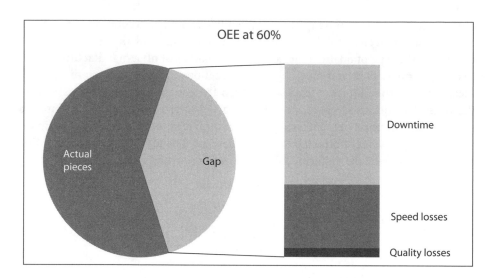

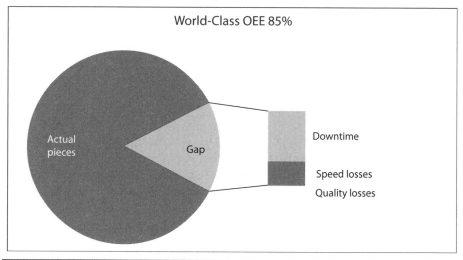

Figure 8.3 Common OEE versus world-class OEE

bar chart. In both examples, the downtime or availability losses are nearly double the speed losses. This relationship will vary in each situation. Understanding the relative impact of downtime, speed, and quality is the key to focusing improvement efforts in the areas that will generate the greatest return. Sometimes tradeoffs are made between downtime and speed to increase OEE. However, it would be unwise to trade off quality—either for gains in performance or for availability. For example, in theory, increasing the speed may improve OEE by gaining 10 percent in speed while sacrificing 3 percent in quality, resulting in a 7 percent overall OEE improvement. The 3 percent OEE quality loss represents a defect or rework rate of 30,000 parts per million, and businesses operating at that level would rarely succeed, regardless of their level of overall equipment effectiveness.

A major value of the OEE metric lies in the fact that it quantifiably captures the total equipment's effectiveness so that floor personnel can easily visualize and understand it. The use of OEE avoids a common failure of improvement efforts that improves one parameter at the expense of another, with the bottom-line result being zero or negative improvement. For example, excessive increases in equipment speed can cause increased component failures or frequent crashes, reducing availability and yielding a lower OEE, negatively affecting the bottom line. Since each metric is actually a comparison of the equipment's current state to its ideal state, the opportunity for improvement is at the forefront. The use of the three categories within OEE is extremely valuable in identifying the areas that offer the most potential for improvement. These three categories are often further divided into major opportunities for improvement. Major opportunities relating to availability consist of reducing time in breakdowns, tool changeovers, and machine adjustments. Performance opportunities include speed optimization, reducing idle time, and eliminating minor stops. Quality opportunities typically involve reducing defects, minimizing rework, and improving the start-up process.

MPM^2 includes the original equipment builder as an integral part of the process and ensures the involvement of other stakeholders as well. Finally, MPM^2 uses the metrics of OEE to set priorities and target improvement efforts. In order to ensure that the results transfer to the bottom line, performance is weighted using volume and based on actual measurement after the improvements are completed.

Process Map. Table 8.1 is the process map for the modified MPM process that results from combining the MPM and Six Sigma methodologies. The first column lists the MPM Six C processes. The second column lists the project management processes as a reminder of their contribution in MPM. The Six Sigma DMAIC processes are listed in the third column. The result of blending these processes together yields the MPM^2 configuration listed in the fourth column. The tight correlation between the Six Sigma and MPM Six C processes identifies *measurement* as the only added process group that yields the resulting MPM^2 process. The existence of an ongoing operation necessitates the need to measure status, amount of improvement opportunity, and final improvement results.

In actual practice, the measurement activity in an improvement parallels the engineering activity in an MPM project. Measurement is a critical part of the strategic assessment that occurs before the project begins, similar to the specifica-

Table 8.1 MPM² process map

MPM Six C	Project management	Six Sigma	MPM² process steps
Cooperate			1. Cooperate
Communicate	Initiate	Define	2. Communicate
		Measure	3. Measure
Coordinate	Plan	Analyze	4. Coordinate
Complete	Execute	Improve	5. Complete
Control	Control	Control	6. Control
Celebrate	Close		7. Close

tion and proposal activities prior to project initiation. Then, a more detailed measurement provides the data needed to establish the improvement goals, similar to the engineering required for the installation team to perform its work. Finally, the measurement activity determines the amount of improvement achieved similar to engineering verifying final project performance to specifications during buyoff.

STRATEGIC ASSESSMENT

Before implementing MPM in projects, it is necessary to ensure that the project meets the definition of strategic as defined in Chapter 1. When dealing with MPM projects, the four factors of size, opportunity, risk, and complexity determine the strategic value. In MPM projects, size measured in terms of project cost for the customer and sales for the supplier is the easiest and most common factor. An operations improvement is expected to be low-cost and short; thus, project cost is the least likely to define a strategic project. Instead, improvement scope replaces project cost as the key strategic indicator. Improvement potential and manufacturing demand determine opportunity and becomes the second factor in establishing an improvement project's strategic value. Finally, financial risks are minimal since the equipment is in place operating at some level of acceptance. However, the operating environment determines risk of failure and complexity in achieving success. MPM² works best when applied to an organization with a lean environment consisting of supportive leadership, effective teams, good workplace organization, ongoing continuous improvement activities, structured planned maintenance, flexible work rules, a willingness to learn, and established standardized work practices. The operations environment forms the foundation for implementing the MPM² process. When revising the definition of *strategic* to fit an operations improvement situation, you must consider the three factors of scope, opportunity, and environment.

Scope. In order to be strategic, systems selected for improvement must represent significant scope to the customer in terms of operating performance and to the supplier in terms of sales. For the customer, a good rule of thumb is at least 10 percent of the operating budget or output of the enterprise. For the supplier, the original value of the equipment adjusted for inflation to present-day values should ideally represent at least 10 percent of the supplier's annual capacity to represent sufficient scope. In the case study, the two blanking systems represented 100 percent of the customer's operating budget and output while representing a little more than 10 percent of the supplier's annual equipment capacity. Thus, it met the opportunity scope requirement to be strategic.

In many cases, the customer can identify a group of systems for improvement, meeting the 10 percent rule of thumb. But the supplier base for the systems may be so diverse as to not hold much value for the individual suppliers. In this case, the customer must initiate the project and may negotiate some compensation with critical suppliers to secure their participation. Senior management participation will depend on the customer's influence with the supplier. This is where having a history of prior successful MPM projects and previous relationships with the supplier can pay dividends to the customer.

Opportunity. After establishing appropriate customer and supplier scope, the next step in assessing the strategic value is evaluating the opportunity in terms of improvement potential and expected demand to use that potential. Improvement potential determines whether an opportunity for improvement exists at a given facility to protect the customer and equipment supplier from investing time and resources into a process that does not achieve results. The expected demand must be of sufficient magnitude to allow the organization to take advantage of the improvements without the need to make major cuts in the workforce to generate bottom-line results from the improvements. This protects the workforce from eliminating their jobs, avoids major disruptions to the operating organization after MPM^2 is complete, and ensures motivation to sustain the improvements. The dramatic step change double-digit improvement in MPM^2 versus the gradual slow rate of change in continuous improvement drives the demand consideration in MPM^2.

The customer and equipment supplier conduct the evaluation of the improvement potential jointly, which MPM^2 refers to as an *opportunity assessment*. In the opportunity assessment, the customer provides all the data to determine the current state, and the equipment supplier uses the equipment specifications and design knowledge to determine the ideal state. Typically, an individual from the initiating company or a consultant with the appropriate skills provides facilitation to develop the OEE metrics from the data and conducts the opportunity assessment. The opportunity assessment is completely confidential. The assessors only share it with the customer's and supplier's key executives. Any further disclosure of the opportunity assessment is at the discretion of the key executives.

Since the opportunity assessment design protects the interests of all participants and both parties benefit even if the decision is not to proceed, everyone participates in the assessment on a no-cost basis. The customer benefits by gaining insight into the strengths, weaknesses, and opportunities of the systems studied. The equipment supplier builds relationships outside the normal purchasing arena, learns more about how its equipment is actually performing, gains an opportunity to promote the advantages of its equipment and services, and potentially creates an interest in future upgrades or new equipment.

The opportunity assessment determines the gap between the equipments' ideal capacity and the current output, which identifies how much potential there is for improvement. If the gap is 15 percent or less, the equipment is functioning at world-class levels, the potential for improvement is minimal, and process initiation terminates. For additional capacity, investing in existing equipment upgrades or new equipment is a better course of action. A gap in the 15 percent to 25 percent range is marginal, and the MPM^2 process will generate improvements but may not achieve double-digit levels. If the gap is in the 25 percent to 40 percent range, the process is ripe for application of the MPM^2 process.

The opportunity assessment is a high-level analysis of the process equipment's ideal capacity versus the current operating capacity achieved to determine the gap. It is measured in terms of total pieces or tons produced for a specific period (shift, day, week, or month). The ideal capacity must be volume-weighted, reflecting the actual part volumes anticipated by the customer for the study period to generate bottom-line performance. In the joint assessment, the customer provides all of the actual performance information and the supplier provides the equipment capabilities.

To determine the ideal capacity, first the basic equipment specifications are entered that cover speeds, feeds, raw stock changes, finish stock changes, tool and die changes, etc.. Next, customer part-specific information referred to as Level I is gathered. The sample data sheet, Table 8.2, is for a blanking system. This information provides the following part, coil, and line setup information details:

Part info—Part number; description; feed length; die feed angle; run quantity; mix; run volume; sequence; volume per month, quarter, or
year, average net pieces per hour produced
Coil info—Width, gauge, weight

Table 8.2 Customer Level 1 part information data

Part number	Part name	Feed length	Feed angle	Run quantity	Volume	Net SPH	Width	Gauge	Coil weight	Stack size	Stack mode	SPM
Part 1	Desc 1	1955	270	400	8800	1400	1578	0.71	25000	300	D	16
Part 2	Desc 2	2044	270	750	16500	950	1438	0.73	25000	300	D	12
Part 3	Desc 3	1549	270	300	6600	1500	1629	0.71	25000	300	D	18
Part 4	Desc 4	1549	270	250	5500	1200	1629	0.71	25000	300	D	22
Part 5	Desc 5	1245	270	1250	27500	1150	1810	0.71	25000	300	D	28
Part 6	Desc 6	1125	270	1800	39600	1050	1808	0.6	25000	300	D	32
Part 7	Desc 7	1435	270	790	17380	950	1587	0.71	25000	300	D	17
Part 8	Desc 8	3114	270	540	11880	670	1737	0.71	25000	300	D	21
Part 9	Desc 9	3114	270	660	14520	800	1737	0.71	25000	300	D	19
Part 10	Desc 10	1395	270	880	19360	650	1540	0.76	25000	300	D	15

Table 8.3 Opportunity assessment data analysis table

	Column												
A	B	C	D	E	F	G	H	I	J	K	K	M	N
		Pieces/shift					Annual volume			Volume adjusted			
Part number		Actual	Ideal	Gap (absolute)	Individual part opportunity		Annual production	% of Total product by volume		Actual pieces/shift	Ideal pieces/shift	Gap	Gap % contribution by part
Part 1		3,865	5,459	1594	29.20%		173,152	7.21%		279	394	115	1.68%
Part 2		4,264	6,367	2103	33.03%		172,302	7.18%		306	457	151	2.21%
Part 3		6,454	9,440	2986	31.63%		131,220	5.47%		353	516	163	2.39%
Part 4		6,454	9,440	2986	31.63%		134,202	5.59%		361	528	167	2.45%
Part 5		4,814	6,363	1549	24.34%		353,582	14.73%		709	937	228	3.34%
Part 6		3,295	4,665	1370	29.37%		643,880	26.82%		884	1251	367	5.38%
Part 7		4,800	6,908	2108	30.52%		270,174	11.26%		540	778	237	3.48%
Part 8		4,800	6,943	2143	30.87%		207,471	8.64%		415	600	185	2.71%
Part 9		3,800	5,205	1405	26.99%		156,298	6.51%		247	339	91	1.34%
Part 10		4,855	15,582	10727	68.84%		158,182	6.59%		320	1027	707	10.36%
Total							2,400,463	100.00%		4414	6826	2413	35.34%

Line Setup—Stack size, stack mode (single station, side out, etc.), press
speed, feed speed, etc.

The headings for the Level I datasheet will vary depending on the type of manufacturing operation. But conceptually, the same type of data will be required to
detail the equipment's capabilities. With the above information, the ideal capability is computed and expressed in terms of pieces produced or tonnage processed
for the specified equipment and timeframe. After calculating the ideal capacity, it
is compared to the actual results achieved for the specified period to determine the
opportunity gap for each part. There will always be a gap, since the ideal capacity
represents everything at optimum performance—no breakdowns, no quality
issues, maximum speed, etc.

In line with the requirement to maintain confidentiality, Table 8.3 is a sample
data-analysis table for a hypothetical blanking system rather than the actual case
data. The following four paragraphs explaining the chart is a bit tedious, but shows
the logic necessary to volume adjust the productivity of any activity so that
improvements relate directly to bottom-line results.

Pieces per shift (Columns C through F)

To understand the chart, follow the Part 1 data. From production reports, Part 1
runs at the rate of 3865 pieces per shift (as shown in Column C). Based on engineering calculations from the supplier, the ideal rate is 5459 pieces per shift
(depicted in Column D). The difference between the ideal rate and the actual rate
is 1594, and is known as *the absolute gap* (Column E). The gap divided by the ideal
rate (Column E divided by Column D) expressed as a percentage equals 29.2,
representing the percent improvement opportunity for Part 1 (Column F).

Annual Volume (Columns H and I)

Column H lists the annual volume for each part, which are then summed at the
bottom of column H, equaling 2,400,463. This sum represents the total part volume of the systems in the improvement project. Dividing the annual volume of
Part 1 (173,152) by the total of all parts (2,400,463) converts this to 7.21 percent—
the percent that Part 1 contributes to the total volume (Column I).

Volume Adjusted (Column K through N)

Multiplying the actual pieces by the Part 1 percent of the total volume (Column C
multiplied by Column I) yields 279, the volume adjusted actual pieces (Column K).
Multiplying the ideal pieces by the Part 1 percent of total volume (Column D multi-
plied by Column I) equals 394, the volume adjusted ideal pieces (Column L).
Subtracting the Part 1 volume adjusted pieces from the ideal volume adjusted pieces
(Column L less Column K) equals 115, which is the volume adjusted gap (Column M).

"Dividing the adjusted Part I gap by the sum of all ideal gaps (Column M divided by sum of Column L) converted to a percentage yields the volume adjusted gap contribution by Part I (Column N)."

Total Gap

The actual volume adjusted total pieces per shift is 4414 (total of Column K) and the ideal volume adjusted total pieces per shift is 6826 (total of Column L). Dividing total volume adjusted actual rate by the ideal rate $\left(\frac{4414}{6826}\right)$ yields an OEE of 65 percent. Subtracting the OEE from 100 percent yields a gap of 35 percent. Another approach is simply to add the individual part gap contributions (Column N) to get a total gap of 35 percent (total of Column N).

The chart in Figure 8.4 is a graphical representation of the last column of the sample data analysis table. The total operational gap is approximately 35 percent with Part 10 having the greatest impact of more than 10 percent, Part 6 has the next most significant impact of more than 5 percent, and so on. This provides an excellent tool to establish priorities to maximize results. Volume weighting the data is critical in this process to impact the bottom-line results. Taking Part 1 as an example, the individual part opportunity gap was 29.2 percent, but when the volume was adjusted, it made up only 1.7 percent of the 35.3 percent total operations gap. The MPM^2 project is not strategic if the total operational gap is less than 15 percent, and is only marginally strategic with a 15 percent to 25 percent gap.

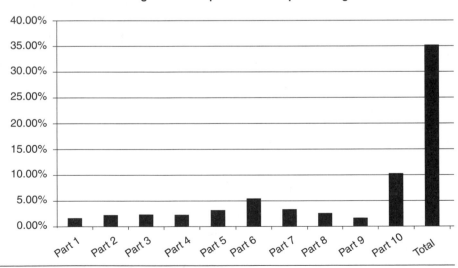

Figure 8.4 Gap by part to total equipment gap

When the gap is in excess of 25 percent, the opportunity is strategic, making a double-digit improvement possible.

It is also helpful to quantify the various areas creating the gap, which becomes the responsibility of the measurement team after the leadership team formation. However, it is possible during assessment to create a comparison by using subjective information and best guesses from the customer to identify the differences caused by actual speeds, feeds, raw stock changes, finish stock changes, tool and die changes as well as quantifying breakdowns and quality losses based on customer reports. This is Level II information and is collected whenever possible. However, this is not critical to the opportunity assessment and is addressed later by the measurement team during the actual MPM^2 project.

The other part of opportunity is the demand aspect. The significance of the customer's ability to take advantage of the improvement has both negative and positive consequences that must not be underestimated. The negative consequence relates to the ability of the improvements to drive bottom-line results. In addition to labor improvements, bottom-line results can take many forms in areas such as productive material, quality, service, spare parts, utilities, etc. However, in simple terms, an improvement generates more output with the same workforce or the same output with a smaller workforce. Significantly reducing the workforce after a joint improvement project due to lack of demand demoralizes the workforce and jeopardizes future improvement efforts. The disruption to the ongoing operations caused by the workforce reduction and subsequent demoralization of the remaining workforce may hinder the improvement of bottom-line results, or the results may even deteriorate as a result of the disruption. The positive consequence of using the improvement to meet increased demand (beyond increasing operating performance), is that it eliminates the need for additional facilities and equipment. This capitol cost avoidance significantly increases the value of the improvement to the organization. Some may argue that cost avoidance is contrary to the supplier's objectives of selling equipment. However, in my opinion, the supplier is proving the value of its equipment that was sold originally and frequently has the opportunity to sell upgrades for that original equipment; this greatly improves the chances of securing future business from the customer.

Demand simply involves looking at the current operating times and future demand projections. If the operation is regularly working a lot of productive overtime to meet schedule requirements or to counteract lost production due to unplanned downtime, then demand exceeds performance. If expectations are for this demand to continue, this indicates a good opportunity for MPM^2. This was the case in the internal GM transfer press improvement project discussed earlier. If the current operation is meeting demand, but outlook in the near term (6–18 months) is for demand to increase (10 percent or more), then an MPM^2 project is a good fit. Added volume in existing products due to market demands or new business opportunities drives increased volume expectations. In the case study, Kasle Metal Processing was looking at new business opportunities in the form of additional blank processing, which they expected to win through competitive bidding. Thus, the MPM^2 project represented a proactive approach to their capacity issue to avoid performance problems after securing the new business.

Environment. The final step in determining a strategic improvement project involves a review of the operating organization and procedures to determine the risk and complexity associated with implementing an improvement project. MPM^2 refers to this as an operational assessment. The operational assessment evaluates forty characteristics spread across eight essential parameters that support the MPM^2 process. These parameters are as follows:

Supportive leadership	Effective teams
Continuous improvement	Basic PM process
Standardized procedures	Flexible work rules
Workplace organization	Willingness to learn

The operational assessment is a highly subjective evaluation of an organization's readiness to successfully implement MPM^2. It occurs over a 24-to 36-hour period with only a small sampling of input from a cross section of the organization's personnel over all shifts. The company initiating MPM^2 is responsible for conducting the assessment. To carry out the assessment, the initiating company usually employs a third party who is acceptable both to the customer and to the supplier. All assessors must be highly skilled in interpersonal communications, knowledgeable in lean manufacturing, and familiar with the particular manufacturing environment. Based on the interviews and observations, one or more assessors draw general conclusions regarding the forty operating characteristics. They record the findings using a *pass-improve-fail* (P-I-F) format. Next, the assessors use the set of characteristics identified to a specific parameter to reach their overall rating for the parameter, which uses the same P-I-F format. The overall rating of each parameter is not a pure average of the characteristics, but rather a subjective decision by the assessors based on those characteristics. After review of the parameter ratings with the customer's and supplier's key executives (and with their concurrence), the assessors establish the total operational assessment. Table 8.4 is an assessment sheet with each evaluation characteristic, a summary rating for each parameter, and an overall rating for the entire operational assessment. Just as with the opportunity assessment, to protect confidentiality, this is a hypothetical

Table 8.4 Operational assessment summary report

Environmental parameter	Assessment rating		
	Fail	Improve	Pass
Supportive leadership			Pass
Meet regularly with the workforce			X
Actively engaged in improvement efforts		X	
Thorough knowledge of process & issues			X
Positive attitude toward change			X
Effective teams			Pass
Defined team structure			X
Regular team meetings			X
Documentation of activities		X	
Individual opinion and feedback		X	
Health and safety priority			Pass
Performance record			X
Performance regularly tracked and posted			X
Regular safety reviews			X
Adherence to lockout procedures			X
Use of personal protective equipment		X	
Visitor protocol	X		
Individual opinion and feedback		X	
Workplace organization		Improve	
Layout, cleanliness, and lighting		X	
Organization of storage and shipping areas		X	
Organization of productive process			X
Labeling of material, tools & equipment	X		
Visual controls, alerts, and status indicators		X	
Ease in identifying process flow		X	
Continuous improvement activities			Pass
Floor improvement groups established			X
Data gathering and reporting in place			X
Problems identified and posted			X
Problems prioritized and analyzed		X	
Action plans to correct defined and tracked		X	
Performance tracked and improving			X

(*continued*)

Table 8.4 Operational assessment summary report (*continued*)

Environmental parameter	Assessment rating		
	Fail	Improve	Pass
Basic PM process			Pass
PM scheduling process in place			X
PM performance measurement		X	
PM documentation of findings			X
Flexible work rules			Pass
Contractual lines of demarkation			X
Job classifications			X
Experience and precedent			X
Overtime sensitvity and procedures			X
Willingness to learn		Improve	
Workforce age profile			X
Workforce education profile		X	
Workforce stability		X	
Experience of trainers		X	
Current training status		X	
Individual opinion and feedback		X	
Overall readiness for MPM^2			Pass

assessment that could apply to any manufacturing facility. The following general guidelines establish the P-I-F rating:

P—Characteristic meets desired requirements for MPM^2
I—Characteristic with only limited success requires further improvement
F—No evidence of the characteristic or failure to achieve desired results

MPM^2 requires a firm manufacturing foundation to ensure success. A failed effort significantly increases the barriers to a successful MPM^2 in the future. It is far better to delay MPM^2 implementation long enough to implement all the parameters before proceeding. If any parameter receives a *fail* rating, the overall assessment rating is *fail* until all parameters move out of the *fail* category.

In retrospect, the use of this operational assessment prior to an equipment installation could identify potential weaknesses in the operation that might affect the installation and start-up teams. Identifying this up front could provide an opportunity for the MPM project team to implement contingency plans to offset the weaknesses. However, as of the publishing of this book, operational assessments have only applied to MPM^2 improvement projects.

## 9

IMPROVEMENT INITIATION

After completing the opportunity and operational assessments, the customer and supplier make a joint decision regarding the merit to proceed. If the decision is to go forward, a contract is established and the supplier or customer—with the involvement of the other—begins planning the formation of the leadership team. The multi-company project management (MPM²) leadership team defines the configuration for the balance of the team structure including timing, assignments, and deliverables. Together with the project manager, the leadership team becomes the monitoring and control authority for the project. They are also responsible for reviewing and evaluating the improvement teams' achievements.

Improvement initiation covers the modifications to the first three MPM process groups: *cooperate*, *communicate*, and *control* and the new measurement process group required for MPM². Since the prior MPM process description is complete, the discussion covers just the modifications and the new measurement process group in a single chapter. The chapter has four sections: *organization and schedule*, *initiation*, *measurement*, and *planning*.

ORGANIZATION AND SCHEDULE

MPM² consists of a leadership team that drives the overall process, a measurement team for data gathering and analysis, and multiple short-term improvement teams. The leadership team and the individual short-term goal-specific improvement teams are the core elements of the process. The short-term improvement teams correlate to the project work teams and provide a high degree of flexibility. This allows tailoring the process to fit the needs of any manufacturing situation in terms of resources, equipment accessibility, and urgency since they can be scheduled to overlap each other, to follow one right after the other, or to be done all at once. The leadership team makes decisions on the priorities, resources, equipment access, and improvement team authority required by the teams. The improvement teams are assigned resources for specific goals, and each team is given two separate event time slots to execute their assignments. Time intervals separate events to allow for completion of the required homework assignments as defined by the team.

The initial strategic assessment reports to all parties that the opportunity for improvement is sufficient to warrant the effort and ensures the effective integration of MPM² with the operations environment. With the addition of measurement, the Six C process groups provide a structured approach that dramatically increases the results of any improvement process. MPM² success requires the following seven key ingredients:

- Leadership support
- Alignment with organizational strategy
- Performance tracking and accountability
- Linkage of improvements to the bottom line
- Allocation of human resources
- Avoidance of overemphasizing approach or technical tools
- Availability of equipment time and materials

Leadership support is an obvious requirement for establishing the MPM² improvement project and sustaining implementation. The strategic project definition discussed previously assures alignment with organizational strategy. Performance tracking and accountability is necessary to drive results in any project. Linking the improvements to the bottom line prevents them from creating offsetting losses, which detract from total performance. An improvement project depends on the availability of the appropriate resources. The customer and supplier are responsible for making these resources available as needed to plan and implement the improvements. In plant operations, bureaucracy and not-invented-here (NIH) syndrome inhibit improvement teams. Project managers must make sure that the formal MPM² approach and technical tools do not create a similar problem. Finally, the entire project relies on providing the teams with the required equipment time and material availability to allow for the diagnosis of problems and implementation of improvements. The project schedule created from the leadership planning session ensures the fulfillment of this requirement by detailing equipment timeslots as well as scheduling and tracking material orders.

A specific team has primary responsibility for the deliverables in each of the seven MPM² groups with one exception: When using multiple improvement teams, fulfilling the *complete* and *control* steps requires consolidating their deliverables. The process groups identified in the MPM² process map and team responsibility align as follows:

- Cooperate   Leadership team
- Communicate   Leadership team
- Measure   Measurement team
- Coordinate   Leadership supported by measurement
- Complete   Improvement team event I
- Control   Improvement team event II
- Close   Leadership team

The following outline details all activities and team assignments from assessment to closeout.

- Improvement scope—developed jointly
- Opportunity assessment—conducted jointly; identifies potential and demand
- Operational assessment—completed by assessor
- Contract—between customer and supplier to implement MPM^2
- Leadership team formation—MPM^2 awareness, measurement team, priorities
- Measurement team—formation, measurement of current state
- Leadership team improvement planning—set goals, organize teams
- Multiple improvement teams (simultaneous, overlapping, or sequential)
  - *First onsite event*—analyze and make improvements
  - *Homework*—complete assignments
  - *Second onsite event*—verify, adjust, standardize
- Leadership receives event reports—gives team recognition
- Validation—measurement team tracks performance to validate results
- Leadership closeout—summarize results and lessons learned

The Gantt chart in Figure 9.1 displays a generic timeline for MPM^2 implementation. This example involves two improvement teams with overlapping implementation timeframes. Approximately two weeks are devoted to the strategic assessment and contract agreement. Although the actual team formation event is one day, preliminary work and participant scheduling takes at least four weeks. One month is devoted to measurement team activities, which vary depending on the information available and the amount of time to gather that information. Leadership team improvement planning meeting is a one-day event that establishes the specific goals, improvement teams, and project macro timing. The Gantt chart shows one week to cover preliminary work prior to the meeting. The next approximately three months covers the teams' execution of improvement team event I, improvement event II, and completion of homework. This time will vary depending on the number of teams implemented, the ability to provide the required equipment availability for the improvement events, and the availability of the improvement

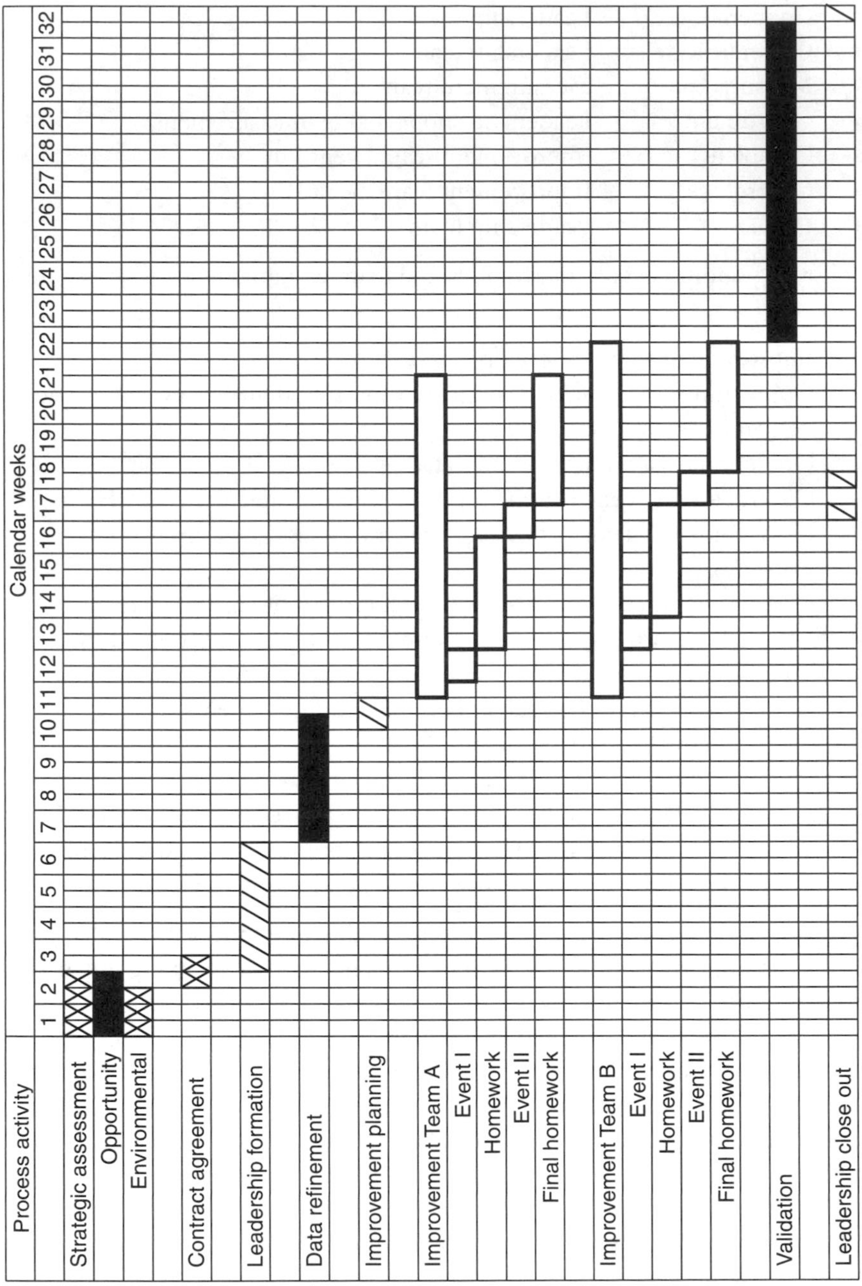

Figure 9.1 MPM² overall process Gantt chart

team's resources. Running all improvement team events simultaneously or sequentially will shorten or lengthen the overall timeframe. The final leadership closeout meeting occurs about three months later to allow validation of the results.

Elements in the Gantt chart are similar to the project phases, which become the Level 1 in the work breakdown structure of the schedule. Table 9.1 lists the initial work breakdown structure with two improvement teams; this serves as a good template or starting point for developing new project schedules. The underlined and italicized items within the work breakdown refer to forms, checklists, or agendas available to support MPM². There are two parts to the schedule. The

Table 9.1 Initial work breakdown structure

1.0 Strategic assessment
    1.1.0 *Identify preliminary scope*
    1.2.0 Opportunity assessment
        1.2.1 Gather equipment specification data
        1.2.2 Site visit and observations
        1.2.3 Gather performance history
        1.2.4 Compute ideal performance
        1.2.5 *Create opportunity assessment report*
    1.3.0 Environmental assessment
        1.3.1 Site visit, interviews, and observations
        1.3.2 *Environmental assessment summary report*
2.0 Customer and supplier MPM² contract
    2.1.0 Review assessments
    2.2.0 Determine opportunity
    2.3.0 Finalize improvement scope
    2.4.0 Negotiate pricing
    2.5.0 Issue contract
3.0 Leadership formation
    3.1.0 Set date, time, place, and duration
    3.2.0 Identify and invite participants
    3.3.0 *Leadership formation agenda*
    3.4.0 *Complete team formation checklist*
    3.5.0 Conduct leadership meeting
    3.6.0 Initiate measurement team
    3.7.0 Publish minutes
4.0 Data refinement
    4.1.0 Identify and compile available data
    4.2.0 Plan and acquire missing data
    4.3.0 Analyze and report

(continued)

Table 9.1 Initial work breakdown structure (*continued*)

5.0 Leadership improvement planning

    5.1.0 *Improvement planning agenda*

    5.2.0 *Complete team improvement checklist*

    5.3.0 Conduct team improvement meeting

    5.4.0 Initiate improvement teams

    5.5.0 Publish minutes

6.0 Improvement team A

    6.1.0 Organize team

    6.2.0 Site prep

    6.3.0 *Event I Agenda*

    6.4.0 Homework

    6.5.0 *Event II Agenda*

7.0 Improvement team B

    7.1.0 Organize team

    7.2.0 Site prep

    7.3.0 *Event I Agenda*

    7.4.0 Homework

    7.5.0 *Event II Agenda*

8.0 Validation

9.0 Leadership closeout

    9.1.0 Team A Event II report recognition

    9.2.0 Team B Event II report recognition

    9.3.0 *Leadership closeout meeting agenda*

project manager for the company initiating MPM^2 develops a schedule for strategic assessment through leadership-team formation with buy in from the other participant. This provides the leadership sufficient lead-time to plan for the meeting while conducting the assessment. It is a good idea to minimize additional planning until the assessment is complete and leadership decides to proceed. Following the leadership formation, the leadership, measurement, and improvement teams provide input on the tasks for which they are responsible to develop the balance of the schedule. Unlike in MPM where each team develops their phase of the project, in MPM^2, the plan develops as one integrated plan from the beginning with each team adding their particular detail to the plan as required. The leadership team establishes the basic timing of the improvement event activities and each team details appropriate work breakdown activities and identifies any conflicts with the original Level I timing. No further details are made to the improvement events in the project schedule. Instead, each team develops their own schedule using their daily lineup meetings. This provides greater flexibility and avoids a forced schedule format on the team. However, tracking homework items adds value, particularly the items that involve others outside the team in the project schedule.

Leadership Team. The plan for the leadership team formation starts with an overview of the MPM^2 process and a review of existing improvement processes and existing team structures. Next, the customer and supplier agree on participants and on a timeline for leadership team formation that fits their needs and expectations. The supplier representation on the leadership team consists of an executive team member and a sales or engineering representative. The customer portion of the leadership team includes a key executive with full authority for the customer site, an operations manager such as an area manager, along with production, maintenance, and quality personnel. The leadership team sets all goals, allocates resources, establishes macro timing, gives recognition as appropriate, and closes out the formal process.

The leadership team formation and improvement planning events each generally take six to eight hours. These two one-day events correlate to the two-day team-building event in MPM. There is usually a desire to combine the leadership team formation and improvement-planning events into a single meeting. This minimizes travel for the participants and expedites the initiation of the improvement events. However, experience indicates that it is better to separate these events to allow formation and task completion of a measurement team to provide detail and insight into the performance issues. This is a critical difference distinguishing MPM^2 from MPM and requires a two- to four-week gap between the leadership formation and improvement-planning events.

The leadership and project managers are responsible for overseeing the improvement teams and for ensuring MPM^2 process consistency. The leadership team meets a minimum of four times during the course of an MPM^2 project. If there is a need for more than one set of improvement events, additional leadership meetings are a good way to monitor the process and give recognition to the teams. The four leadership meetings are formation, improvement planning, team recognition, and closeout. The following outline details the leadership deliverables from each of these meetings:

1. Leadership team formation deliverables:
    A. Participant or contact list
    B. Team norms
    C. Build relationships
    D. Resource and results matrix
    E. Prioritized improvement areas
    F. Charter measurement team

2. Leadership improvement planning deliverables:
    A. Set improvement goals
    B. Charter improvement teams
    C. Macro timing
    D. Define site prep for each improvement team
3. Team recognition deliverables:
    A. Receive improvement team report
    B. Give recognition to improvement team
4. Leadership closeout deliverables:
    A. Evaluate results
    B. Lessons learned

The prior Gantt chart describing overall implementation of the MPM^2 process shows the leadership meetings as striped bars. There are five leadership meetings in the example since the two teams receive recognition at different times. The first two meetings are formation and improvement planning. The other three meetings appear as part of closeout consisting of two team-combined report and recognition events and the final closeout meeting.

Measurement Team. The measurement team starts as a few individuals from the customer and supplier assigned to perform the opportunity assessment prior to MPM^2 initiation. All or selected individuals from the opportunity assessment become part of the leadership team. These individuals usually become the measurement team that works as a subset of the leadership team with the responsibility to refine the initial data from the opportunity assessment and conduct a validation assessment after improvements are complete. Refining initial data involves sorting the data into specific segments, parts, or areas for improvement with sufficient clarity to allow the leadership team to set meaningful goals. Improvement planning uses the measurement team "report out" to establish areas for improvement and set the goals. Once this is complete, the leadership team determines the number of improvement teams, assigns resources, and establishes macro timing for the improvement events. After completion of the improvements, the measurement team monitors and reports the performance over an agreed upon time as final validation of the results. The MPM^2-process Gantt chart shows the activities of the measurement team as solid bars in three different time intervals: opportunity assessment, data refinement, and validation.

Improvement Team. Ideally, the leadership team should assign an improvement team for each goal they establish. However, when resources are limited or the improvement goals target the same system, a single team can tackle multiple goals. The team is usually a little larger to ensure it has all the required skill sets but uses fewer total resources than would be required by multiple teams. When all goals apply to the same system, the single team simplifies coordination and minimizes conflict. A single team tackling several goals may require additional events, perhaps an event for each goal.

The improvement teams are generally made up of a facilitator, a specialist from the equipment supplier; operator, maintenance, quality, and tech support from the customer; and the customer's supplier or end user personnel as appropriate. The improvement teams have priority access to the equipment during two intervals of time called improvement Event I and Event II. These events generally last one-week and the improvement team personnel are free from their other assignments to focus exclusively on the assigned improvement goal. This does not entirely remove the equipment from production during the week. A typical schedule of equipment availability might require three and one-half shifts such as afternoon on first shift Monday and all of first shift on Tuesday, Wednesday, and Thursday. On Monday morning and Friday, the improvement team plans their week and reports the results. After meeting the production needs on the second shift, corrective actions identified by the improvement team and the set up for the next day's activities are completed.

When dealing with multiple improvement teams, the timing of events for each team occur simultaneously or sequentially, or overlap. The method selected must consider resources, interactions on the equipment, and local equipment availability. Ideally, the equipment is in a running mode but with sufficient open time to allow problem diagnosis as to root cause and then permanent correction. The idea is for the improvement team to determine and implement solutions to improve performance during Event I. Recognizing that some solutions require added time, the interval between Event I and Event II is designed as homework assignments for the team members to implement the longer solutions. The time interval between Event I and Event II is usually one to two months depending on the defined homework and equipment availability. The purpose of Event II is to validate all the solutions, make any necessary adjustments, and ensure procedure standardization to sustain the improvements. The final homework after Event II is to correct any issues discovered in Event II that require more time to correct. The MPM^2 Gantt chart depicts each improvement team with an overall clear bar for all team activities and four smaller clear bars representing the next breakdown level showing the events and homework intervals.

Team Deliverables and Tools. Table 9.2 details participants, responsibilities, and deliverables for the leadership, measurement, and improvement teams. In addition, the table lists the tools used by each type of team to meet their responsibilities and fulfill their deliverables. This table is strictly a guideline for team structuring. The complexity of the organization, sophistication of the manufacturing process,

Table 9.2 MPM² team structures and tools

Topic	Leadership team	Measurement team	Improvement team
Participants	Key executive Area manager Maintenance Production Financial representative Project manager Equipment supplier representative Consultant	Financial representative Production Equipment supplier representative Project manager Consultant	Production operator Maintenance Quality Technical support Equipment specialist TBD End user Project manager Consultant
Responsibility	Improvement initiation Leadership Team closeouts	Refine current state data Gap analysis	Assigned goal
Deliverables	Group norms Set improvement goals Roles/org charts Establish improvement teams Define team authority Improvement team timing Evaluate project execution Improvement event site prep Oversee team events	Define roles of participants Current state report Average part change over times Average stock change times Equipment speed/feed by part Speed loss Pareto by part Pareto of downtime causes First-time quality Scrap losses	Participants roles defined Adhere to goals Daily report outs Final report out Maintain daily logs Track goal performance Plan/coordinate activities Visual log on site
Tools and techniques	Team checklists Group norms Personal history Organizational chart Situational matrix Resource/results matrix Goal setting Gantt chart Pre-event checklists MPM² process survey	Brainstorm Categorization Capacity planning tools Responsibility chart Automated data collection Current state data checklist Pareto chart Run charts Histograms	Group norms Personal history RASIC Fishbone diagram Network analysis Lean tools as required Gantt chart Site visual control board Daily summary Task list Report out

or issues identified in the opportunity assessment may drive different or additional representation on the teams.

INITIATION

The following section covers the initiation of the improvement project, focusing on the leadership formation, data refinement, and improvement planning. If all parties agree to implement the MPM² project, the customer and equipment supplier select personnel for participation on the leadership team after completing the assessment. Some key considerations during the participant selection process are the various roles and responsibilities of the participants as well as the participant's availability for the initial formation and improvement-planning activities. Thus, during this selection process, it is best to perform the task of setting the dates and location for both activities at the same time. The MPM² structure and tools table identifies the following eight functional roles for participation on the leadership team:

Customer key executive	Equipment supplier executive
Area manager	Maintenance representative
Project manager	Production representative
Financial representative	Consultant

Customer and Supplier Executives. As indicated previously, the user or supplier of the equipment initiates the process. Just as in MPM, the side that initiates the process must have an executive that understands the process, sees the strategic value of the process to the initiating company, and is committed to leading the process by example. In MPM terms, this executive is the project sponsor and fulfills the following responsibilities:

- Provides the financial resources for the project
- Has the final say on scope modifications
- Is the main recipient of project deliverables
- Serves as the project manager's direct boss
- Makes certain that the project remains aligned with the company's strategic direction

The executive from the initiating company is the one who recruits the other executive to participate in the process. Once these two leaders have agreed to proceed based on their views of the process and its strategic importance to their respective organizations, the balance of the participants can fall into place very smoothly. The key role of these two executives is their vision and desire to work together for mutual benefit. A secondary value of the executives is their experience and big-picture perspective that covers all the opportunities that are available to leverage other projects, technology, and lessons learned from their respective organizations to help the MPM^2 process.

Project Manager and Consultant. The project manager and consultant are responsible for leading the process, like the black belt in the Six Sigma process. Unlike the MPM process, in which multiple companies supply project managers, in MPM^2, there is only one project manager who typically comes from the organization that initiated the MPM^2. The project manager and consultant fulfill similar roles on the leadership team. The intent is for the consultant to develop self-sufficiency in the organization by transferring individual process knowledge to the project manager during the first MPM^2 project execution, allowing future implementation without the consultant. Ideally, the consultant functions as a coach for the project manager and helps support the project manager with facilitation, organization, and planning skills. The project manager and consultant responsibilities are:

- Manage knowledge, skills, tools, and techniques in the MPM^2 process
- Organize all communications and meetings
- Facilitate all planning and improvement events
- Facilitate formation of the leadership team
- Monitor and adjust to keep the process on target
- Hold accountable for results

The success in making the client organization self-sufficient directly relates to the skill sets of the project manager. The ideal project manager warrants respect and has an overall understanding of the organization's formal and informal networks. This project manager possesses strong interpersonal skills and a high level of communication and organization ability. Ideally, the project manager is well educated, experienced, and believes strongly in the project management and Six Sigma methodologies. Finally, the project manager requires sufficient time to manage the process and commitment to the overall concept.

Other Leadership Participants. In addition to the key executive, the equipment owner or user—also referred to as the customer—provides maintenance, production, and finance representatives, along with an area manager, who are responsible for all the disciplines involved in the studied system. Frequently, engineering or quality personnel supplement or substitute for maintenance or finance personnel. Depending on the organization, hourly personnel from the studied system may fill or supplement some of these functions. If hourly personnel are used they should be selected based on their system knowledge and ability to influence the other personnel. With the exception of the key executive and project manager, the leadership team membership is not set in stone and adjusts to fit the organizational structure and culture.

Beyond the key executive and project manager, there are no other participation requirements from the equipment supplier for the leadership team. A lot depends on the equipment supplier executive's and project manager's technical and application knowledge of the equipment. Usually, the equipment supplier executive draws in one or more sales, engineering, or service representatives to supplement this technical knowledge. It also gives the equipment supplier a great opportunity to build relationships with the customer. The involvement of the sales, engineering, and service personnel at the leadership level in the win-win environment of the MPM^2 process builds relationships that can prove valuable in future issue resolution and new business opportunities.

Initial Leadership Meeting. The project manager and the consultant are responsible for ensuring the solid planning and execution of a leadership team. Figure 9.2 is a preleadership meeting checklist used to verify the completion of each aspect of the leadership team formation as each task is completed. Figure 9.3 is a standard agenda for the leadership formation. To ensure maximum value from the meeting and to ensure the meeting of its deliverables, it is a good idea to prepare participants and make agenda item assignments ahead of time.

For the initial team formation, it is important to assign an individual to facilitate each of the elements listed under presentations. Usually the customer's key executive handles the introductions and agenda review, a customer representative presents the opportunity assessment, and the customer's operations manager presents the customer perspective. The customer's or supplier's key executive facilitates the formation and tasking of the measurement team. The consultant or project manager is responsible for the MPM^2 process overview, resource and results matrix, and wrap up. The project manager distributes the other items among the participants based on their knowledge and facilitation skills.

Introductions and agenda review, norms, and personal history follow the MPM process. The use of the MPM company single-line organization chart and situational matrix exercises will depend on the existing relationship between the customer and supplier. In the case study, Automatic Feed Company and Kasle Metal Processing were partners and knew each other very well. Usually, the leadership team consists of representatives from only two companies with a close relationship, perhaps from a prior MPM project. Thus, they do not require these exercises. Use of the organization chart and situational matrix exercises is appropriate when three or more companies are involved or the participants do not have strong prior relationships. The MPM^2 process overview, resource, and results matrix topics follow standardized content established from the initial pilot

Improvement title _____

Customer _____ **Supplier** _____

Key executive _____ **Key executive** _____

Project manager _____ **Consultant** _____

Equipment scope _____

#	Activity	✔
1.	Define preliminary scope	
2.	Complete opportunity assessment	
3.	Complete environmental assessment	
4.	Customer and supplier review assessment results and reach agreement to proceed	
5.	Customer and supplier contract established	
6.	Review customer team structure and improvement efforts	
7.	Agree on leadership team participants	
8.	Agree on place, date, and duration for leadership formation meeting	
9.	Verify meeting facility and equipment	
10.	Arrange refreshments, lunch	
11.	Customer and supplier finalize agenda	
12.	Prepare and send invitations	
13.	Secure customer assignments to present introductions, agenda review, and customer perspective	
14.	Assign balance of the agenda items to leadership participants	
15.	Review presentation materials with assigned personnel	

Figure 9.2 MPM² Preleadership formation checklist

improvement project plan. The opportunity assessment and customer perspective require that presentations be developed for each specific project. The operational assessment normally does not appear on the standard agenda since any deficiencies are minor and are handled internally by the organization outside the MPM² process. The last two items are placeholders for the identification of key opportunities and initiation of the measurement team, which are the result of the decisions, assignments, and action plans formulated by the leadership. It is critical to capture these in the minutes and resulting project plan that is developed. The project manager is responsible for developing and communicating the project schedule to all parties. In addition, he is responsible for detailing all associated action plans with individual assignments and due dates following the MPM open-issues list process in projects.

Agenda
Leadership team formation

Introductions and agenda review	Customer key executive
MPM^2 process overview	Consultant/project manager
Norms	As assigned
Personal history	As assigned
Opportunity assessment report	Customer tech representative
Customer perspective (Issues and opportunities)	Customer operator manager
Resource/results matrix	Project manager
Identify key improvement areas	As assigned
Form and task the measurement team	Customer/supplier key executive
Wrap up	Project manager

Address any open issues

Review assignments and action plans

Set next meeting date

Set responsibility and deadline for distribution of minutes

Figure 9.3 MPM^2 leadership team formation agenda

Resource and Results Matrix. In MPM, initial leadership team-building spent a great deal of time on mission and goals. This used brainstorming, categorization, and exercises to develop the mission and goals. In the case study, this process proved to be non-value added. When dealing with an operations improvement effort, the mission is already set and requires selection and quantification of goals. Instead, use the resource and results matrix exercise to select the goals in the MPM^2 project. The resource and results matrix is a core deliverable from the leadership formation that drives the actions of the measurement team. The matrix uses the three improvement categories defined previously associated with OEE consolidated with a fourth category called *upgrade potential* to reflect the interests and value of the outside supplier. These four categories each contain three subcategories of improvement, which make up the following 12 opportunities for improvement:

Availability	Performance
1. Reduce breakdowns	4. Speed optimization
2. Reduce changeover	5. Reduce idle time
3. Minimize adjustments	6. Eliminate minor stoppages

	Quality		Upgrades
7.	Defect reduction	10.	Functionality
8.	Minimize rework	11.	Performance
9.	Start-up impact	12.	Reliability

These opportunities are numbered 1 through 12, and are evaluated by the leadership team based on the data generated and the team's experiences. Next, the posting of the opportunities in a matrix creates the resource and results matrix as shown in Figure 9.4. From this matrix, the measurement team creates the data necessary to support the goals associated with the items that fall within the shaded squares, representing high-low, high-medium, and medium-low values of the results and resources respectively. These squares are essentially those areas where the results are greater than the required resources. In this example, items 1, 2, 4, and 11 in the upper right corner receive top priority, delivering high results and requiring low resource levels. Items 8 and 10 receive secondary priority.

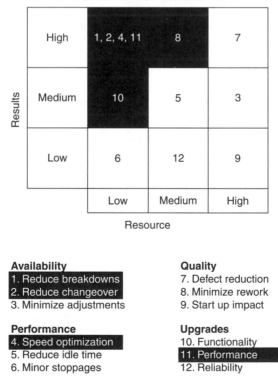

Figure 9.4 Resource results matrix

The main deliverables from the leadership team formation are team norms, greater trust and respect among team members, prioritization of improvement opportunities through the resource and results matrix, initiation of the measurement team, and preliminary project and related action plans. At the end of the meeting, the arrangements and agenda for the next leadership improvement-planning meeting are established, and a person responsible for publishing the minutes with a due date is designated.

MEASUREMENT

Once the leadership team has identified the key improvement areas from the resource and results matrix, they need accurate data on the current and ideal states in order to establish goals for the improvement teams. This data replaces the brainstorming list that MPM used. The acronym SMART discussed previously is a useful tool to use in developing these goals.

The amount of data and accuracy required to establish SMART goals is greater than that needed for the opportunity assessment. Thus, goal establishment requires additional data gathering and analysis. The leadership's selection of key improvement areas from the resource and results matrix exercise allows the measurement team to focus their efforts in specific areas for better efficiency and quality of the analysis.

In the case study, the opportunity assessment gathered the following Level I information by part number to compute the ideal state and to compare to the current state to determine the opportunity for improvement:

Part info—Part number; description; feed length; die feed angle; run quantity; volume per month, quarter, or year; average net pieces per hour produced

Coil info Width, gauge, weight

Line setup—Stack size, stack mode (single station, side out, etc.), press speed

The difference between set press speed and the engineered press speed explains a portion of the opportunity gap for a blanking process. The balance is attributable to the following Level II information on performance, work schedule, and downtime issues:

Line performance—Die change time, pallet change time, coil thread time, tail out blank time

Work schedule—Start, break, lunch, cleanup times

Downtime—Equipment downtime, quality-check time, minor adjustment

The opportunity assessment may attempt to gather information on the Level II areas, but limited time constraints and resources usually result in ballpark estimates and averages that are not part specific and downtime information that lacks frequency and duration by causes. Although this information is helpful in assigning improvement areas to the resource and results matrix, it is not detailed enough to set goals. The measurement team's role is to gather the additional Level II data and conduct the required analysis.

By selecting the measurement team from the leadership group, team formation elements such as norms, relationship building, and role definition are complete, allowing the measurement team to begin working on their assignment. Another benefit of making the measurement team a subset of the leadership team is that it builds confidence and validity in the results they generate, which helps to expedite the subsequent goal setting activity.

The measurement team generally has a brief planning session at the conclusion of the leadership formation, and then handles subsequent communications via conference calls or e-mail. In some instances, they find it necessary to schedule one or more site visits to gather additional data or test assumptions in the manufacturing operation. Following a project management methodology when developing the schedule and requirements for these visits ensures the accomplishment of the desired observation and measurements in the most efficient manner with minimal disruption to the customer operations. For example, identifying the specific jobs and functions for observation allows the customer to arrange the required materials and schedule the jobs to run in the desired sequence during the visit. The measurement team may also develop specific forms for the equipment operators to record data beyond the measurement team's visit. For example, downtime recording can provide very useful data if collected and reported properly. The measurement team might provide a report format for all downtime with a set of causes for coding the downtime by the operators. The measurement team gathers the downtime sheets weekly, summarizes the lost time by cause, and creates a Pareto chart to prioritize problem resolution efforts.

In addition to defining the current state, the measurement team also looks at the ideal state to ensure it properly reflects the equipment capabilities. After validating the current and ideal states, the measurement team must do a comparative analysis and generate a report that presents the information in a clear and concise manner that is appropriate for the leadership team to use to establish goals. The fact that the measurement team is a subset of the leadership team significantly aids in this objective.

The measurement team uses the results of the resource and results matrix evaluation of the 12 improvement opportunities to set their priorities and focus their measurement efforts. Opportunities in the availability, performance, and quality categories generally require developing detailed information from the floor operation, while the upgrade opportunities generally take the form of a longer-term business case development. In some cases, the improvements achieved through working in the first three categories can reduce the business case for upgrades. However, many of the corrections implemented to improve the current OEE are critical to realizing the benefits in any proposed upgrades. Spending money to upgrade a poorly performing operation (not operating at its true potential) rarely meets expectations. The operating issues that prevent a machine from reaching its potential will have a similar effect on any upgrades.

The availability issues tend to relate primarily to the equipment, while performance issues are a combination of equipment and part-specific tooling. Quality issues usually tie back to part-specific tooling and productive materials. Resolving pure equipment issues can benefit all the parts running in the equipment and thus tend to have a multiplying effect on performance. In the availability category, the information is generally broken down into equipment areas or causes. Pareto charts showing both frequency and durations are the best way to display this information. In the performance and quality category, the detailed information often takes the form of part-specific information. Figure 9.5 is a plot showing each part's

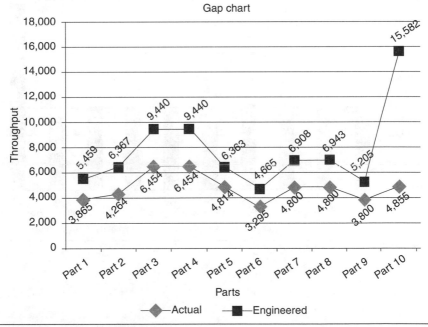

Figure 9.5 Throughput/shift part gap

actual rate (plotted with diamonds) and its ideal or engineered rate (plotted with squares) with the difference being the individual part gap. Figure 9.6 shows the individual part gaps as percentages ranging from 23.4 percent on Part 5 to 68.8 percent on Part 10. A priority based on this way of looking at the gap puts Part 10 first with Part 2 next. In order to convert this opportunity by part into a bottom-line performance impact, the data must be volume adjusted to weigh the impacts of each part on the total performance. Figure 9.7 represents the volume-weighted gap percentage plotted in a Pareto chart showing Part 10 first followed by Part 6 second with Part 2 in the eighth position.

It is important for the measurement team to present their report using Pareto and other techniques that allow the leadership to quickly understand and prioritize the issues. It is critical for the measurement team to complete its assignment including the final report before conducting the leadership improvement planning. If the measurement team falls behind in completing its assignment, it is better to delay the leadership planning session until the measurement team is ready.

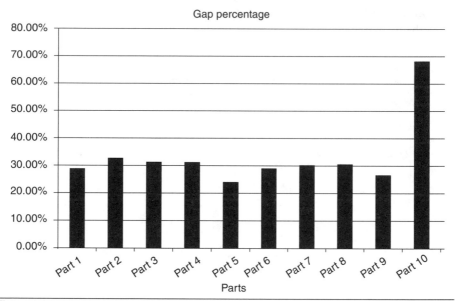

Figure 9.6 Part gap as a percentage

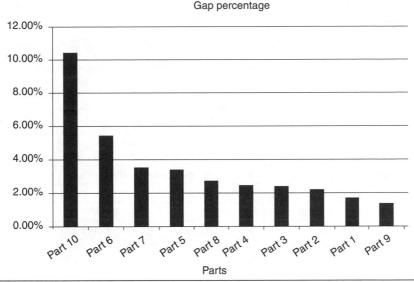

Figure 9.7 **Volume weighted part gap Pareto**

PLANNING

Improvement Plan. The date, place, duration, and tentative agenda is established for the improvement planning meeting at the conclusion of the leadership team formation event. The project manager and consultant working in conjunction are responsible for completing critical preparatory elements for the leadership improvement planning meeting ahead of time. These consist of measurement team assignments, meeting arrangements, and agenda finalization with assignments. The checklist in Figure 9.8 provides a detailed list for reference and the recommended agenda in Figure 9.9 displays key topic assignments.

No matter who initiates the process, it is important when finalizing the agenda to involve the customer to the maximum extent possible in presenting and facilitating the improvement-planning session. Note the following recommended agenda items assigned to the customer in the preceding agenda:

- Review norms from first meeting
- Measurement team report
- Improvement team assignments
- Improvement events macro timing
- Agenda for first improvement Event I

This helps increase the customer's participation and ownership in the plan. The above topics provide the proper involvement of customer personnel making

Improvement title _____

Customer _____ **Supplier** _____

Key executive _____ **Key executive** _____

Project manager _____ **Consultant** _____

Equipment scope _____

#	Activity	✔
1.	Publish minutes from leadership formation meeting identifying key areas of improvement and measurement team assignments	
2.	Create a PowerPoint chart of norms developed by leadership team	
3.	Measurement team completes assignment	
4.	Measurement team prepares presentation	
5.	Agree on place, date, and duration for leadership improvement planning meeting	
6.	Verify meeting facility and equipment	
7.	Arrange refreshments, lunch	
8.	Finalize agenda with customer and supplier	
9.	Customer to identify presenters from their organization for each of the following agenda items: • Review norms from first meeting • Measurement team report • Develop improvement team assignments • Set macro timing for improvement events • Prepare agenda for first Improvement Event I	
10.	Assign balance of the agenda items to leadership participants	
11.	Review presentation materials with assigned personnel	

Figure 9.8 Preimprovement planning checklist

presentations and facilitating discussions. Even if the customer initiates MPM^2 and provides the project manager, this approach increases buy in within the customer's organization. In each case, when assigning agenda topics, the presentation and facilitation skills of leadership participants must receive careful consideration. The consultant or project manager helps ease the customer into these roles by preparing an initial set of slides covering the agreed upon norms and a summary of the measurement team report to help the customer in their presentations. The team assignments, macro timing, and improvement Event I agenda are pure facilitation activities; these results are recorded on a flip chart or white board in front of the team. The consultant or project manager may play the role of scribe to assist the customer in facilitation if necessary.

Agenda
Leadership Team Improvement Planning

Welcome	Customer key executive
Review norms from first meeting	Customer key executive
Review action plans from first meeting	Project manager
Measurement team report	Customer numbers representative
Establish improvement goals	Supplier representative/consultant
Develop improvement team assignments	Customer operations manager
Define requirements for each improvement event	Supplier representative/consultant

- Equipment
- Material
- Manpower

Set macro timing for improvement events	Customer representative
Leadership participation and review process	Project manager

- Daily improvement team status
- Improvement team summary reports

Prepare agenda for Improvement Event I	Customer representative
Wrap up	Project manager/consultant

Figure 9.9 Leadership improvement planning agenda

Generally, the customer's key executive handles the norms review as part of the welcome at the start of the meeting. This demonstrates the executive's support and commitment to the norms. The person viewed as the numbers expert from the customer that participated on the measurement team is the ideal individual to present the measurement report since it gives greater credibility to the data. In addition, the extensive knowledge of the numbers expert regarding the customer's perspective maximizes both understanding and impact within the customer organization. Use of the area (operations) manager to make team assignments secures support since the bulk of the improvement team's resources are the area manager's responsibility. The project manager assigns the remaining improvement team items to customer representatives from the improvement teams with appropriate facilitation skills.

When backed up by the consultant, utilizing the equipment supplier's executive to facilitate the establishment of goals and the delineation of improvement event requirements frees the project manager and all the customer's personnel, allowing them full participation. This also facilitates buy in on these two critical topics. The supplier's representative or consultant is more objective in the facilitation of the goals and can encourage the team to put more reach in the goals. In

MPM, cross-company, cross-functional subgroups provide a means for building relationships, thus increasing collaboration and efficiently dealing with a large number of issues. In MPM[2], the project manager designs these concepts into improvement planning for the topics of establishing goals and event requirements based on an individual assessment of the participants, issues, and a variety of functions to complete the topics most efficiently and with the highest commitment.

The project manager typically handles the review of the action plans from the first meeting and facilitates the development of the plans regarding leadership's participation in reviewing the improvement team's daily status and end-of-event summary reports. The project manager supported by the consultant handles the session wrap up and makes sure that someone has the responsibility of creating and distributing the minutes. The project manager also builds all the plans into the project schedule and incorporates appropriate leadership-assigned actions into the open-issues action plan.

Goal Setting. In MPM[2], the leadership team sets goals at two levels. They establish the goals in terms of an overall big picture for the leadership team and in more task-specific terms for the improvement teams. The use of the overall goals at the leadership level keeps the emphasis on bottom line and overall equipment effectiveness, while the task goals help to focus the improvement teams and provide immediate feedback to the teams at the end of each event. For example, the leadership team establishes the goals that relate to bottom-line performance and require significant time intervals (one to three months) to measure effectiveness. In the case study, leadership set an overall goal to close the OEE gap as follows:

Leadership's overall goal: 40 percent closure in OEE performance gap

In our opportunity analysis example, the volume adjusted total gap is 35 percent. Reducing this gap by 40 percent reduces the gap by 14 percent, yielding a 21 percent gap or an OEE of 79 percent, which is 6 percent below world class. Closure of the final 6 percent gap requires minor improvements best achieved through continuous improvement efforts. From another perspective, increasing OEE from 65 percent to 79 percent represents a 21.5 percent improvement in total productivity, which is in line with the MPM[2] vision of double-digit improvement.

To establish the task goal, leadership uses the resource and results matrix from the leadership formation session that prioritizes the areas for improvement. The matrix, together with the added data gathered, compiled, and analyzed by the measurement team, forms the basis for the task goals. The case study matrix identifies reductions in breakdowns and changeover durations, optimizations in speed, and upgrades focused on performance as the top priorities for improvement. To achieve the gap closure, leadership set task-specific goals for downtime, die change time, and system strokes per minute as follows:

Task Goals

- Eliminate the top three causes for downtime
- Achieve a die change time of 10 minutes
- Achieve a 30 percent speed increase on the top 10 gap-contributing parts

In the case study, leadership determined the performance upgrade to be an issue, requiring a business case and project funding. As a result, leadership took on the assignment of pursuing this option themselves. They identified a specific project opportunity, began the business case development, and set a deadline to complete the business case and make a decision regarding funding.

At the conclusion of the Improvement Event II, the achievement of task goals are immediately apparent and the team can be recognized accordingly. However, some homework issues may still linger that require adjustments, training, procedure documentation, or other attention. As in the case study, implementation of the performance upgrades, typically requires additional time as well. Once everything is complete, the measurement team measures performance over a period of possibly three months to determine if these task goals achieved the desired 40 percent gap closure. This also has the benefit of ensuring sustainment of the improvements over time and verifying that no adverse effects are present on other variables.

The MPM project phase scorecard described in Chapter 5 requires modification to fit the needs of an operations improvement. The scorecard is not a good fit for the improvement team, since each improvement team maintains focus and tracks their respective goal daily via the visual control board. The measurement team is just a subset of the leadership team, and leadership has a scorecard consisting of the operations bottom-line performance. Thus, the scorecard is optional, and the short timeline dictates a single scorecard for the overall improvement project rather than one for each phase.

Table 9.3 is a blank scorecard for the *blanking case study,* created by replacing the activity-specific items such as timing and cost with specific goals set by the leadership. Retaining safety monitoring as a critical element in the improvement process keeps safety awareness at the forefront. Making changes creates potential safety issues that require anticipation and resolution. In their enthusiasm to make improvements, employees may be tempted to take shortcuts that put them or others at risk; this is to be avoided at all costs. The process description defines meeting requirements with just a little fine-tuning by leadership, and leadership must establish open-issue targets depending on the needs of the improvement project.

Table 9.3 Improvement scorecard

Start date: Data as of:	Goal	Current four-week trend				Project cumm
		Week	Week	Week	Week	
Safety						
Near misses	0					
Recordables	0					
Lost time days	0					
Improvement goals						
Gap closure	40%					
Remove downtime issues	Top 3					
Die change time	<10					
Top 10 parts speed increase	30%					
Communications						
Mtgs/conf planned	27					
Mtgs/conf held						
Variance	0					
Open issues						
Opened						
Closed						
In process	<5					
Older than two weeks	0					
Current week variance explanation:						
Comments and concerns:						
Status code:	●	On target				
	▲	Corrective action implemented				
	✗	Corrective action required				

The scorecard is first used in the leadership formation by getting commitments on the safety goals, total quantity of meetings, and acceptable number and age of the open issues. This requires modification of the agenda previously discussed. In the case study, the meeting estimate of 27 consists of five leadership meetings, four measurement meetings, and nine meetings for each improvement team. The target number of open issues and the age of open issues is lower to reflect the shorter timeframe and smaller project size. The second leadership meeting sets the goals, which makes the scorecard complete, but the other three categories will already be underway, allowing for status reports to help the project manager control all stakeholders.

## 10

IMPROVEMENT RESULTS AND MPM CONCLUSION

Formation of the leadership team establishes the key customer and supplier relationship, identifies the target areas for improvement, and builds an expectation and excitement toward the improvement opportunities. Companies should avoid the tendency to go directly to the improvement event. The measurement team requires time to gather additional data and the leadership team requires time to set goals, plan for the specific improvement events, prep the facility, and prep the improvement teams. Taking the time to complete these activities makes the improvement events run smoothly and ensures that the improvement event fully utilizes all resources to maximize results. This chapter covers the *complete, control,* and *close* MPM^2 process groups in an improvement project. Part II covers these topics thoroughly as they apply to a normal project. This chapter covers all the modifications to these process groups to fit an improvement project. The chapter contains four sections: *Event Requirements, Event Completion, Closeout,* and *Conclusion,* which includes final remarks concerning multi-company project management (MPM) overall.

EVENT REQUIREMENTS

When making team assignments for the improvement events, personnel are carefully selected from those who have the skills needed to support the specific event objective. The teams should have representation from both production and maintenance personnel working the systems under study. Finally, it is useful to draw in a third party who does not know the specific equipment as well as the customer's or equipment supplier's technician to gain a fresh perspective of the process. Possible sources for this third-party perspective are suppliers, sister plants, or final customers. At the time of the leadership improvement planning meeting, team assignments are tentative subject to follow-up on individual availability. Thus, during the time between assignments and the actual event, business and personal circumstances of the various personnel can change, causing the need for substitutions to meet agreed requirements. In the most severe situation, it may be necessary to retime the event to ensure that key personnel are available. The project manager must monitor this situation closely and communicate any deviations to the entire team.

The topic of defining equipment and material requirements is critical to ensuring that each improvement event delivers maximum results for the resources invested. Production equipment availability needs must clearly define the extent to which the improvement team can disrupt normal production by shutting down to diagnose issues, pushing speeds to the limiting point, testing and practicing improvement ideas, and changing run sequences to meet the specific needs of the improvement team. Prior to the event, everyone involved in the process receives a notification requesting support for the improvement process. One part of the team planning is selecting parts for each event, followed by issuing material orders to ensure that the material is available. Material will be a function of the event objective. For example, when conducting a speed improvement event, part priority selection is required if all parts listed in the gap analysis cannot be run. For speed improvements, the part selecting follows these priorities:

1. Study all equipment conditions by selecting parts that yield the greatest variety of operating conditions. In a blanking process this would include such options as exposed and nonexposed; developed and straight cut; long, medium, and short progressions; special setups (i.e., side-out stacking)

2. From the above parts, select the parts that contribute the most to the performance gap (volume adjusted opportunity found in opportunity assessment report)

3. Pick problem parts identified by the customer after filling the above priorities (may already be covered in above)

The proper selection of resources together with the availability of equipment and materials will determine the level of success achieved by each improvement event. The project manager plays the lead role in coordinating these elements, ensuring the communication and understanding of all goals by everyone. The project manager also is responsible for following up to ensure that everyone meets their commitments.

The leadership improvement planning meeting establishes general improve-ment-event requirements in terms of equipment, labor, material, and macro tim-ing. The project manager's role is to work with the teams to provide additional detail as required for the project schedule and to document all this information in the project plan and action items. Then, the project manager must track the proj-ect plan and action items to ensure conformance. The Pre-Event I checklist in Figure 10.1 and Pre-Event II checklist in Figure 10.2 are tools to assist the project manager in preparing for the subsequent improvement events.

EVENT COMPLETION

Each improvement team consists of a project manager or consultant; an equip-ment supplier specialist; an operator, maintenance, quality, and tech support from the customer; and the customer's production material supplier or end-user per-sonnel as appropriate. The equipment supplier's specialist provides the technical expertise for the equipment. The project manager or consultant provides MPM^2 knowledge, Six Sigma skills, and team facilitation skills. The customer's personnel provide intimate knowledge of the specific equipment, the operating environment, and historical performance. Involving the customer's floor personnel in the improvement's development process builds ownership and creates a synergy that generates exceptional improvement solutions. The involvement of raw material suppliers and end users provides two other critical perspectives that can help to create out-of-the-box thinking when brainstorming solutions. A side benefit is that the material supplier gains a greater understanding of how their product affects the process; the end user gains insight into the effort and commitment their source puts into improving the process.

During the leadership team's improvement planning session, specific goals were set, team assignments were developed, and a macro time line was established. Prior to the start of the improvement team Event I, individual team members receive all the background information on MPM^2, data developed by the measure-ment team, and the assigned goals. This is generally the responsibility of the operations manager, but the project manager, consultant, or some other member of the leadership team can fill in if required. The operations manager asks indi-vidual team members to give some thought as to how they might meet the assigned goals and to clear their schedules to participate in the improvement events.

Event I Activities. The agenda in Figure 10.3 lists the daily activities typical of an Event I scheduled over a five-day period. Each improvement event kickoff starts with a presentation of the challenges and goals to the team by the customer's key executive. Any leadership team members on site that day should attend the

Improvement title _____

Customer _____ **Supplier** _____

Key executive _____ **Key executive** _____

Project manager _____ **Consultant** _____

Equipment scope _____

#	Activity	✔
1.	Publish minutes from leadership improvement planning meeting identifying improvement goals, improvement team assignments, and macro timing for Events I and II	
2.	Members from leadership team to meet with all assigned improvement team personnel to review overall MPM^2 process and results of two leadership meetings	
3.	Members from leadership team to meet individually with each improvement team participant to detail expectations, review their role, and ask them to begin thinking about improvement ideas	
4.	Verify equipment requirements defined during improvement planning and subsequent discussions with improvement personnel are all in place	
5.	Verify material requirements defined during improvement planning and subsequent discussions with improvement personnel are all in place	
6.	Verify personnel requirements defined during improvement planning and subsequent discussions with improvement personnel are all in place	
7.	Prepare contingency plans to address any potential weaknesses in the above equipment, material, or personnel requirements	
8.	Conduct a Pre-Event I conference call with key planners and participants to review preparations and agenda for Event I	

9.	Insure a full time facilitator is identified for Event I to help the team in the following areas:
	   • Brainstorm improvement ideas
	   • Select best solutions
	   • Develop improvement plan
	   • Monitor plan execution
	   • Assist in preparing "report out" to leadership
	
	Note: Facilitation role may be fulfilled by a qualified project manager or 3rd party	

10.	Set time, date, and place for Event I report out	
11.	Identify and confirm leadership participants for Event I report out	

Figure 10.1 Pre-Event I checklist

Improvement title _____

Customer _____ **Supplier** _____

Key executive _____ **Key executive** _____

Project manager _____ **Consultant** _____

Equipment scope _____

#	Activity	✔
1.	Publish Event I report and distribute to all participants and involved personnel	
2.	Members from leadership team to meet with all assigned improvement teams to insure understanding of results and clarify homework assignments from Event I	
3.	Monitor progress of customer homework assignments and verify all assignments will be completed prior to start of Event II	
4.	Monitor progress of supplier homework assignments and verify all assignments will be completed prior to start of Event II	
5.	Verify equipment requirements defined for Event II are all in place	
6.	Verify material requirements defined for Event II are all in place	
7.	Verify personnel requirements defined for Event II are all in place	
8.	Prepare contingency plans to address any potential weaknesses in the above equipment, material, or personnel requirements	
9.	Conduct a Pre-Event II conference call with key planners and participants to review preparations and agenda for Event II	
10.	Insure a full time facilitator is identified for Event II to help the team in the following areas: • Brainstorm control ideas • Develop control plan • Monitor plan execution • Assist in preparing report out to leadership Note: Facilitation role may be fulfilled by the PM if qualified or a 3rd party	
11.	Set time, date, and place for Event II report out	
12.	Confirm leadership full participation in Event II report out	
13.	Plan appropriate recognition for the improvement team at completion of Event II	

Figure 10.2 Pre-Event II checklist

Monday	Time	Location
Daily improvement team meeting	???	Conference room
Introductions and MPM^2 process overview		
Norms, history, roles		
Brainstorm improvement Ideas		
Select best solutions		
Develop improvement plan		
Lunch	???	
Separate into team activities to execute plan	???	Plant floor
Daily update meeting	???	Conference room
Assign follow-up items to 2nd shift		

Tuesday		
Daily improvement team meeting	???	Conference room
Review 2nd shift follow-up		
Adjust plan based on previous day's results		
Separate into team activities to execute plan	???	Plant floor
Lunch	???	
Separate into team activities to execute plan	???	Plant floor
Daily update meeting	???	Conference room
Assign follow-up items to 2nd shift		

Wednesday		
Daily improvement team meeting	???	Conference room
Review 2nd shift follow-up		
Adjust plan based on previous day's results		
Separate into team activities to execute plan	???	Plant floor
Lunch	???	
Separate into team activities to execute plan	???	Plant floor
Daily update meeting	???	Conference room
Assign follow-up items to 2nd shift		

Thursday		
Daily improvement team meeting	???	Conference room
Review 2nd shift follow-up		
Adjust plan based on previous day's results		
Separate into team activities to execute plan	???	Plant floor
Lunch	???	
Separate into team activities to execute plan	???	Plant floor
Daily update meeting	???	Conference room
Begin preparing report out presentation		

Friday		
Finalize presentation	???	Conference room
Event I report out	???	Conference room

Figure 10.3 Event I–Schedule of daily activities agenda

kickoff. It is a good idea to show the improvement team how these improvements can help to increase their security, income, environment, or any other issues important to the individual team members. With the input of the improvement team, a schedule for daily updates and an end-of-week report out are established. The leadership details the authority of each team, identifies equipment availability, and offers their support if they encounter any roadblocks. They solicit questions from the team and answer them to the team's satisfaction. Other leadership members present during the kickoff assist with the question-and-answer period and offer their support as well. After the customer's key executive completes the kickoff and after all the questions have been resolved, anyone not part of the improvement team departs and the facilitator begins leading the improvement process.

The development of norms is identical to that used by the leadership team. Building relationships uses the personal history exercise or some other form of introduction process that allows for the sharing of information across a broad range of topics. The roles and responsibilities are defined by constructing a RASIC matrix, with contributions from the entire team. The improvement team may further subdivide the goals provided to them by the leadership team. The purpose of the Event I report out is to explain the results achieved and present a schedule of activities that the team agreed to complete prior to Event II. During the period between the two events, the individual team members complete the activities per the schedule and communicate with the project manager to keep the schedule status up to date.

Many of the tools and methods used in MPM require modification before they can be effective problem solvers or improve processes. The MPM process description in Parts I and II discusses brainstorming as it pertains to leadership goals and action plans, scheduling for coordination and control, and visual control for floor activities. The next three sections titled *Fishbone Diagram*, *Network Analysis*, and *Operations Visual Control Board* discuss how these methods apply in operations during the improvement events.

Fishbone Diagram. The fishbone diagram, also known as the *cause and effect diagram*, starts by using a modified brainstorming technique similar to that used by the leadership to generate a set of causes affecting goal achievement. As the group identifies each, the facilitator records the item on a fishbone diagram within the appropriate category listed on the fishbone. Thus, identification and categorization occur at the same time and is a major deviation to the methodology used with brainstorming by the leadership. Although MPM did not discuss this topic, this approach is also valid for the project work teams in root-causing project problems and formulating solutions.

Figure 10.4 is an example of a fishbone diagram for a hypothetical blanking system with a few possible causes listed for reference. This particular fishbone

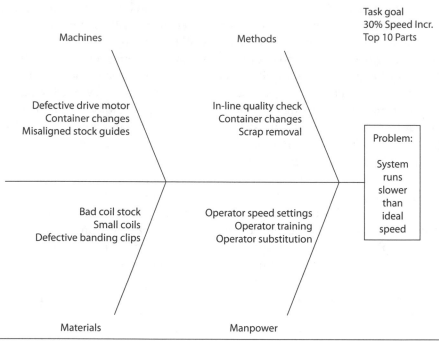

Figure 10.4 Fishbone diagram

relates to the task goal of optimizing speed, as listed in the upper right corner. The problem in the box on the right states, "System runs slower than ideal speed." The categories of causes are above and below the elements of the fishbone with the individual causes on the elements. The four categories commonly used are *machine, methods, materials*, and *manpower*. These can be changed or supplemented as the situation dictates. If an item applies to two categories, it appears in both categories on the list. In the example, *container changes* appear as a problem cause in both the *machine* and *method* categories.

In a large blanking system with many different parts cycling through one system, performing this approach on the system as in the example identifies problems common to all parts and is a good first step. In the case study, the task involved improving the top 10 parts. Therefore, a next step might be to repeat the fishbone for each part, yielding part-specific causes. Breaking the team into subgroups that are responsible for specific parts and pulling them back together for an overall review improves efficiency, and comparing results can add value to the brainstorming. Downtime issues are an excellent fit for this process as well.

After completing the fishbone with all causes, the team uses a consensus process to identify the root causes. Teams may use data from the measurement activity, set up a floor test, or collect additional data to verify the root causes. After root-cause identification, the group collaboratively develops corrective actions. Finally, the project manager incorporates these corrective actions to eliminate or reduce the root causes into the team's improvement action plan. The team implements the improvement action plan when they get access to the equipment. Using a formal work breakdown structure, identifying dependencies, creating the network, and computing the critical path generally is not required. It is best to keep the plan simple with a listing of the steps, the assignments for each step, and the ballpark timing. The final step is to ensure that the entire team is committed to the schedule—this should be accomplished for some if not all issues on the first day in addition to providing some floor time for the team. The improvement planning works best when it is not overly complicated. The listing of action steps, assignments, and checklists on large flip-chart paper works well and provides good visual tools for the floor. The visual control board is a good place to post current plans. At the end or beginning of each day, plans are modified based on lessons learned and new plans emerge as required. If a corrective action proves ineffective, the team must search for alternative solutions, and then they must try again. Oftentimes learning what does not work can be as valuable as learning what does work.

Network Analysis. In manufacturing, repetitive processes such as product changeover, changing raw stock, quality checks, and removing finished parts are processes that affect machine availability (assuming they require equipment downtime to complete). Network analysis is a tool that is very effective in defining a plan for process improvements. The product changeover—spanning the time from the last good part to the next new good part—is an excellent application for this tool. Network analysis is really just applying the schedule development and critical path methods from the coordination and control process groups to analyze a process for improvement.

First, while observing the process, it is necessary to detail all the tasks required. As a first step, the team organizes tasks into subgroups. For example, the blanking die change team might group the tasks as coil change, coil feed, die change, and end-of-line change. These subgroups become level one of the work breakdown structure. Just as in MPM, these subgroups are divided into detailed tasks, but the detail is at a micro level. MPM^2 differs from MPM because the task descriptions are at a micro detail level with time elements of the tasks in seconds or minutes rather than days or weeks. After creating the work breakdown structure of the actual process, each task is analyzed to determine if it is value added and if it requires equipment downtime to complete. Nonvalue added tasks can be eliminated. Tasks that do not require downtime are scheduled external to the product change, which effectively removes them from the process.

Next, for each task in the resulting WBS, the dependencies are identified and the network diagram is created. The use of manually generated network diagrams is practical since the number of tasks is less than 100 and subgroups can reduce it to multiple networks of 20 tasks or less. The manual approach using sticky notes on a large white board works well with floor personnel. Extreme care should be taken when defining the dependencies to avoid introduction of discretionary dependencies, as this will distort the improvement opportunities. For example, Operator A might be performing two tasks in sequence because the operator can only do one at a time, but the use of a second operator allows the two tasks to occur simultaneously.

Unlike the schedule development process derived from estimates, the time and resource information comes from the actual observed times of people performing the tasks. Time from stopwatch data is in the form of seconds or minutes rather than in the form of days or weeks. Since these processes are short (less than one hour), videotaping the process and replaying it is the best way to generate the data to capture all the tasks, dependencies, labor assignments, and times. This network gives a picture of the current process, and assuming unlimited resources, the calculated critical path is the best time the process can deliver; this time is usually far better than the actual videotaped version.

If a company opts for scheduling software such as MS Project, they should recognize that minutes are the smallest increment of time. Recording tasks in seconds with scheduling software will require the use of a two-tier timeline where minutes represent seconds and hours represent minutes. Of course, with this approach, the *minutes scale* (which in reality is in hours) repeats after 24 minutes. Scheduling software is beneficial because of its computation of the critical path, its identification of over-utilized resources, and its ability to show the effects of what-if scenarios on the total time.

The resource loading report reveals over-utilized resources. For resources, any overutilization can be resolved by reassignment within the workgroup, resequencing, or by introducing added resources to yield a valid process network and achieve the critical-path time. Organizations that employ many different work classifications within the process targeted for improvement restrict their ability to reassign tasks to achieve the desired improvement. If the task driving the overutilization cannot be reassigned and additional resources are unavailable, a mandatory dependency is introduced into the network to eliminate the overutilization. If this occurs on the critical path, it increases the best time accordingly. This network is the true picture of the current process and its critical path is the best time with the defined resources. To this point, the network analysis identified tasks for elimination, externalization, reassignment, resequencing, and resource additions.

Implementing these process changes using the network description and achieving the previously recorded times for each task yields the calculated critical path's best time. This represents the true potential of the process in its current state. The final step is to analyze the specific tasks on the critical path to determine ways to reduce the task times further with methods, tools, equipment, training, or added resources. Resource addition in this context is to reduce a specific task time while the resource addition in the prior paragraph was for overutilization. The brainstorming using the previously discussed fishbone diagram can prove very useful in identifying causes and actions to reduce the task times. As in prior discussions of critical path, any time reduction in the critical path elements requires a recalculation of critical path to ensure that the reduction did not create a new critical path. The multi-company perspective in this part of the process is particularly effective since equipment suppliers and other participants outside the customer organization offer a variety of perspectives that help to break down barriers that prevent the normal workgroup from seeing all the possibilities. This final network is the improvement objective.

The improvement team implements all changes identified from the analysis, tests functionality, and measures the actual process improvement time. In the case of changeovers, a series of practice changes are run on each shift on the actual equipment with assigned personnel to fine-tune their skills and to build a routine within the workforce. Their participation in developing the changes, determining the critical-path times, and testing the results builds commitment. The final network with all the improvements documents the process and becomes the baseline for any upcoming continuous improvement. This information is converted into specific job instructions for each individual in the workgroup to maintain the process integrity during personnel changes and in between shifts. The network and job instruction documentation combined with organizational discipline to follow and monitor instructions provides the control to sustain the process improvement.

Operations Visual Control Board. At the start of each day, the team meets briefly to ensure that everyone agrees on assignments and makes any necessary adjustments to the project plan. The team should plan a brief report out at the end of each day to a leadership representative covering their findings, accomplishments, and any roadblocks encountered. The project manager records the results daily and summarizes them at the end of the week to make up the final report out for Event I. The facilitator structures the start-of-the-day coordination meeting and the end-of-the-day report out as standup meetings using a flip chart or white board to keep it simple, short, and efficient. The facilitator employs the following tools during the improvement events to document and manage the MPM^2 process: site visual control board, daily summary and report, open-issues list, and project Gantt chart.

MPM borrowed the visual control board concept from lean manufacturing and adapted it to projects to visualize the project activities. Thus, the manufacturing operation may already employ an operations form of the visual control board. An operations control board displays the team-specific performance parameters (i.e., safety, throughput, quality, on time, customer feedback, etc.), tracked versus time, team continuous improvement issues and action plans, and overall plant objective performance. The MPM² improvement fits in well with this operations information, but may require a temporary additional board on the floor to display all the information from the MPM² project. This board will contain improvement plans, daily and event reports, homework, and goal performance status. Once the final team homework is complete, appropriate adjustments are made to the existing control board format, appropriate MPM² data is incorporated and the temporary board is removed. If a control board did not exist prior to MPM², use the MPM² control board as the nucleus to evolve into an operations visual control board.

Event II Activities. Event II starts with the improvement team reviewing their project status and making any necessary adjustments. The focus is on ensuring that all gains meet expectations, processes are in place to sustain the gains, and any newly completed items receive validation. A key point is that the improvements must be permanent. A primary way to ensure permanency is to build the change into the process documentation. Just as lessons learned are integrated into the project documentation and procedures, process improvements are integrated as well. The main difference is the type of documentation. For improvements, the team uses planned maintenance procedures, job instructions, job setup, training manuals, spare parts records, daily team routines, reporting tools, modified or new checklists, material requirements, material ordering—essentially any systems in operations that document the improvement. Failure to build process changes into the documentation and lack of discipline in following the documented process is one of the major causes of quality and productivity loss. Failure to document and enforce discipline is the nemesis of any continuous improvement process.

Figure 10.5 lists typical Event II activities based on a four-day event duration. Since team formation occurred in Event I, the team can begin working immediately on the project following the same routine of meeting at the start of each day and reporting out at the end of each day. At the end of the week, the final report is made to the entire leadership team, and the leadership team plans and executes a recognition activity to thank the improvement team for their efforts.

Reviewing each improvement team's activities daily with summary reports at the end of each event ensures process consistency and fulfills the requirement to oversee improvement events. Daily activities during Events I and II are monitored by having the team report to the customer's operations manager so that any issues

Monday	Time	Location
Planning session with team leaders and facilitators	???	Conference room
Tuesday		
Daily improvement team meeting	???	Conference room
Review homework results		
Brainstorm control methods		
Plan week's activities		
Separate into team activities to execute plan	???	Plant floor
Lunch	???	
Separate into team activities to execute plan	???	Plant floor
Daily update meeting	???	Conference room
Assign follow-up items to 2nd shift		
Wednesday		
Daily improvement team meeting	???	Conference room
Review 2nd shift follow-up		
Adjust plan based on previous day's results		
Separate into team activities to execute plan	???	Plant floor
Lunch	???	
Separate into team activities to execute plan	???	Plant floor
Daily update meeting	???	Conference room
Begin preparing report out presentation		
Thursday		
Finalize presentation	???	Conference room
Event II report out	???	Conference room
Improvement team recognition	???	Plant floor?

Figure 10.5 Event II schedule of daily activities agenda

can be addressed immediately to keep the team on track. At the end of Event I, a summary report is made to the customer's key executive. The project manager folds any homework into the project schedule or action-plan tracking sheet as appropriate to ensure that there is proper follow-up on these items between Event I and Event II. At the end of Event II, the entire leadership team is present to evaluate the results and give the improvement teams recognition for their efforts.

CLOSEOUT

The MPM² closeout process is less complex than MPM's since there are only a few deliverables to deal with and the improvement contracts are relatively simple. Still, it is important to provide recognition, conduct a formal closeout meeting with the leadership, conduct a process survey, develop lessons learned, and review results to ensure customer and supplier satisfaction.

Recognition. Team recognition is an important element of the MPM^2 process. It is a good way to thank the teams for their efforts and to highlight team accomplishments for the entire organization. The recognition of accomplishments helps to integrate the changes into the organization and fosters a positive atmosphere to support future improvement efforts. Team recognition follows the principles explained previously in MPM consisting of keeping it simple, applying it equally to all teams, and requiring the leadership to participate in a serving capacity to acknowledge the accomplishments of the team. As in the MPM philosophy, no improvement team ever fails since they all gain something or discover new information regarding the operation. The recognition can be a single event after all teams have completed their Event II report out recognizing all the teams, or separate events at the completion of each team Event II report out. Separate events are preferred, and whenever Event II report outs are more than a few weeks apart, a separate recognition is preferable to keep it timely. If multiple improvement teams report out over a time interval, the leadership attends each Event II report out.

Closeout Meeting. Upon completion of the final Event II wrap up, there may be several homework items still open. This includes such things as applying the lessons learned during the improvement events to the balance of the parts in the gap analysis, implementing corrections identified during the events, incorporating improvements across all shifts, and implementing any training associated with the improvements. Leadership closeout should not occur until sufficient time has elapsed to button up most homework items and generate performance data to measure goal attainment. Project managers should allow 30–60 days to complete the homework before gathering performance data for a specified time interval. A three-month period with minimal equipment changes, no new product introductions, and stable schedules is ideal for the measurement team to gather performance data. Thus, leadership closeout occurs 4–5 months after the last Event II. This timing provides accurate measurements of bottom-line results and confirms sustainment of the improvements.

The final closeout meeting summarizes all the results achieved during the process and measures the overall satisfaction of the customer and supplier. The focus should be on quantifying the results to provide justification and validation of the process for the customer and supplier. The checklist in Figure 10.6 is a tool to help the project manager in preparing for the final closeout meeting and for ensuring that all aspects of the MPM^2 process have been completed. This is a good time to verify proper documentation and fulfillment of leadership expectations.

Improvement title _____

Customer _____ **Supplier** _____

Key executive _____ **Key executive** _____

Project manager _____ **Consultant** _____

Equipment scope _____

#	Activity	☑
1.	Insure improvement teams have received appropriate recognition	
2.	Quantify and summarize all results in final report to customer	
3.	Insure reported results relate directly to the initial goals established by the leadership team	
4.	Measure customer and supplier satisfaction using standard reporting forms from each	
5.	Supplier to generate a lessons learned list	
6.	Customer to generate a lessons learned list	
7.	Agree on place, date, and duration for leadership close out meeting or conference call	
8.	Verify meeting facility/network and equipment	
9.	Finalize close out meeting agenda with customer and supplier covering the following items: • Lessons learned review and discussion • Customer satisfaction • Future follow-up actions and opportunities	
10.	Conduct leadership MPM² process close out meeting	
11.	Publish minutes of close out meeting detailing follow-up actions and potential business opportunities	
12.	Distribute and collect MPM² process evaluation surveys from all leadership personnel	
13.	Summarize MPM² process evaluations and distribute to all leadership personnel	

Figure 10.6 MPM² closeout checklist

The MPM² process survey and lessons-learned exercise identify what-went-wrong and what-went-right from a process and hardware standpoint. The results of the survey and exercise can be used to improve the MPM² process. As always, the customer is encouraged to discuss future opportunities where they would like the equipment supplier to assist them. Figure 10.7 is a generic agenda for the close-out meeting.

Agenda
Leadership MPM² close out meeting

Welcome and review of norms	Customer key executive
Review improvement goals	Supplier key executive
Review validation results	Customer representative
	(From measurement team)
Overview of MPM² survey results	Project manager
Identify and detail any follow-up actions	Project manager
Lessons learned review and discussion	Consultant facilitates
Customer lessons learned	Customer as assigned
Equipment supplier lessons learned	Supplier as assigned
Discussion of key lessons	Team discussion
Discussion of future opportunities	Customer as assigned
Wrap up	Consultant
Verify all issues are closed	

Figure 10.7 MPM² closeout meeting agenda

Process Survey. The consultant and project manager are responsible for distributing, collecting, summarizing, and reporting the results of the process survey back to the leadership team. Figure 10.8 is the survey summary from the case study MPM² process. As the figure shows, the process survey form from MPM requires only modification of the parameters to fit the MPM² needs. Roles and communications are common to both surveys. Equipment performance and utilization parameters loosely relate to performance specifications and supplying a better product. The MPM² parameters of focus on improvement efforts, teamwork, and financial results replace the MPM parameters of timing requirements, recognizing risk and problems, and maintaining and adjusting schedules. The case study project achieved a 95.7 percent positive rating without negative scores. The Pareto chart in the survey summary identifies the top process strengths as the focus on improvement efforts, teamwork, and equipment performance. In the case study, the financial results reflected a lower rating since the closeout meeting preceded the validation measurement. Thus, actual bottom-line performance data was incomplete. This is item 11 in the lessons-learned list discussed in the next topic.

Lessons Learned. The lessons learned comes from the improvement suggestions on the process survey and the leadership lessons-learned discussion during closeout. Figure 10.9 is the list of lessons learned from the case study MPM² process. As indicated previously, it is insufficient to generate a list of lessons learned for the next implementation. To really be effective and add value, the lessons learned must be built into the process or specifications so they become a part of the baseline and

Improvement title: Blanking Throughput
Customer: Kasle Metal Processing

Start Date: 9/19/2007
Supplier: Automatic Feed Company

1)   Did the MPM^2 process improve the following:

		Help +2	+1	No 0	-1	Hurt -2
A.	Clarity of roles and responsibilities		6	1		
B.	Focus on improvement efforts	4	3			
C.	Communications	2	5			
D.	Teamwork and enthusiasm	4	3			
E.	Equipment performance	4	3			
F.	Equipment utilization	2	4	1		
G.	Financial results		5			

Overall Survey Rating 95.7% Positive with Zero negative
Pareto of Survey Results:

KMP Blanking Throughput Results Pareto

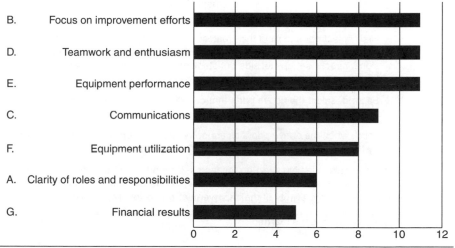

Figure 10.8 Case study survey results

MPM² Lessons Learned

1. Environmental assessment should focus on standardized work instead of health and safety. Use health and safety items as a portion of the standardized work effectiveness.

2. Brainstorming is not an effective tool to focus the leadership group. Instead, use a results/resources matrix plotting MPM² key areas to determine priorities to set goals.

3. Expand the elements of MPM² to include equipment upgrades in addition to the sub-headings of functionality, performance, and reliability.

4. Define two levels of data requirements from the customer: one for opportunity assessment and one for measurement and analysis.

5. Use readiness checklists to insure preparation is complete for key steps in MPM².

6. Establish a conference call to coordinate readiness prior to Events I and II.

7. Develop a generic schedule of daily activities to better regulate the activities of the improvement teams during Events I and II.

8. Assign a project manager/facilitator to organize and manage the complete process and insure full time facilitation support for the improvement team events.

9. Perform part selection for each event as a part of the team planning and order material to insure it is available for the event.

10. Part priority selection is required if all parts listed in the gap analysis cannot be run when performing a speed improvement. Select parts according to the following priorities:

    a. First, select parts to yield the greatest variety of operating conditions: show and exposed; developed and straight cut; long, medium, and short progressions; special set ups ie: side out stacking. (Insures all equipment conditions are studied.)

    b. Second, select the above parts that contribute the most to the performance gap. (Volume adjusted opportunity.)

    c. Third, when the above priorities are complete, pick problem parts identified by the customer. (May already be covered in above.)

11. Schedule final leadership wrap-up meeting 4–5 months after the final Event II. This allows one month to finish homework items and 3 months of stable operation to measure the effects of the improvement on bottom line performance.

Figure 10.9 Case study lessons learned

establish a new level from which to improve. Leaving this integration of lessons learned to the next project results in key nuances of the lessons becoming lost due to the passage of time and potentially different players. Lessons are integrated into the documentation to avoid duplicate effort and different approaches that lack standardization and efficiency. To realize the full value of the lessons learned, they should be integrated immediately after identification, as was done in MPM. In accordance with this approach, this text incorporates all lessons learned from the case study into the preceding process description.

Case Study Results. This case study reduced changeover time by 63.9 percent, generating an additional one hour of production time per day; it also eliminated two of the three top downtime items. Specific-part speed improvements averaged 31 percent, generating a volume-weighted average speed improvement of 18 percent across the entire blanking enterprise. The expected overall improvements should generate a bottom-line savings potential of $1 million annually and represents significant capacity cost avoidance potential. The supplier submitted new equipment and upgrade proposals totaling $870,000, which the customer figured had a business case payback of less than a year. The customer expects these projects to drive another double-digit year of improvements. In summary, the $1 million in annual improvements generated from MPM^2 created the funds needed for new equipment and upgrades from the supplier resulting in a win-win for both parties.

The following two lists summarize the benefits the customer and supplier derived from applying MPM^2 in the case study.

Customer advantages:

1.   Assessment provides excellent analysis of organization's strengths, weaknesses, and opportunities
2.   Helps to increase focus and model team behavior in improvements
3.   Equipment corrections made during the process help to eliminate future service calls that might otherwise have been required
4.   Double-digit performance improvement in the bottom line related to system or systems selected for improvement

Supplier advantages:

1.   Assessment provides excellent analysis of equipments' strengths, weaknesses, and opportunities in manufacturing environment to aid future designs
2.   Lessons learned from this process enables them to market a similar service to other customers
3.   Provides opportunity to promote training, service, spare parts, and other technology the supplier offers
4.   Increase utilization of suppliers' engineering and service personnel
5.   Increased understanding and customer feedback of suppliers' equipment in production to help value and prioritize future performance, functionality, and reliability improvements

6.   Create immediate business opportunities through identified upgrades
7.   Create future business opportunities for new and replacement capacity

This case study generated significant results for both customer and supplier. It validates the benefits of MPM with modifications in an improvement project.

MULTI-COMPANY PROJECT MANAGEMENT (MPM) CONCLUSION

Multi-company projects are a special set of projects with strategic value to multiple companies. In the project hierarchy, they fall between projects and programs since programs may contain traditional single company or multi-company projects. Programs and multi-company projects require organizational structures, management considerations, and project methodology that go beyond the typical single company project.

Conventional thinking views most projects from a single company's perspective. They are viewed as internal and are executed within the company's project management process by an assigned project manager. On larger projects, the project perspective expands to include companies contributing major content as well. Beyond the project customer, this could include an engineering design house, original equipment manufacturer (OEM), architect, general contractor, software designer, and their key suppliers. When the content represents sufficient strategic value in terms of size, complexity, risk, or opportunity, they will assign their own manager and project organization. Each of the project organizations is simply a subset of the overall project. Projects involving multiple companies have the added dimension of cross-company cooperation and require a means for integrating the various project organizations to manage their overall effectiveness and maximize project success for all participants. The integration of multi-company management and project management techniques and principles yields a process referred to as MPM.

MPM is easily adapted to projects in manufacturing, construction, retail, finance, information technology, or any other business or industry environment. It integrates well with other tools, techniques, and philosophies available to help improve results, such as Lean and Six Sigma. Either the supplier or customer may initiate the collaboration process in the project or operation lifecycle phases. The initiation of MPM requires the voluntary commitment of the participating companies and their senior executives. Since the participating companies are independent, the project organization uses a team structure to maximize effectiveness. The team structure allows the multiple companies to operate as a single cohesive project team and results in extensive collaborative opportunities among the participants building synergy that maximizes business results.

The core of the MPM methodology is the Six C process consisting of process groups representing *cooperation, communication, coordination, control, complete,* and *close* processes. Team formation consists primarily of the first three process groups with a heavy emphasis on group interaction skills and building relationships among the participants while creating the project charter, organizational structure, and baseline schedule. Team formation, whether in a single company or multi-company environment, frequently lacks structure and discipline. The MPM process provides specific direction and tools to ensure the establishment of a fully functional, stable team.

The project implementation involves the *control, complete,* and *close* process groups. It places emphasis on the project management processes since the team skills and procedures are in place and only require maintenance and reinforcement to sustain them. The multi-company aspect of MPM allows expansion of the traditional close activities to build greater business value in the project for the customer and the supplier.

Effective project organizations involving multiple companies require a joint leadership structure, full collaboration of key companies, and utilize a consensus style decision-making approach. The MPM process provides a solid foundation to build on in establishing a multi-company project or operations improvement. It defines a basic interorganizational structure to coordinate and integrate all the project activities in a unified manner to achieve business results for all participants. MPM is a perfect fit in the project hierarchy and a great opportunity whenever multiple companies see strategic value in the same project or operations improvement.

Thank you for reading this book. Hopefully, the detailed, practical, and straightforward processes and techniques provided in this book for creating and managing multi-company project organizations will enable you to maximize your project, program, operation, and overall business results. Your feedback, questions, and inquires are always welcome. Feel free to visit my website at www.teamimplementers.com or to send me an e-mail at dabaker@teamimplementers.com.

BIBLIOGRAPHY

Barkley, B., and J. Saylor. *Customer Driven Project Management: Building Quality into Project Processes.* 2nd ed. New York: McGraw Hill, 2001.

Boston, L., C. Keller, and J. Rooney. "Two Sides of the Same Coin: Using Teams in Customer-Supplier Relationships." *Journal for Quality & Participation* 25(3), 4–8 (Fall 2002).

Fleming, Q., and J. Koppelman. *Earned Value Project Management.* 3rd ed. Newton Square Pennsylvania: Project Management Institute, 2005.

Gido and Clements. *Successful Project Management.* 3rd ed. Mason, OH: Thomson South-Western, 2006.

Gray C. F., and E. W. Larson. *Project Management: The Managerial Process.* 3rd ed. New York: McGraw Hill, 2005.

Griffith, A., and G. Gibson Jr. "Alignment during Pre-Project Planning." *Journal of Management in Engineering* 17(2), 69 (March, 2001).

Harrington-Mackin, D. *The Team Building Tool Kit: Tips, Tactics, and Rules for Effective Workplace Teams.* New York: AMACOM, American Management Association, 1994.

Hersey, P., K. Blanchard, and D. Johnson. *Management of Organizational Behavior: Leading Human Resources.* 9th ed. New Jersey: Prentice Hall, 2008.

Kerzner, Harold. *Project Management: A systems approach to planning, scheduling, and controlling.* 9th ed. New Jersey: John Wiley & Sons, 2006.

McCarty, Tom. "Six Sigma® at Motorola." *Motorola,* September, 2004. http://www.motorola.com/mot/doc/1/1736_MotDoc.pdf (accessed February 26, 2008).

Nicholas, John. *Project Management for Business and Engineering.* 2nd ed. Oxford, UK: Elsevier Butterworth-Heinemann, 2004.

Project Management Institute. *A Guide to the Project Management Body of Knowledge.* 4th ed. Project Management Institute, Newton Square, PA, 2008.

Sanborn, Mark. *Team Built, Making Teamwork Work.* New York: MasterMedia Limited, 1992.

Scholtes, Joiner, and Streibel. *The Team Handbook.* 3rd ed. Madison, WI: Oriel, 2003.

Shuman, J., and J. Twombly. "Collaborating with Suppliers for Innovation and Growth." The Rhythm of Business, 2006. http://www.rhythmofbusiness.com (accessed March 22, 2008).

Soderquist, Don. *The Wal Mart Way: The inside story of the success of the world's largest company.* Nashville, TN: Thomas Nelson, Inc., 2005.

INDEX